Man's Divine Nature

Jivolae James Harris

Copyright © 2021 Jivolae James Harris
All rights reserved. No part of this publication may be reproduced, distributed, or transmitted in any form or by any means, including photocopying, recording, or other electronic or mechanical methods, without the prior written permission of the publisher, except in the case of brief quotations embodied in critical reviews and certain other noncommercial uses permitted by copyright law. For permission requests, write to the publisher, addressed "Attention: Book Rights and Permission," at the address below.
Published in the United States of America
ISBN 978-1-953904-90-4 (SC)

Jivolae James Harris
222 West 6th Street
Suite 400, San Pedro, CA, 90731
www.stellarliterary.com
Order Information and Rights Permission:

Quantity sales. Special discounts might be available on quantity purchases by corporations, associations, and others. For details, contact the publisher at the address above.
For Book Rights Adaptation and other Rights Permission. Call us at toll-free 1-888-945-8513 or send us an email at admin@stellarliterary.com.

To Muhammad Ali, the greatest of all time

Table of Contents

Chapter 1: Introduction — 6

Chapter 2: Rise Up — 26

Chapter 3: Herculean Effort — 49

Chapter 4: Act Like A Champ, Think Like A King — 99

Chapter 5: Profiles of Some Champs — 125

Chapter 6: The Power of Life — 132

Chapter 7: COVID 19, We Must Not Surrender — 141

Chapter 8: Persevere the Pandemic and Strive for Greatness — 154

Chapter 9: Hope — 163

Chapter 10: The Physical, Mental, and Spiritual — 174

Chapter 11: The Call of the Universe — 193

Chapter 12: Blast Off — 219

Chapter 13: Survival — 230

Chapter 14: To Become Great — 240

Chapter 15: The Theory of Lay Epistemics — 252

Chapter 16: Have a Job 265

Chapter 17: Infinite Greatness 283

Chapter 18: My Story 293

Chapter 19: The Master of Home Life 305

Chapter 20: I Remain 315

Chapter 21: Apotheosis – Man Elevated to the Divine 324

Acknowledgements 330

Chapter 1:
Introduction

◇◇◇◇◇◇◇◇◇

The realization of greatness will give you your wings.

- Jivolae James Harris

Being divine, somewhat supernatural is the first step toward being what you were intended to be. We have a God in us. You are divine at birth; you become supernatural when your full powers emerge. Human nature is to be what you were intended to be. This book is the anecdote to the pandemic. The pandemic is 360 degrees away from our intended world. We have to coalesce, we have to unite now.

Like activist and multi-faceted genius, Paul Robeson said we must try to bring the world together. We must write books that will be our manifesto to live on. We need to be inspired by our heroes. Like Gauss said we need mathematics. Muhammad Ali said be the greatest. That is the premise of this book – amidst the pandemic we must still strive for greatness.

The divine man, those who reach greatness, makers of the Heavens and Earth, the deliverer of man are indeed the saviors of us all. Philosopher Christopher Hitchins said God doesn't exist. The Cosmos is the sun, moon, and stars. The Big Bang expanded the Universe. To Hitchins, I say – divine persons led the Jews out of bondage in Egypt. Divine persons freed the African slaves from slavery. Divine persons of greatness invented a cure for tuberculosis, a treatment for cancer and AIDS, and now a vaccine for the Corona Virus. Divine men helped me overcome a brain disorder to become a great scholar-athlete and professor. The pandemic does the opposite of apotheosis, it doesn't bring out the god in us, it brings disease, death, poverty, and depression.

Apotheosis is man's elevation to the divine. It was said that George Washington experienced apotheosis. I believe Dr. Martin Luther King, Jr. experienced it as well.

The achievements of man are infinitesimal. The mystery of creation baffles us. If you are to be godly, you must know the way of the chosen. A way to awaken the god in you is to act like a champ and think like a king. Make like Thutmose, king of Egypt in the 15th century b.c.. He was an intelligent ruler. This philosophy is tantamount to what the chosen do.

Awaken the God within. Equalize human beings. Roar like a lion. Make like a rocket ship. Make like Moses in Egypt. Let there be light. Let the stars shine luminescently. Activate your highest self. Like the boxing of Ali, like the quarterbacking of football star, Patrick Mahomes, like the basketball of Jordan, be great. Like the superb broadcasting of Oprah Winfrey, be great. Like Akenaton, like King Menelik of Ethiopia, like Jay Z, be great. Like philosopher Dr. Cornel West, like Dr. Neil deGrasse Tyson, astrophysicist, be great. Like the first respondents of COVID 19, be great. Like my mother, Theresa, who gave birth to me and took care of me in my childhood, be great. Fly above the clouds and be great. Like Barack Obama, chosen to govern the people, you must lift us up. Grab hold of the wind like a sailor and breathe freely. The metaphysical is that you must transform your mind by prophesizing the right thoughts. Ali thought he was the greatest, so he became the greatest. King Akenaton thought he was majestic, so he ruled a kingdom. You must be like Ali and act like a champ, you must be like Akenaton and think like a king. That is the philosophy of this book written by a man who received a master's degree from an elite university after being told by a doctor that because he had a brain disorder he would never graduate college. He received that master's and went on to be accepted into a Ph.D program. This man had effervescence and light. You will be divine.

Apotheosis during the pandemic is still possible. Infinite greatness, like divine greatness, is the idea that your greatness will have an infinite impact on others. My personal story is offered as I was born with a brain disorder that stymies me a thousand times over. You are man. You are Heaven. You have wings. You can fly high as the sky. You just need to adjust to illness and be healthy. Illness can clip your wings. You must adjust. My love of people antithetical to evil supercedes anything I accomplished. But I still strive for greatness.

In mathematics, infinity is defined as lacking limits or endless. Every individual must examine the possibility of his own greatness. The multiplicity of your mind determines your greatness. Your greatness is not silent. The Universe has an effect on the protoplasm of man. As a man thinketh, so shall he be. In order to be great man must transform the way he acts and the way he thinks. The quest for greatness is in essence a quest for freedom. Much like a caterpillar larvae, man's mind undergoes a metamorphosis. Man must be bold and confident like a champ and majestic and wise like a king. Man can't let potential lay dormant; he must ascend to the highest. In this book our champs are the following: a king, a heavyweight champ, a president, a valedictorian, a CEO, and a PhD.

In this book we bring you into the mind of a champ and king in order for you to emulate them and develop strategies for infinite greatness. You must make like a rocket ship and blast off. You will face adversity as you try to succeed. We're in the midst of a storm. The storm is not as powerful as man; he can overcome the storm of adversity with the use of his mind. So we ask in this book, "What is the formula for success and how do you become great?" Each neuron in your brain works for you to be great. Greatness doesn't lapse. Greatness is within your reach and it is within the laws of nature. Man is connected to the Universe. His brain is a microcosm of the Universe, billions of brain cells like billions of galaxies.

You must reach for the stars. In other words, be ambitious. Be determined. Have a burning desire to be great. Follow your passions. Passion is *passus* in Latin meaning fervent devotion. Find an area in which you can achieve greatness. In order to be great it takes courage and imagination. Be innovative like King Dsojer, Pharaoh of Egypt. Be wise like Ramses II and Akhenaton. Being great is preferred to being mediocre. I am giving you the following foresight: once you have ambition and you follow the philosophy of greatness that is outlined in this book, you will reach greatness.

You do not need a telescope to see the stars, you can be among them. That's because, in life you have to shoot for the stars. You have to be ambitious in every endeavor. When you make an attempt, attempt for the highest, the ultimate, the most. The galaxy is full of stars. You have to desire to reach your constellation. There are many who became doctors, lawyers, singers, actors, and professional athletes. They were people who believed in shooting for the stars. The greatest of all time, Muhammad Ali shot for the stars. Paul Robeson, athlete, actor, singer, linguist, lawyer, and activist shot for the stars. He was the mightiest river known to man.

You must dream with the sky as the limit and you must act upon the dream. You must be fierce like the talented and beautiful songstress and megastar, Beyonce. Furthermore, you must have hutspa. For example, if you are an actor, shoot for an Oscar, if you are a footballer, shoot for the Super Bowl, and if you are a scientist, shoot for the Nobel Prize. Hence - hutspa. Do not settle and never accept mediocrity.

It is not a confabulation that the brain has the capacity and wavelength to be illuminated. Likewise, man can be skyrocketed from an unwanted set of circumstances, a state, or condition when he desires. This is called blasting off; blasting out of a state of mediocrity, of just existing, to being great. This book brings light to the subject of mediocrity vis-à-vis greatness. "Blasting off" also means reaching your full potential. One must not be complacent about one's state. Looking through the lens of a champ, life is about achieving and living up to one's own design like a flower reaching full bloom. In this case achievement is synonymous with success. The closest distance between two points is a straight line. This book offers a formula for success and blasting off that is a straight line. It is about resounding greatness. It is aimed to be progressive and a document about human progress. One of the formulas recommends the reader to be a possibilitarian, a person

who always thoroughly examines the possibilities around him.
In life, like as in a car, man needs a spark. It can be anything – another person, an idea, a cause, or in this case the desire for greatness, the desire to be a champ. He must follow his dreams and fantasies, aspire, reach his high, climb mountains, and blast off, fly high, and soar. A quarterback has to throw the ball, a messenger has to pass his message, a doctor has to cure his patient. Pick something and be the best in the world at it under all circumstances. You have to have ambition, an ambitious spirit. Chalk up victories and be fruitful, prolific, successful, and extraordinary. Be productive for the rest of your duration. If you want to be a star, then pursue being a star. Pursue your goals with the might of a king.

One must elevate his thoughts, actions, and consciousness. To climb Mount Everest you need the mentality and mode of thought needed to climb Mount Everest. Reach the summit. Expand yourself. To blast into space you need the mentality needed to blast into space. To be lion of the jungle you have to do everything it takes to become lion of the jungle. To become infinitely great you need to want to become infinitely great. You may be entrenched in your state and desire to be removed from it. You have to have the mentality to be removed from it.

Think beyond the sun, moon, stars, and planets, the Cosmos, the galaxies, the Universe. Rise up! Face your obstacles, move forward, and blast away from the circumstances that hold you down for so long. Through rocket science, rockets blast off into space or to the moon like the Soviet Union's cosmonauts or our astronauts. Metaphorically, you must blast off from the state or condition you are in. You have to get your feet off the ground as the hardest part is getting started and moving out of the state. You may find yourself in a ditch or hole in life, use your talent to get out of it.

Blasting off in track is like separating yourself from the pack, breaking through the wind to run through the finish line. In science blasting off is like discovering the unknown and undiscovered phenomena. In mathematics it is like solving complex equations. In life it is like breaking inertia to accomplish one's goals. Much like a plant rises above the soil to reach sunlight, man must ascend to higher heights. Blasting off includes transformation of the mind and body. Collective greatness will offer us the rise of man. As a child I watched so many of the other Pop Warner football players and how great they were. Automatically I wanted to emulate them. I did. I reached the college level. The power of the imagination goes higher than the clouds.

Hercules was a champ. His brother Perseus who saved Mount Olympus was a king. Zeus, their father, god in Greek mythology, god of thunder and lightning, protector of the people, in essence was a champ. Knowledge, wisdom, and understanding are the key to gaining greatness and freedom. Like a slave on a plantation looking up at the stars for hope, a goal seeker must keep his priorities correct and stay focused to obtain success. Blasting off is a special human need, psychological and idiosyncratic. A person blasts off the way a plant blossoms. Hope leads to the blossoming of man. In order to think and act like a champ and king, you must blast off both mentally and physically. Being great is empowerment of the spirit.

Describing a champ can absorb a lot of metaphors, but the primary adjective to describe him is passionate. He has passion for being at his best and living up to his full potential. The great passion of this entity does not stop. The passion of a CEO is remarkable, as is the passion of a studious valedictorian. The passion of a heavyweight champ is relentless, as is a PhD or president.

There is something inside a champ that makes him want the most out of life. His values are powerful as are the principles that he lives by. Passionate about life and the pursuit of happiness, a champ strives more than everyone else. He is working on his art form more than everyone else. His passion leads to his intensity. His intensity leads to his success.

Flying in with the wind, a champ's passion is best manifested by his climb from the bottom to the top – his journey. He begins as a willing participant and ends up a star. He has stumbling blocks but he overcomes them. He falls but he gets back up. He masters his environment and his possibilities. He stumbles forward until he can reach his destination. He astounds people along the way.

Your mind is a force, a powerful force. You must program it to meet your physiological and psychological needs. The best way to program is to act like a champ and think like a king. Think of life as a mountain. Know that the mountain is steep. You must be prepared to climb. Life is about pluses and minuses. You just have to make adjustments. In other words, you must adapt to what life gives you. You have to know when to roll with the punches and when to go against the grain.

Be courageous like a champ. Be bold like a king. Think big like a king. Be strong minded like a king. Like a king, like a champ, use your imagination. The possibilities are endless. The greatness you seek is there for you to take. The success you desire is within you. You just have to maximize the way you think and act. In 600 B.C., Buddha wrote, "All that we are is the result of what we have thought. The mind is everything. What we think, we become." Tap into all the secret valleys of your mind. It's mind over matter.

What determines our trajectory in life? The outstretched arms of destiny grab you tightly. The infinite ways of life baffle you. You're perplexed. You have to dig deep inside of yourself. This is the greatness of man. Complete darkness surrounds you. You can't see the stars in the dark distant sky. You must shed light. This is the greatness of man. The soul of man is his infinite mind. His mind illuminates the darkness. This book is the story of the transformation of my mind. Everything is everything. It is what it is. I am talking about life. You must make the most of it by acting the way a champ acts and thinking the way a king thinks. Learn from your past, live in the present, and look toward the future. This is where you have been, where you are, and where you are going. Know what it takes to get from where you are to where you're going. You must make strides. Progress is forthcoming.

Be able to make successful transitions along the path. A champ has blasted off, separated himself from the rest and earned the right to be called "champ". He has the mentality of a champ, he performs like a champ for the people, and thinks like a king. Shakespeare was a champ of literature because he acted, thought and performed like a champ. Beethoven was a champ of classical music because he performed songs like a champ and acted like a champ. The Russian poet, Alexandre Pushkin was a champ at an early age because he acted and thought like one. They each had the mental edge to be different from everyone else. They had tenacity and let their education, training, hard work, practice, persistence, and perseverance help them blast off and be luminous and separated from the rest. They left legacies for us to follow and blueprints for us to emulate. That blueprint was, "think like a champ, act like a king." So you want to fly, you want to float over the laws of the Universe, you must rehearse your vision in your head. The dispersion of effort makes a champ a champ. A champ like a king hopes for a high position, greatness, anything but mediocrity. A king must stand taller and climb higher. If you are determined enough, you will succeed.

As you move forward in your endeavor, be inspired. Like being inspired by the majesty of a king, be inspired by great people. This will lift you up until that day when you too will be great. Be inspired by the beauty of the Earth, the blue sky, the Cosmos, the amazing grace of man. Be inspired by success. Being inspired by greatness sparks a greatness in you. Inspiration has a psychological effect on you. This book aims to inspire you to be great and live up to your full potential. It informs you what you must do to climb the highest of mountains and reach your peak. It brings to light my own self-actualization or my full bloom. The goal is to flourish. Take matters in your own hands. It's your world. Be the exception not the rule. Live up to your destiny.

To the highest of mountains and the deepest of seas, we seek inspiration. With inspiration we become excellent. Many are called upon by the Universe to do amazing things and they answer the call. It is with this inspiration that they are lit up like a light to do the impossible. They advance the cause of mankind, of civilization. Our intention is to lift you to your highest level. It is to inspire you to be intense and to overcome whatever is in your way of reaching your plateau.

The motion that you make defines your chances. Inspiration invigorates your spirit, your human spirit. Your spirit carries you through the world. Your mind needs a spark to do intense things. This is inspiration. Watching others do amazing things transcends to you and you wish to emulate them. Like in Rome, Cicero told the children to emulate the achievements of their ancestors and Rome was saved. You have to use inspiration as a force. This is a force that drives you to grab hold of your destiny.

Inspiration awakens the giant within. It has a chemical effect on the brain, its impulses, its reaction to the external world. When a man runs 100 meters in a mere 9.5 seconds, he inspires the world, when a man composes beautiful music without the benefit of sight, he inspires the world, when two brothers invent a way for man to fly throughout the sky, they inspire the world. When we complete a journey of our own, we inspire the world. A poet inspires the world with her verses, a doctor inspires the world with his medicine, an architect inspires the world with his pyramid. We look to others for inspiration in our daily lives. The great Pharaohs of Egypt left monuments in Egypt to inspire generations to come. We writers like Mark Twain leave written words for people to be inspired. Scientists like Albert Einstein, creator of the theory of relativity, inspired us to discover more than we now know.

Elevate your thoughts. Think better cognitive thoughts. Think positively and progressively. You are a product of your thoughts much like plants are a product of the seeds that produce them. If you think positively, the way you act will be positive. If you think negatively, the way you act will be negative. In order to be a champ, you must think on your highest plane.

The king is the champ of his kingdom. The CEO is the champ of her corporation. The president of a country is the champ of that country. A valedictorian is the champ of her class. This concept is applicable to a myriad of fields and categories. People look up to a champ. He is automatically a symbol of excellence, the standard, the bar. A champ brings light to our life where there was darkness. He has the superior mentality, the mental edge, wit. The champ makes a believer out of people. He is the best. In your life you will face challenges. Reflect on your previous experiences to get through them. This is what a champ does to meet his challenges. A champ goes through life's rigorous curriculum, the obstacles and adversity, the training to be great, the hard knocks of life, the competition, the race against mediocrity.

In life a person achieves a proportion of his potential. His ideal situation is to actualize his full potential. There is no exact science to reach such, but a person must first desire the highest proportion of his full potential. In journeying to your full potential, it will require patience. A plant doesn't grow in one day; a caterpillar doesn't become a butterfly in a day. Rome wasn't built in a day. You must wait until your time has come for you to flourish. Acting like a champ and thinking like a king may require a metamorphosis to occur similar to that of a caterpillar larvae. A caterpillar crawls slowly for some time before it spins a cocoon where it builds the foundation for becoming a butterfly. After coming out of its cocoon, the caterpillar is ready for flight. Man is similar. He goes through stages of maturation and development before coming into his own. This development changes the content of his thinking and the mode of his actions. From thinking comes thought. Focused thought leads to drive and determination. To be the man that you want to be takes thinking, drive, determination, desire, and dedication.

Adversity will try to clip your wings. You must maintain your flight and succeed against the odds. The Egyptians from 3100 B.C. were successful, the Roman Empire under Constantine was successful, the Persian civilization was successful, the Chicago Bulls with Michael Jordan were successful. But like Jordan, these civilizations weren't built in a day. Success requires development over time. Beautiful things come to those with a mastery of development and time. Your time will come like a volcano erupting and you will succeed.

In life you have two choices – live or die, sink or swim. You have to dedicate yourself to a principle and live by it. You must escape the mundane. Elevation to a higher self is essential. Human progress is powerful much like a plant breaking through the soil to reach sunlight. Life is about ups and downs. Success is an extension of oneself. Love allows for the resurrection of the spirit. Hope is the mainstay of human life.

My analysis of life leads me to believe that life is supposed to be easy. It has been made to be difficult. It does have its ups and downs. You set goals and you achieve them. Success comes when you proliferate Herculean effort and perseverance. Achievement makes life more livable. Adversity must be endured. Man must adapt to his environment in order to survive the way a giraffe grew a longer neck to reach the fruits of higher growing trees. When man fails, he must learn from his mistakes. Success comes as a result of something you learned when you failed. Thomas Edison failed 10,000 times before successfully inventing the light bulb.

The purpose of life for man is likewise – to be lit up. Man must be uplifted and raised from his state. His state of mind must be uplifted. He must have consciousness and awareness of himself and his environment. He must be raised over his circumstances; he must be greater than his circumstances. Man must not yield to the negatives of his surroundings. The rise of man depends on his mind. The root of success is his mind. The root of mobilization from his state is his mind.

Man must engage in the discovery process. We discovered outer space and the moon. We must engage in intellectual discourse. We must wrestle with fact and fiction. Additionally, we must continue the course of civilization and we must educate ourselves. There must be advancement of the collective psyche as much as there is advancement in technology. We must keep pushing forward the cause of humanity. He must make things possible. He must know his purpose; it's a compass to guide you.

Man must have self-knowledge in order to be removed from an unwanted state. He must know his peculiarities, his wants, his strengths, and weaknesses, his motivations and desires. The Greek philosopher Socrates said, "Know Thyself." Knowing thyself is a process that doesn't occur overnight. A champ learns more about himself as he pursues his championship. He learns about himself as he trains and learns about himself after he becomes a champ.

Conquering lands wasn't enough for man. He had to conquer minds. A champ's mind is unconquerable. He can not be taken. He can not be subdued. He is larger than life. His ambition is astounding. He is remarkable. His courage is unwavering. His resilience is long lasting. He pales in comparison to nothing. He is a giant.

Proliferate with Herculean effort and greatness will appear. Being a champ is psychosomatic; it involves the mind acting upon the body. The power comes from *abintra*, Latin for within. Every champ needs an awakening of some type – an epiphany. He must awaken within. He must see the world through new lens. Whatever is inside of him must come out. He must be a new man, superior to his former self. Shine like you're supposed to.

A champ has the intensity of a light bulb. A light bulb works because of scientist Lewis Lattimer's carbon filament. What makes a champ work? It's the way of his mind – the way his mind works. It does not settle for less. It desires a great deal. It desires intensity. It desires being the best. Regardless of the arena, a champ wants full wattage of his ability. You see the mind of a champ is not a real mystery. He is tenacious, believes in hard work, is ambitious, wants to succeed at whatever he does and wants to triumph. He doesn't mind overcoming difficulty to get to his destination. He set his goals high and has every intention on fulfilling them. He has a nact for competition. In fact, he strives on it. It makes him better. He knows how to take charge and unlike the mediocre he knows how to get started on his endeavors. He has that psychological edge.

When Moses led the Jews out of Egypt and out of Pharaoh's grip, he was, above all else, a champ. He retorted, "Let my people go!"

He led them out of bondage. His mind was full of power and he had a great desire to be free. I had dreams all the time that I was the heavyweight champion of the world. I actually trained as a boxer for a while before being interrupted and I rehearsed a vision of having a champion title fight in my head over and over. I ate, drank, and slept boxing and I wasn't going to settle for less than people calling me "champ". Being called champ is an honor. I had the desire, ambition, the dream. Now that that dream has not come to the surface, I desire to be a champ of a different kind, both a PhD and CEO. I can relate to champs of this nature and the desire is there. I just have to apply the blast off formulas in this book. The purpose of greatness is feeling alive.

What makes a champ great is his ability. Yes, he works hard and perseveres, but simply put it is his ability that makes him who he is. His ability separates him from the rest and gets him out of his unwanted state. It takes struggle and sacrifice to blast off and be successful. It takes struggle and sacrifice to overcome obstacles and reach pivotal points of your journey. Much like animals in the jungle, man goes through struggle and sacrifice in his transformation process. Man must fit himself to his environment. Charles Darwin's research attests to this. He wrote "Natural Selection", later coined "Survival of the Fittest." Man must adapt to his environment and changes in his environment.

Once a person reaches greatness, his soul is at ease. It is a psychological and idiosyncratic human need. Feeling like a champ is amazing and the relief that you have achieved your goal is immense. When we think of champs, we think of the psychological makeup of an Evander Holyfield, the psychological edge of Roy Jones, Jr. the will and perseverance of a Muhammad Ali, the desire of a Lennox Lewis. These heavyweight champs had training and preparation and were inspirations to us all. President George Washington was a champ during the Revolutionary War. President Theodore Roosevelt was a champ in bringing us the Panama Canal. President Abraham Lincoln was a champ when he ended the Civil War.

What was Superman but in essence a champ. He fit all the characteristics that we have described. What was the Incredible Hulk but a champ? He overcame a force of some kind and reached greatness. What was Zeus but a champ? What was Paul Robeson, singer/actor/athlete, but a champ. What was Alexander The Great but a champ? What was Napolean Bonaparte but a champ? What was King Tut but a champ? What was philosopher Aristotle but a champ? What was Bruce Lee, martial artist, but a champ? What was Magic Johnson but a champ? What was Rocky Marciano but a champ? You are your own rock. You are your own mountain. You are your own foundation. Act like a champ and think like a king.

Now, a king strives to be a god. Don't have a peasant state of mind. You can not reach the palace thinking like a peasant. Have a king state of mind, have self-esteem. The Pharaohs for instance looked up to multiple gods such as Osiris, Thoth, Isis, Horus, and Ra. The Pharaohs were intermediaries between the people and the gods. The gods looked out for the people as did the kings. King Akhenaton likened himself to a god. In Greek Mythology, King Perseus saved Mount Olympus from the evil Medusa. Perseus was Zeus' son. Apollo and Atlas were gods. As was Poseidon. A king acts like a god and in turn you must think like a king. Keep your eyes on the prize and take your throne. As your author I want the best for you. I look to the sky for my best; to the stratosphere. Greatness awaits you. This book is sufficient to get you there. Blast off like singer, Beyonce as her chords ring loud and clear throughout the world, like the great actor Denzel Washington, like the brain surgeon, Dr. Ben Carson, or the great Toni Morrison, or the great philosopher and professor, Dr. Cornel West. Make like the great track runner, Usain Bolt – lightning. Make like the great astrophysicist, Dr. Neil DeGrasse Tyson and the great heavyweight champ Vladimir Klitko. Make like the great NFL quarterback Drew Brees and the great NBA star Lebron James. Also make like the great talk show host and actress, Oprah Winfrey or the great computer whiz Bill Gates. Greatness is a plateau that can be reached, but you must want it. The verses in this book are designed to transform you and make you successful. If you can see it, you can do it. You can have glory and glory is triumph of the spirit.

Destiny awaits you. The treasure of life is yours for the taking. You just have to crystallize your goals and converge on your dreams. The centripetal force of your goals is unstoppable and your spirit is unbreakable. Master the elements. Master the psychology of success. The trick is that you have to understand life. This is a mysterious concept, but you can delineate it or make it much simpler with wisdom or sophism. Boldness is the way to your fulfillment. Success is predicated on the way you act and think. Trade in your old thinking with the forms of a champ and king – confident and majestic. Lift the veil from society with high thinking and progress. There is nothing more inspiring than human progress. A man who couldn't walk is inspired when he is able to once again walk.

The night pervades. I look up in the dark sky and know that I can be great. Kings have come before me looking up at the same sky wondering what's out there for them. In the darkness I see a glimpse of light. It illuminates my mind like an incandescent light bulb. There is a spark. I have an idea. I can be a great writer much like I was a great athlete, scholar, and mentor. I can write about my philosophy on greatness, what it takes to become great and more than just mediocre. King Menes looked at the same dark sky and saw the glimpse of light of a new civilization. Frederick Douglass looked up at the dark sky and saw a vision that he could one day be free. Dr. Maya Angelou looked up above and saw that she could win the Nobel Prize in Literature. Adhere to the philosophy on greatness that is outlined in this book and look up at the dark sky and know that you too can become great and masterful. Know that you can be the light of the world.

Chapter 2:
Rise Up

◇◇◇◇◇◇◇◇◇◇

"I am a mountain. I am a tall tree. Oh! I am a swift wind sweeping the country. I am a river down in the valley. Oh! I am a vision and I can see clearly. If anybody ask you who I am – just stand up tall, look em' up in the face and say: I'm that star up in the sky, I'm that mountain peak up high, hey I made it. I'm the world's greatest and I'm that little bit of hope when my backs against the ropes. I can feel it, I'm the world's greatest."

- The World's Greatest

As man lives his essence lives. As he dies his essence still lives. As he wins his battles in life, his essence wins also. When he loses, his essence loses as well. He is nothing without his essence. His essence is his incandescent light. His essence makes things happen. His essence has a certain speed, a certain power. When we see man glow, we are seeing his essence shine through. We can feel his essence. Ever so effervescent, he is very much alive. This is his essence asunder. A champ is the concept of the essenced man, his energy, his movement, his strength, his power, and his liveliness. There are men and women who exemplified great essence during their lifetime and serve as a model to us all. Michael Jordan and President Bill Clinton are just to name a few.

Ultimate means the highest, the best, the most. This is the ultimate motivational book. David was able to slay the giant Goliath because of an ultimate inner feeling that he possessed. In this book we aim to achieve the ultimate inner feeling for the reader. The aim is to teach the reader how to persevere and succeed and be great. Although this is a deep analysis, the reader can psychologically inherit ultimate characteristics that will lead him to be a champ.

The Promised Land is not a geographical destination, rather it is a state of mind. Mentally, a reader must acquire the mindset necessary for perseverance and success to come to the surface. Illumination or being lit up like a light is the goal. The 4D's of greatness must be applied. They are desire, determination, drive, and dedication. A person must desire to win. If he wants to climb Mt. Olympus, he must be determined to do what is needed to climb Mt. Olympus. This also takes a level of commitment or dedication. For any goal in life, one has to also have drive or a magnetic push toward something.

Michael Jordan is the quintessential poster child of the 4D's of greatness. He had an inner drive that propelled him past defenders onto six championships, into NBA Hall of Fame, and now owner of his own NBA franchise. Michael did not even start for his high school basketball team, but he persevered and eventually made it as a college basketball star. His determination and spirit led him to the NBA where he became an All-Star and eventually MVP and leading scorer. This book discusses the importance of self-esteem, patience, perseverance, peace of mind, hutspa, and more. It will include profiles, anecdotes, and lessons so that you can achieve an inner feeling commensurate with success and greatness.

The night sky is illuminated by a constellation. Man's mind is illuminated by bright ideas. The configuration of ideas in your mind determines your destiny. Let's shed light on this concept of illumination in an otherwise dark world. The brain is the most complex entity that exists. Made of protoplasm and billions of brain cells and white matter, the brain stores all of man's ideas. Excitement lights the brain up. The cerebral powers of man allow him to do amazing things. He conquers his obstacles and progresses upward in civilization. People shoot information at you; your brain takes on this information like an oncoming train and gives it meaning. You learn. You move forward. You pass the test of life.

When I first learned the power of my brain, I wanted to light it up like a light bulb. I wanted to use it as a mind is a terrible thing to waste. The rise of man depends on this. There is nothing more inspiring than human beings progressing. I was inspired by the likes of Garret Morgan, inventor of the traffic light and gas mask apparatus, Lewis Lattimer, inventor of the carbon filament that makes the incandescent light work, or the Wright brothers who gave us flight. These men had their minds illuminated with bright ideas. What gave them their inspiration?

Their minds were illuminated. They were inspired by greatness, coming up with something that doesn't exist until their minds thought of it. It was the dawn of a new day once they came up with their brilliant ideas. What would make a man fly a kite in the middle of a thunder storm? Ben Franklin flew that kite first in his mind and went on to invent electricity. What gave the Pharaohs of Egypt the inspiration to design the pyramids? What inspires a man to want to make something of himself? He knows where he doesn't want to end up and under what conditions he doesn't want to live under. He knows he doesn't want to be poor and wanting and that he must meet his needs. It starts with the mind. The mind moves you from where you are to where you can be. Knowledge is power; you must feed your mind the way a mother feeds her baby. You must feed it knowledge. Everyone won't master physics the way Einstein did, but everyone must master their environment to survive. When survival is at stake, the mind must be illuminated. He must spring up ideas that will put him in position to succeed.

He must have willpower and focus. He must have drive and determination. It's fascinating to see how a woman like Harriet Tubman could free hundreds of slaves by following a star in the sky. It's fascinating to see how Matthew Henson climbed several feet of snow to find for the first time the North Pole. It is indeed fascinating to know how Dr. Charles Drew invented blood plasma, a substitution for blood. Think of how Dr. Martin Luther King, Jr. made his dream a reality. We remember his prodigious mountains and heightening Alleghenies and his dream that illuminated his mind. He knew where he didn't want to end up and under what conditions he didn't want to live under.

Grab the greatness of an idea from the clouds. Get inspiration from the blue sky above. Be a thinker. Be inspired to do great things. Let your mind wander off into places far away. Let your mind generate power like a windmill or a steamship. The glory of man is the glory of ideas. Every man gets an idea once a year that can gain him riches. There's nothing like an idea whose time has come. It's time for you to perform what your brain can perform. Thus, you can make something out of nothing and be great. Whether it be the sun, moon, stars, the Cosmos, that inspire you or a person of great latitude, make light out of every dark situation and be great. Illuminate.

Rise up. Make like that plant rising above the soil to reach sunlight. Measure up to your own standards. Live the life you want to live. Be free. Never be sedimentary, always be moving. Rise up like that giraffe stretching its neck to reach the fruit of tall trees. Never succumb to adversity. Grow. Move with the speed of enthusiasm to take on life's greatest challenges. No matter how tough the challenge, you be tougher. Advance to your greatest intellect. When the weight of the world is against you, rise up. When you can not beat the odds, rise up. When there is thunder and lightning in your life, weather the storm and rise up. Be greater than your conditions. Be greater than your greatest fears.

Barack Obama wanted to be the nation's next president. He was against a wall of challenges. He dug deep inside of himself and rose up. He became the nation's next president. Rising up against one's circumstances is a mental engagement. Such an enterprise requires one to dig deep inside looking for inner strength and will to overcome their obstacles. A young boy grew up in a tough inner city neighborhood with gangs, drugs, and violence. He had a desire despite this to make something of himself. He rose up excelling in school and in football and eventually graduated from college and obtained his masters degree from a prestigious university. That young boy was me. Time and time again when I had nothing and things were stacked up against me, I had to rise up. My mind was made up to do something about my circumstances, my challenges. I chose to be greater than what was in front of me.

Steveland Morris was born blind. This was an obstacle of tremendous magnitude. Relying on his ability to hear well, Steveland rose up and became Stevie Wonder, a great musician that the world admires tremendously. His example for the world was that you can do amazing things despite adversity. One of the ingredients that allow you to rise is desire – wanting something really badly. Gabriel Douglass was a young gymnast who wanted to succeed at her sport. She worked tirelessly on her craft in the gym until she perfected her skill. Her sheer desire and determination led her to win two gold medals in the Olympics. Having desire is a positive psychological state. Once you achieve the mindset, the next step is to carry out your vision.

If you believe in something strong enough, nothing can hold you back. Desire can spring one into action like a burning flame. It can help you rise up against hindrances in life no matter how difficult. Philosophically rising up against adversity is not just human nature. It involves a psychological process of the mind in which a person recognizes a need to mobilize his inner forces to overcome circumstances and achieve a better state of being. This does not automatically occur with every individual. Often a person has a disposition to want to a better state or is bred or taught to want more for himself. Often the suffering forces man to act in some way.

We have to achieve in life in order to prolong life. It takes destiny and conviction but often starts with adversity. The right mindset builds correct action. A champ has the right mindset. This is required to succeed. Every action prompts an equal positive reaction. Nothing in the Universe can be destroyed. Certainly Herculean effort can not be destroyed. It is a necessity for success. Rising up when the time comes is a necessity. When the darks sky is lit up it is the stars way of rising up and answering the call of the Universe.

Answering the call of the Universe is the task of a champ. He must act and react to the positive and negative. His result must match his effort. His diligence must not falter. His swagger must be present at all times. A champ is someone who overcomes a force of some kind. He is someone who beats mediocrity and separates himself from the pack. Also, a champ is anyone who is being the greatest he can be. He is someone who has blasted off like a rocket ship.

One has to have a strong feeling about oneself. In other words, one must have self-esteem. Part of having self-esteem is believing in yourself – believing that given any situation you can succeed. You can do it. You have to believe vehemently in the positive traits that make you *you*. It is a tremendous deficit in one's character not to have self-esteem. If you want to be a star, then be a star; but you must first believe you can be a star. Much like a lion roars, you must roar. You must allow your talents to come to fruition. When I played college football, I had to believe in my positive traits in order to be successful. I won a NCAA league championship. As a masters student my belief in myself allowed me to master the curriculum and graduate from a top graduate program.

Self-esteem is a psychological state of mind or condition. It is built in a person over time by their upbringing and their environment, especially how they respond to both. A person must formulate a positive feeling or orientation of himself. Philosophically, a person will develop a positive feeling of himself if the people around him are positive toward him.

Self-esteem goes a long way. It helped Jesse Owens win four gold medals in a mere forty-five minutes at the Berlin Olympics. It helped Dr. Martin Luther King, Jr. win a Nobel Peace Prize.

Self-esteem led Dr. Condeleeza Rice to obtain a PhD from a prestigious Stanford University and serve as a cabinet member for the president of the United States. It helped Lebron James go from a young eighteen year old high school basketball star to a NBA legend. This section will discuss many who had self-esteem and how it propelled them to great feats in life. It will also discuss self-esteem in general as possessed by a champ with personal stories and lessons from the author and others. Finally, a profile of Paul Robeson, the all-American, will be offered to show how one man armed with self-esteem achieved so much in his illustrious career as an actor, singer, lawyer, linguist, and activist. The hope is that the reader will likewise arm himself with self-esteem to meet many of the challenges they will face.

If you think positively about yourself, then you will likewise act positively. Additionally, positive things will happen to you. As James Allen said, "As a man thinketh, so shall he be." His prophetic words are words to live by. If a plant has healthy roots, then most likely the plant will be healthy too. The root of all personal achievement, whether it be like that of Theodore Roosevelt or John F. Kennedy, is self-esteem. These presidents made their mark on the history of this world by having a positive view of themselves to begin with. They faced adversity during their climb to the top, but armed with self-esteem, they were to overcome these much like a bird or airplane overcoming gusty winds to fly ahead to their destination.

My belief is that young children who exhibit self-esteem will do better in school than those with low self-esteem. The low achievement levels of many of our youth are rooted in low self-esteem. As a youth I was able to master self-esteem as I was an elementary student and a Pop Warner football player. My grades reflected this. I was an 'A' honor roll student throughout elementary school. My outstanding performance on the football field also reflected this positive self-esteem that I possessed. The teachers around me as well as the coaches were positive toward me as were members of my family.

As a youngster I had positive role models to look up to. My older brother was a private in the army and a former football player. He was a good student in school. He and I had a good relationship – playing football together in the streets. He was my #1 fan and promoter too; always bragging about my football skills to his friends. I also looked up to a lot of NFL players and some NBA players as well. The Pittsburg Steelers had the great Terry Bradshaw, Franco Harris, and Lynn Swan as well as "Mean" Joe Green. I was inspired by their play and it made me feel good about myself. The rival was the Dallas Cowboys. This Super Bowl team had Roger Staubach, Tony Dorsett, and Drew Prearson. I also looked up to Earl Campbell of the Houston Oilers and Lawrence Taylor of the New York Giants. In the NBA, there was Dr. J, Moses Malone, Darryl Dawkins, Magic Johnson, Larry Bird, and Kareem Abdul-Jabar. I got a great feeling from watching these greats. In business I looked up to real estate mogul, Donald Trump and in politics one day, Jimmy Carter came to my city. I was astonished. These great role models helped me by inspiring me to want greatness myself.

Self-esteem for me as a child meant being able to manage my life and solve arising problems. Being a precocious child, my mother left me to my own devices. I knew how to go to school, go to football, basketball, and baseball practice, work to help the family with day-to-day issues. All this culminated into the greatest accomplishment of my young life – at 13 years old I was named Pop Warner National Scholar. I was one of only thirty-five to be named such honor in the country. For this I received several accolades including a Mayor's Proclamation. This really boosted my self-esteem and was positive reinforcement. I truly believed in myself and my ability to write as the criteria was essay writing, grades, and football performance.

When developing a personal view of myself, I looked at my impact on other people. As a scholar-athlete on an early path of achievement, I brought joy and excitement to a lot of people. My volunteer work in the community with those younger me and also older than me saw me bringing light to the lives of many. I felt the self-efficacy and value in it all. My self-esteem was positively reinforced because of my ability to impact others.

A seamstress by the name of Rosa Parks had self-esteem. One day after work and being tired, Rosa refused to give up her seat on a bus and this led to the largest boycott of the civil rights movement. Rosa believed in herself and her action made history. A man by the name of Jesse Jackson had self-esteem enough to run for president of the United States. His platform was "Keep Hope Alive" and although he did not get elected, he made significant strides speaking at the Democratic National Convention. Flying in with the wind, Bill Russell won eleven championships with the Boston Celtics of the NBA. He believed in his talent, intelligence, skill, and himself.

Bill Clinton, a Rhodes Scholar, who obtained a Masters in History from the prestigious Oxford University in England, became president of the United States of America. His great self-esteem was apparent as he had the strongest economy in U.S. history. By the age of 32, Ben Carson became one of the nation's leading brain surgeons. He was also known for his speaking to audiences about pride and self-esteem. My personal favorite was Paul Robeson, valedictorian of Rutgers University in 1919, who spoke 20 languages. His story will be profiled later in this book. His self-esteem was immense.

My personal success did not occur overnight. It took a process of overcoming economic dislocation, athletic injuries, illness, loss of loved ones, and more. But my self-esteem was relentless like Robeson and I was able to overcome my obstacles for the most part. Now I am an author, businessman, mentor, and world traveler. My greatest accomplishment to date was being accepted into a PhD program in Marketing after obtaining a Masters of Business Administration from Purdue University.

Self-esteem is a psychological trait. You either have it or you don't. It can be taught; that's the good news, but if a person is not in a positive environment conducive to his development, self-esteem is negligible. When a person receives positive feedback from other people it positively affects their self-esteem. When its constantly negative feedback, then a person may view himself negatively in relation to others.

Writer Maya Angelou wrote a poem entitled, *Still I Rise*. This is a positive poem and the person narrating has a positive view of herself. She has self-esteem. Maya herself is a writer with great self-esteem and skill. Toni Morrison, a Nobel Prize in Literature Laureate writes with confidence and an apparent self-esteem. They follow the footsteps of the Pulitzer Prize winning author, Ralph Ellison who wrote the novel, *Invisible Man*. Princeton professor and acclaimed author, Dr. Cornel West, has a great deal of self-esteem as his writing has touched academia in large proportions.

My younger brother, Darryl, was fourteen years old and a freshman in high school. He had little experience at the running back position prior to high school, but had the self-esteem inside of himself to start running back for a large group four high school varsity football team. The first time he touched the ball he ran for over 50 yards. When I was fourteen I played for my high school's football team. The team was full of big, strong, and talented players. I was talented but not as big and strong. However, I believed in myself from prior games in Pop Warner football and was able to secure the back up tailback position as a freshman. I went on later to be captain of the team and leading scorer. After high school I earned a position on a college football team. These successes could not be achieved without a saturation of self-esteem.

50 Cent was a drug dealer who wanted more than just this lifestyle. He hustled for years and made money as a dealer, but wanted to enter the music industry as a rapper. He had the talent and the self-esteem to transfer his skills as a drug dealer to the music industry as a rapper. He signed with Dr. Dre and Eminem and became a major success. He changed the way a rapper's career was managed by doing things unconventional, his own way. 50 Cent later succeeded as an actor and businessman and now has an empire worth over $250million.

Desire something out of life; be ambitious. Know that there is light at the end of the tunnel and a pot of gold at the end of the rainbow. Create a life for yourself or as Anthony Robbins, a motivator says, "Design a life for yourself." You must make your mark on history, carve out your own niche like 50 Cent. Stand for something. If you don't stand for something, you'll fall for anything. Desire is something that transcends beyond boundaries. There is no limit to what you can desire. Maybe you want to be a millionaire or even billionaire or maybe you want to own your first home or become a doctor. There is no limit. In fact, the Cosmos is not even the limit. Go beyond the stratosphere, the luminous sky. You stand out like that. Be peculiar. Have expensive tastes. Want the most out of life for yourself and your loved ones. Have relentless self-esteem.

Michael Jackson grew up in Gary, Indiana with his parents and siblings. They were poor and lived in a tiny house. However, with self-esteem, Michael led his family to the music industry, forming the Jackson 5. They desired fame and fortune and would shoot for the stars. After hard work and dedication, Michael and his brothers along with Motown Records, became stars in their own right. Michael launched a solo career in which he performed the best selling album of all time, "Thriller" with Quincy Jones. Michael performed on tour and at the Grammy Awards and took the world on by storm. His bright light was shined on the music world for many years as he amassed great fame and fortune. He became an international icon. Michael believed in himself and his abilities to get to the top and he never looked back. He reached the Promised Land.

When I was eighteen, I was an accounting intern at the Fortune 500 corporation, Johnson & Johnson. There I worked with accountants, accounting managers, controllers, and financial analysts. Only eighteen years old and with just two years of high school accounting, I had to believe in myself every time I stepped into the building. My self-esteem allowed me to flourish in my immediate environment. I received a great evaluation for my first internship and was invited to come back that winter.

Elizabeth Taylor was a very beautiful actress. She starred in movies and became a star. She won numerous awards for her acting as leading lady with an impressive list of co-stars. In addition to being beautiful, she had a great deal of self-esteem that propelled her like an airplane to stardom. Like Michael Jackson, Elizabeth Taylor became an international success. Everything she touched seemed to turn to gold. She is a great example of drive and determination and a great role model for us all; she was a great actress.

Track and field star, Michael Johnson is blazin'. One of the fastest men ever to live, Johnson has the Olympic world record in the 400 meter dash. He formerly held the world record in the 200 meter dash as well. Johnson is a bolt of lightning across a track. He now is a track and field analyst. He possessed an inner feeling un-daunted by the tough competition. He had great self-esteem. Johnson was widely known for blasting his competition or breaking away from the pack by a sizable margin. He was amazing. The gold medalist had an ambition to be the very best, to be the champion, and his self-esteem allowed him to follow such an ambition.

Self-esteem is an aspect of character and character is an important virtue for any man. We remember Dr. King's "content of his character." The content of man's character is his most important characteristic. The positivity within himself is a major part of his virtue. Positivity must flow in his mind and there must be no room for negativity. A man must be a quality individual who thinks with an open mind. A parent who takes care of her young has character. A teacher who bestows knowledge onto his student has character. A faithful wife has character. A president who acts in the interest of his fellow citizens has character. You too must have character.

Believing in oneself or having self-esteem is no new phenomenon. 2500 years before the Greek Hippocrates, known as the Father of Medicine, existed, a priest, architect, and medicine man by the name of Imhotep existed. Imhotep was around during the time of King Dsojer, Pharaoh of Egypt. In fact, it was Imhotep who built the first pyramid at Saquarra for King Dsojer. Imhotep, was a multifaceted-multitalented genius and was responsible for the discovery of blood circulating in the veins. He was associated with the quote, "Eat, drink, and be merry." He was known as the God of Medicine prior to Hippocrates. He was also a philosopher and wise man. He had a positive self-esteem and his achievements reflect this.

Eleanor Roosevelt, wife of President Franklin Delano Roosevelt was a champion of the people. The first lady assumed many leadership roles while her husband was in office for twelve years. She dedicated herself to many causes including equal rights and was known to have helped get the Tuskegee Airmen their chance to fly. Eleanor was outspoken and very visible as first lady. She supported her husband during times of peace and times of war. She had excellent self-esteem and her actions showed this. She was instinctive and ambitious and had a desire to improve the lives of people and she did.

My mother, Theresa, was a single parent of eight children. If it were not for her self-esteem she would not have made it. Working two jobs in which at times she had to walk several miles to and from work, she took on the challenge with tenacity. She wanted better for her children than what she had. She was very involved in her children's education and extra-curricular activities. After years of relentless effort and strong will, she was successful in raising her eight children. Her achievement is often overlooked, but worthy of admiration. She did it by believing in herself and having a positive feeling about herself.

Contrary to the fallaciousness of our perceptions, people with self-esteem do succeed. People with self-esteem can fly. If they conceive it, they can achieve it. It is the absence of self-esteem that causes underachievement. The absence of self-esteem correlates with the absence of greatness. It takes a lot to be great. There is no one formula or algorithm, but perseverance, self-esteem, and determination are a common denominator for those who do become great. When Tiger Woods became great at golf at an early age, he possessed perseverance, drive, and tenacity. His upbringing and environment had built a strong self-esteem and self-image within him.

They say birds of a feather flock together. Thus, people who have self-esteem often are around like-minded people. This is transcendence. A bright star can be so bright that it makes other stars in the constellation appear bright as well. When I played high school and college football, I hung around the teammates that I wanted to like the most. I rubbed elbows with them, learned from them, and depended on them. It is a heuristic that if you hang around people with positive attributes, their positive attributes will become your positive attributes. So if they are driven and they have self-esteem, this will have a positive effect on you.

The sun shines its rays on those with self-esteem. Your chances in life are increased when you are armed with self-esteem. The tortoise was able to beat the hare in a race to the finish line because he had a good feeling about himself. When your time to shine comes you must be ready. Your mind must be ready and ready to tackle any challenge and overcome any obstacle. This requires positive self-image. When you look in the mirror each morning, you must feel good about what you see because as they say if you look good, you feel good.

Let us take a step back to Self-esteem 101. If you are good at something, more likely it will increase your self-esteem. At 32, Serena Williams was the oldest #1 ranked tennis player in history. She won more major tournaments than any other player ever. This U.S. Open champion and Wimbledon champion is good at what she does and as a result has tremendous self-esteem. It's not just her athletic ability that allows her to win, but her inner feeling about herself – a mental edge. Off the court she is a fashion designer and actress as well as businesswoman.

Patti Labelle is a legendary soul, R&B, and rock & roll singer. Her inner feeling about herself has led her to a career in music that lasted five decades. She had numerous hits from her many albums and has received several awards. Her soul-stirring voice is known throughout the world and she is known for her vibrant and lively performance. Off stage and out of the studio, Patti is a humanitarian. You can hear her vocal chords ring loud and clear all over the atmosphere.

Much like a caterpillar larvae, man goes through a metamorphosis as well. Remember a caterpillar spins a cocoon when it's ready. This cocoon is a shell that protects itself from its environment. It matures in the cocoon and develops wings needed to fly as a beautiful butterfly. A man goes through different developmental stages as well. He matures over time and rises to be a beautiful adult. However, if in the developmental stages, he doesn't develop self-esteem, there is something in the developmental stage that is lacking. So he becomes a butterfly incapable of flying.

When I ran track I was a sprinter. My track coach would always yell while we were running, "Run for time!" She meant even if you do not finish first, second, or third, run for your best personal time ever. This means be the best that you can be. Being the best that you can possibly be and running for time is a part of self-esteem. Not everyone can be Tiger Woods or Michael Jordan, but anyone can succeed at being the best that they can be.

The sky will not always be blue and there will be rainy days. With self-esteem in tact, you can weather the storm. This means that no matter how difficult times get, if you have a strong feeling about yourself, you can overcome difficulty. I had to overcome economic dislocation and loss of loved ones growing up. Many people have to overcome illness like Jackie Joyner-Kersey. She had to overcome serious asthma and other breathing problems to win gold at the Olympics. Her will and self-esteem embodied the spirit of the Olympic athlete.

Mozart was a classical musician. His songs made him internationally famous and his music is widely listened to even today. His music relaxes his listeners and many classical musicians today model their careers after him. Mozart learned classical music and at an early age and with self-esteem, he continued to progress until he became one of the best musicians ever.

Barack Obama was a Harvard Law professor who taught Constitutional Law. He was also a community organizer. It dawned on this intelligent man that he could enter politics and he became a U.S. senator. After just one term as senator, Barack armed with relentless self-esteem and confidence decided to run for president. He had the slogan, "Yes We Can!" After campaigning for months he won the Democratic Party nomination for president. He overcame all the doubt and disbelief. People said he was not experienced enough, but Barack believed in himself. He became president of the United States of America.

One of the best lessons in self-esteem was the story of a person I knew by the name of Jack Jones. Jack Jones was an idiosyncratic youth who got into a lot of trouble growing up. He was an only child and his mother was always working. Jack was not a very good student in school and would get suspended for misbehaving quite frequently. His peers and older people from the neighborhood said that he wouldn't amount to anything. Jack did believe in himself though and was good at something. He was always making something with his hands. Although no one believed in him, he had somehow developed a great deal of self-esteem much of which he got from his mother talking positively to him.

Jack spent one summer as an apprentice at a machine shop. Here he developed a work ethic to go along with his inventive spirit. Jack saved a lot of money at the end of the summer and invested the money into a series of inventions. Over the course of ten years, Jack had fifteen inventions and sold them to corporations for over twenty million dollars. His example was one that showed that with ability, hard work, and self-esteem, one can beat the odds and make something of oneself.

Where can self-esteem take you? Self-esteem can take you to the highest plateau. With no reservations you can climb to the top. When you have self-esteem, you likewise have high expectations for yourself. You set the bar very high for yourself. Your standards are very high. You do not settle and you want nothing but the best for yourself. This is reflected in your career and in your life. You have to be focused on your goals as if you were a periscope protruding the ocean to focus on an object on shore. With the self-esteem and focus of a champ, you can meet expectations in common hours. Ultimately acting and thinking like a champ and king is about one's self-esteem in essence.

We desire greatness. The opposite of greatness is mediocrity. It's not just individuals that can be mediocre, but there can be a state of mediocrity in general. When a nation is at war the way we are in Afghanistan, then we are in a state of mediocrity. As a nation we are not where we want to be or where we can be. We've had World War I and II, Korea, Vietnam, and Iraq in the past. Our nation has been plagued with conflict throughout its history including the Civil War.

A nation experiences mediocrity when it is plagued with crime and violence. Today there are over 1.1million people incarcerated in our country for crimes they committed. A sociological report stated that it was safer to be in the Vietnam War than it is today to live in some U.S. cities according to the homicide rate. Violent crimes are up in the country as is white collar crime. Gang violence is prevalent in this country and police brutality shakes the conscience of this nation at an alarming rate in recent times.

Terrorism such as 9/11 shatters the comfort zone of America. We are victims of terrorism at home and abroad. The bombing of the Boston Marathon rocked our nation as many died or were severely injured. Ferguson, Missouri showed us that we do not value human life the way we should in the 21st century. Nearly a century ago, Harvard scholar, W.E.B. Dubois wrote, "The problem of the 21st century is the problem of the color line." This belief is still applicable today in that we are still a nation that is infiltrated by racism and bigotry across all race categories. In the work force there is still a glass ceiling and there is income disparity based on race as well. We suffer from redlining and gentrification in the housing market.

As a nation we have had to declare a war on drugs. Drug abuse is out of control and many lives are being destroyed. Many go to jail due to drug related offenses while others have mediocre existences because of drug abuse. We are clearly facing a crisis of great dimensions in our nation with respect to illegal drugs. Our youth is experimenting with drugs and its affecting their development as adults.

Our educational system leaves much to be desired as well. We were once a leader in education in the world now this has been compromised. Currently, American students rank only 22nd in the world in mathematics. This is exacerbated by schools that are underfunded and not a priority in appropriations by politicians and leaders. Science and the arts have lagged behind in the American educational system. Many students can not afford the costs of college education and can not enroll therefore. We can only be great as a nation if our educational system is great.

In the richest nation in the world, a superpower, a member of the G-7 nations, we still have a massive amount of poverty. For example, 44% of African-American children grow up in poverty. There are millions of homeless people in the United States and millions below the poverty line. The economy has struggled over the last decade being a recession. In Economics, a recession is defined as two consecutive declines in gross domestic product for the country. Our government faced a possible shut down and the federal trade deficit was excessive.

Our nation is plagued by incurable disease. AIDS is still an epidemic as it affects people in all walks of life and ages. Many of our states have declared a health crisis due to the number of instances. There is still not a cure for cancer as millions die due to this abnormal growth. Breast cancer affects hundreds of thousands of women and hundreds of thousands of men are affected by prostate cancer. Diabetes is a common disease as many people have the risk factors for such a disease. There are also 9 million mentally ill persons in America affected by bi-polar disorder, schizophrenia, and schizoaffective disorder.

Now there is individual mediocrity in addition to the state of mediocrity previously described. This is a situation where an individual is not being everything he could possibly be or is below average. This in turn has a psychological effect on the individual. This individual misses out on the rewards of life including financial, social, and political. His self-esteem may be negatively impacted in addition to his wealth and status. He may have never experienced the glory of the great.

Many have lost their jobs because of COVID 19. Many scramble to make ends meet. He struggles with productivity and excellence. He doesn't get promoted or rewarded for his efforts. He is constantly finishing last in the race of life. He has ignorance where others have knowledge. His problems baffle him and he has no self-efficacy, the ability to do things effectively.

A mediocre state means you do not go the extra mile. You do not receive the respect of others and do not compete well with others. This warrants the name Average Joe. A mediocre man doesn't have "game". He doesn't set high expectations for himself and his standards are not high like the great ones. His mind is unsettled; he must make amends. He is not at peace, he doesn't feel free and he doesn't know himself or like himself either. A mediocre man is an underachiever. He is plagued by dismal performance in the classroom, sports arena, social arena, workforce, and life.

However, there is a reassuring fact: a state of mediocrity for a nation can be temporary as it is for an individual. A nation can rise. It can rise under new leadership or the collective rise in psyche and work ethic of the people. An individual can rise. He can have a transformation of mind and mindset and can become great. He can go from an underachiever to an overachiever. There are thousands of stories about people who were mediocre at one time to become great later. Again, Michael Jordan did not even make his high school varsity basketball team only to later transform into a NBA star. This book is a proponent of the same type of transformation process. It requires that you make like a champ and think like a king.

Mediocrity is undesirable. It is the antithesis of being a champ. They don't exhibit the same qualities and characteristics. Where the mediocre fail, a champ succeeds, where mediocre falls, a champ stands tall. A champ can't stand mediocrity. This is what's in him. This is how he thinks. This is how he acts. He is destined to blast off from mediocrity. He is destined to launch from the ground.

Chapter 3:
Herculean Effort

◇◇◇◇◇◇◇◇◇◇

During COVID 19, we must still strive for success. Success can alleviate us from the burden of mediocrity and illuminate us with a light of value, excitement, and happiness. It is the most sought after process that exists in the Universe. People seek it with varying degrees of desire and perseverance and think about it often. It preoccupies the minds of billions of people and yet we still cannot agree on a single definition of success. What is success? This is an important question to pose even before striving for such a thing.

Success, or *chenggog* as is translated in Chinese, is not just an outcome or result, but rather it is a process. This is a process of putting together the pieces of the puzzle to make all the parts fit. Success in life, career, and sports all involve an individual putting his knowledge, experience, lessons, talent, and skills to meet a goal. Tiger Woods put the pieces if his puzzle together by combining what his parents taught him, his training, talent, lessons, and skills to win several majors in the sport of golf at an early age. Bill Gates combined innovation and focus to found Microsoft Corporation and at one time was worth over $81 billion. Most people would say that he was successful.

Most people would define success in this manner by giving examples and stories of people or corporations that have succeeded.

In the past they cited businessmen like Rockefeller, Carnegie, and Ford and athletes like Babe Ruth, Hank Aaron, or Jackie Robinson. They mentioned events like the discovery of a cure for tuberculosis or Neil Armstrong landing on the moon or the Cosmonauts. Today many define success by giving examples such as Gates, Dell, and Buffet and athletes like Michael Jordan, Tiger Woods, Wayne Gretsky, the Williams sisters, and Lance Armstrong. They cite events such as the invention of the Internet and the advancement of digital technology. Using examples to define success is helpful to paint a picture, but to understand the essence of what success as a process is, one must know what is called the properties of success.

There are six main properties of success. In science, a property is defined as a quality or trait that identifies a substance. The properties of the substance stay the same even if the volume changes. Through nanotechnology, the properties of matter are identified. Matter is anything that takes up space and has mass. It assumes four states: liquid, solid, gas, and plasma. Its properties include purity, density, color, mass, and composition. It has resistance, a boiling point where liquid is turned to gas and a freezing point where liquid is turned to a solid.

Matter is made up of molecules. Gas, another chemical, is a state of matter and takes up space, but not always the same space or keeps the same shape. Analogously, success can be broken into properties that identify its qualities or traits or processes. Like chemicals, the properties of success stay the same. Substances are broken into two kinds of properties: chemical and physical. Similarly, success is broken into two kinds of properties: mental and practical. Success is made up of molecules also: intangible and tangible qualities or elements. Gas is a state of matter and takes up space; success is a state of mind and requires the practical use of space or action. Using this analog, the properties of success are that 1) it is not finite but continuous 2) it involves a cycle or pattern of ups and downs 3) it is not the opposite of failure 4) it is a mental and practical process 5) it involves making necessary transitions and 6) it is not universally measured.

The first property states: Success is not finite, it is continuous. In geometry they teach us the difference between an endpoint and a line. An endpoint is an isolated point in a geometric space and often people have isolated points in time when they are successful. A person being given a promotion, a quarterback throwing a touchdown, or a student scoring 100% on her first exam are examples of success for a point or moment in time. However, like a line, success is a process that is not constrained by a geometric space or moment in time. Success is a continuous process of always striving to gather pieces of the ultimate puzzle and striving to meet goals.

The reason the line continues is that once one goal is met, new goals arise, and new challenges. Also, success begets success and having success for a moment in time or space does not satisfy our growing desire for success. If Tiger would have settled for a finite moment of success by retiring after one major victory, he may not have satisfied his personal standard for success and not viewed as the most successful golfer ever by fans and players.

Even an individual project or goal involves a continuous and not finite process. For example, a heavyweight boxer often comes into the ring looking to get one clean shot and expects success to occur.

Obviously, this is a knockout. However, what if the opposing boxer has a strong chin and endures that punch, you have to keep on fighting. Knowing that success is continuous is a key step in developing the patience necessary to meet goals we set.

I am of the philosophy that success is not at an isolated point. For example, current success is tied or connected to success one has had in the past. The success that Walter Payton had becoming the all-time leading rusher in the NFL was connected to lessons and successes he had even as early as Pop Warner and high school football. Thus, it is a building process over time. One must continuously build on one's progress.

Property #2 states that success involves a cycle of ups and downs. Murphy's Law dictates that things may go wrong and they do. During my journey to become a scholar, I faced many tragedies and obstacles that I simply could not have predicted. When it rained it poured. My economic dislocation, injury, deaths in the family, and serious illness were all difficult conditions to accept and deal with. Successes did occur in between these downs and a cycle seemed to be apparent. In fact, my most devastating tragedy occurred almost right after my most successful period of success as a student, athlete, and world traveler. This is the nature of the success process. Success is rarely a linear process. A person has to climb a hill to success. The reality of it is that a person has ups and downs, peaks and valleys, is successful at times followed by low points. It's like a EKG reading. In competitive situations such as a tennis match, a good serve or volley is often followed by an unforced error or the overplaying of the ball. The very knowledge that success has this property prepares us for such a journey and is the first step in overcoming obstacles. It offers us resilience, tenacity, and the ability to remain focused.

Property #3 states that success is not the opposite of failure. In life I learned just as much from those who had failed than those who had succeeded. Failure is not the opposite of success. Henry Ford said, "Failure is an opportunity to begin again more intelligently." Thomas Edison had 10,000 failures before he successfully invented the light bulb. It was a necessary part of the process. He extracted lessons and value from the failures and put the pieces together. This was his discovery process.

If we are correct in arguing that failure is part of the success process, then one must not fear failure. This would mean that one fears a vital part of success. There is a steep learning curve in many failures and learning is one of the building blocks toward success. Transitively, one should not fear learning, especially from mistakes and failures. As a Pop Warner star, I honed in on what my coaches were telling me what they had done wrong in their careers such as not focusing on school and focusing. When you fail at something you gain knowledge of what not to do and mentally you know where you do not want to end up again.

You can survive failure and take the lessons that will put you in position to succeed. In fact, many of your successes may be connected to or a product of something you discovered when you failed. Thus, it is the rule not the exception that you must fail in order to succeed. You learn from your mistakes. Turn your failures into success of equal or greater magnitude. The knowledge that failure is a part of success or that success is a derivative of failure in many respects allows us to look to learn from our failures and not be mentally crushed by momentary failures before success can be achieved. Failures also help us appreciate when we meet our goals.

Messages flow from the mind. The brain contains billions of synaptic nerves that pass messages from one brain cell to another in a process. The thought precedes the action in a process. Likewise, success is a process and not just the final outcome. Most of us tend to believe that success occurs at the end of the endeavor via the championship, victory, or crown. However, knowledge of the process would lead us to know that the major fertilization of that success occurs when the seed of success is first deeply planted in the mind of the goal seeker. Success can not occur until the goal seeker has a vision in his mind of actually carrying out the act. He has to first see it in his mind. The mind produces the roots of success and the goal seeker must then live out what he sees in his mind.

The victory or outcome is more a reflection of this mental process. Therefore, success has the property of being both a mental and practical process of seeing it, then believing it, and finally doing it. As Napolean Hill, the author with one of the most popular success formulas, put it, "Whatever the mind of man can conceive and believe, it can achieve." My sports success did not occur at the college stage or even high school stage. Its foundation occurred when I first saw someone accidently bite the bone of his Thanksgiving turkey because he was so encapsulated by a football game on television. Almost through osmosis, my mind took this in and I saw myself gloriously playing that game. I visualized it, dreamed it, and became it. Psychologists have found that visualization techniques or what they call creative imagination and behavioral techniques can lead to positive outcomes.

Many Olympic athletes are associated with this mental process. The continuous rehearsal of my vision in my mind gave it depth, strength, and a mental edge and clarity. By the time I stepped on the field it was natural. In my dream I was running the ball, breaking tackles, and scoring touchdowns. When I first started playing, my Pop Warner coach positioned me on the offensive line because I was not the fastest guy on the team. Since I rehearsed my vision so much in my mind I was confident in offering my coach a deal. If he gave me a chance to run the ball one time, I would not bother him any more. He agreed and I ran the ball with both grace and relentlessness, breaking several tackles and refusing to go down. The fullback position was now mine for the season. My success occurred before I physically ran the ball. I was not the most experienced for the position, but I saw it clearly in my mind and believed it. It was not until then that I did it.

The depth and details you have when seeing and visualizing your dream the better for you to flow right into its reality. What is vision but an idea given light? What is success but a vision given wings? The vision starts the process. Next is the belief and actual follow through. Of course, seeing it and believing it was the root of success for him, but Tiger Woods had to also fulfill the practical requirement of this process – training and working on his craft. From an early age he traveled all over the country playing golf, building his skills and confidence. Tirelessly and with the aim of perfection, he practiced and practiced and took in all the education and training that his father and coaches offered. Howbeit, he was mentally and practically in position to win at golf and life.

We had to navigate our thoughts and dreams. We were lit up. Traveling through space with dreams of illumination, our minds fly in places far away. The invention of electricity, the light bulb, and paper started with dreams in the minds of Franklin, Edison, and the Egyptians. The civil rights movement was led by a man who in 1963 declared, "I have a dream." Before Matthew Henson became the first person to reach the North Pole, he had to first see it, then believe it, then climb through feet of snow and gusty winds to place the American flag on the soil. In high school, whenever I wrote a poem or essay and win the academic fair, my mother would ask me, "That came out of that little mind?" Even before high school, as early as kindergarten, the first motivational motto they taught me was, "I think I can." Remember that? *I think* implies use of the mind and *I can* connotes a belief to be able to do something. This is a great way to begin an education, as we need to examine the possibility of our greatness.

I have been a motivational vessel since age 13 and started Intellectual, Inc. at age 20. My messages have evolved over the years, as have the messages of many speakers that I have been exposed to. However, this concept of seeing and believing has been a constant that has simply grown in stature much like my body since age 13. The height of this tall message can be seen by sharing some powerful words of some of the nation's top motivational speakers/coaches. They labor on a daily basis to help educate and inspire people to be great and their research supports our properties. Here are a few examples.

Dr. Wayne Dyer:

When pursuing a goal, the most important thing is to continuously hold in your mind the picture of yourself successfully completing that goal.

Believing in your own ideas, abilities, and decision-making ability is the first step to achieving success in life.

You are a product of whatever thoughts that you have.

Les Brown:

When you have a big dream in your head, you can overcome almost any obstacle.

Laurie Beth Jones:

All significant changes and inventions began with a vision first.

Seeing and believing is the mental aspect of success. The practical aspect involves what Coach K of the Duke University basketball team calls P & P – preparation and planning. When I was a nationally ranked sales consultant for a Fortune 500 company one of the things that they kept reinforcing to us was that people do not plan to fail, they fail to plan. This is applicable to people in all endeavors. One should not whimsically make plans; one should formulate detailed strategic plans and transfer them from their minds to carbon. Planning brings focus as Alexander Graham Bell proclaimed, "The sun's ray do not burn until it has a focus."

Then one should hone in on the preparation needed to mobilize the plan with the ability and preparation one will advance, the verb tense meaning to move forward, and must strive to be advanced, the adjective meaning to be bigger, better, and faster than the rest. With speed, muscles on their shoulders that look like mountains, agility, and size, athletes must master preparation to be the most advanced.

For instance, Grammy Award winning singer, Whitney Houston ascertained that preparation was one of the keys to her success. She gave the following advice to her fans, "It's better to be prepared for an opportunity and not have one, than to have an opportunity and not be prepared." They say practice helps you approach perfection. Preparation involves going through the scenarios that you'll face over until you become familiar with how to respond. Jordan talked about standing at the free-throw line with 10 million people watching him. In order to be poised and not fear failure, he relied on preparation. He describes the process, "So I mentally tried to put myself in a familiar place. I thought about all those times I shot free-throws in practice and went through the same motion, the same technique I had used thousands of times."

Preparation involves education and training as well. Gerald Ford prepared for the presidency by first getting a bachelors degree from Michigan and a law degree from Yale. He then trained in the area of law and politics through various positions. It also involves developing strategies to excel at a particular thing. The first African-American millionaire, Madame CJ Walker was a case in point. She held a job as a domestic and while performing her duties she would work on developing grooming products and services. She worked on this craft for many years and was eventually prepared to start her own million-dollar hair care and grooming company. Now one of America's top African-American businessmen is Sean "P Diddy" Combs. He started out as an intern for BET and while in the shadows of many great producers and managers in the music industry, he dreamed and more importantly worked on his craft at BET. Now he is CEO of Bad Boy.

The mental aspect of seeing and believing is best symbolized by what a basketball commentator said about Shaquille O'Neal. During the 2002 NBA Finals, this analyst said that Shaquille has already won this game in his mind. Believing nurtured a certain spirit in Shaq called the "will to win" and this is what he and his team became known for especially in the face of elimination. Emmitt Smith was told that he was too small to play in the NFL. Despite this, his mental vision and preparation propelled him to be the all-time leading rusher in the NFL. So the mental edge can help one overcome obstacles and beat odds. In the late 1960's Oklahoma Sooner Steve Owens was criticized as being too slow to be successful at runningback. However, a Cincinnati Bengals scout commented, "Owens may have run a 4.8 second 40-yard dash, but he runs a 4.5 in his mind."

Similarly, All-Pro wide receiver, Jerry Rice is not the fastest receiver in the game, but his talent and preparation helped him become the all-time leading receiver in the NFL. People in all areas and fields go through this process. Many of our most intriguing businessmen like Bill Gates, Michael Dell, Warren Buffet, Ross Perot, and Joshua Smith go through this process over and over. The late Reginald Lewis, businessman extraordinaire, describes in his autobiography how he used his mental wits to be among the big boys in business. Oprah Winfrey has mentally processed success. Bill Clinton did the same in creating the strongest economy our country has had in our history. One of his most respected and admired role models was a track star, Edwin Moses. Moses had an amazing determination and it was rooted in his ability to mentally and practically process his goal of being the best hurdler in the world. He did so for several years.

Relentless mental and practical preparation has made the likes of Tom Hanks, Denzel Washington, and Halle Berry top actors. Meticulous focus has helped Dr. Ben Carson become one of the nation's best brain surgeons. Maya Angelou and Toni Morrison are great writers and Anthony Robbins, Dennis Kimbro, and Les Brown are great motivators because they have mentally and practically processed success. Michael Jackson saw himself as a superstar in his youth and followed through on his vision producing *Thriller*, the best-selling album of all time. There are countless numbers of schoolteachers, accountants, firemen, dentists, and other everyday folk who have achieved their particular personal goals as well under the auspices of mental and practical processing.

It is vital to believe that it is possible to achieve intensity in some endeavor, career, or life activity. The depth of this belief largely determines your chances of success. It is not until this belief is deep that you will seek out and practically prepare to conquer these endeavors like you did competition for so long. Like Langston Hughes mentioned in a poem, a goal seeker cannot allow his dream or vision to be deferred. How deeply ingrained is your dream? Believe in the power of believing.

In conclusion, success doesn't occur with the actual winning of the game or the completion of a goal; but rather through the crystallization or end result of a process that occurs in the mind of a goal seeker. Thus, success is rooted in the actual acquisition of the mindset necessary for success to occur. So once you have the mindset needed for your goal, the next step is to prepare for the task and then follow through.

Following through a goal from start to finish was something I learned from completing football season after season through adversity. This built determination, discipline, and persistence. Finally, knowledge that success has this property helps us develop an approach to success. When one's actions are in syncopation with one's dream, one can expect the harmony of result. The purpose of Life is to be illuminated. To rise. In a dark world, one must shed light.

The fifth property of success is that success involves making necessary transitions. Tom Hanks starred in the blockbuster movie "Forrest Gump." In this movie, Forrest overcame a handicap and became an All-American football player. The popular chant of "Run Forest, run" transitioned into a football career in which he ran through his opponents and was invited to the White House. This was an intense feeling, but afterwards he too was faced with the question of "Now What?" he had to make yet another transition. Being exposed to seafood by friend Bubba, Forrest later became a multi-million dollar seafood entrepreneur.

He made a successful transition. Where would he have been had he not been exposed to a formula that helped him transition? How would the movie end then? Transitions are vital to survival. Your reflex, your response, your judgment, your adaptation, your analysis must be transitioned for the purpose of living. Noah Webster, author of Webster's Dictionary defines transition as 1) n. Passage from one place, condition, or stage to another; change. 2) Something as a period of time or a situation, that leads to another. From that definition we define passage as a way through or over; free entrance, exit, or transit; a passing. Condition is defined as – the state or mode in which a person or thing exists; state of health. Finally, the other operative word in our master definition is stage –

a distinct period or step in some development, progress, or process. We apply our definition of transition to our discussion on success.

Transition is passage from one place to another. When the goal seeker is in the prime of his or her career, he or she is in a certain place. This place can be called his comfort zone. They are active and satisfied with their lives at this point. However, when the career is over they are now in another place. This is a new and lonely, unfamiliar, and uncertain place. They miss the other place and are at a disjunction in their lives. Transition is just that, a junction in the lives of all people. They do not know how to get out of this new place but they know they must do so. Transition means getting the goal seeker out of that place and into another that is either home or close to home. Condition is the state or mode the person is in or state of health. Many people in this new unfamiliar place are unsure, imbalanced, out of sync and often have lowered self-esteem.

Transition would then have to be part mental as we said earlier. Their condition must have passage or an exit. Helping dreamers exit from this place and condition is the goal and it is going to require managing change in addition to the mental and practical processing of success. Finally, the word stage connotes that being in this foreign place and having this condition is a distinct period or step in the developmental process. Transition to me meant getting on a different path toward the same ambition or destination. My ambition is intensity and discovery. Football and sports was one path and now I am on another path. Many times, especially when I became ill, there was a need to sift focus or make a turn in my drive toward whatever goal permeated my consciousness. I remember meeting so many students in college who had changed their major two or three times.

They were changing directions or paths quite often but they were still headed to the same direction – a bachelor's degree. I argue that in all the many success stories out there that motivate and inspire us, they each feature a major transition or period of managing change. Managing change or what corporations call change management is an inevitable part of becoming successful over the course of a lifetime and in individual endeavors. Like failure, it is not the opposite of success. When the goal seeker is in that new unfamiliar place with no glory, this is a major change. After all, they have been in a comfort zone for a long time. It is what they know, what they do, what they think, and how they live. Then comes a long this thing called change and crisis can occur. However, as we pointed out, this is only a stage of the developmental process and the root word, transitory is defined as brief or ephemeral, so the goal seeker must believe that this can be only a brief visit to this unfamiliar place if they believe and "play their cards right".

Finally, there is no way in getting around or circumventing transitions. They are necessary. Transitions are required for personal development, learning, focus, and direction. Essentially, transitions are required for progress or a desired condition. Many people want things, but try to get around doing what is necessary to get those things. If you desire a certain condition, you must get used to making transitions and learning from them. When you first leave your parent's nest, you cannot avoid the realities of transition and change. When you graduate college and enter the workforce, there is no way to avoid mental and practical transition. After you get married, you can no longer think for one, you must transition to thinking for two. When a corporation enters a new industry in attempt to gain market share, they cannot avoid a new nature of competition and decision making nuances. They must transition physically, emotionally, financially, and spiritually.

The goal seeker must make the right turns and go in the right direction transitioning toward success. In a musical composition, a transition is defined as the connection of sections of music. If you think of your life as a musical composition, the lack of making transitions or connecting experiences creates a tune or life with no harmony or rhythm. No one wants to hear a flat note or fragmented note. To prevent the decrescendo of intensity it is required to deal with the change. Fully put to your mind this philosophy and knowledge that transitions are necessary to prepare you for such a process. Now what?

The sixth property of success is that success is not universally measured. Like Albert Einstein posited, it's all relative. Bill Gates amassed $81 billion and Michael Dell over $50 billion. Jordan won six championships and Bradshaw, four Super Bowls. Tiger Woods won more majors in a shorter period of time than any other golfer in history, Carl Lewis matched Jesse Owens' 1936 feat with four gold medals of his own at the 1984 Olympic games, Dan Marino threw 48 touchdowns in a single season, Wilt Chamberlain scored 100 points in a single game, Jesse Berkett hit over .400 two times and Cy Young won 511 baseball games. Michael Jackson's *Thriller* went platinum multiple times.

When I worked at Johnson & Johnson in the early nineties they were grossing annual sales of over $11 billion and a net profit of over $1 billion. In these cases we are talking about a lot of money, great accomplishments, and honors. Are these automatically good indicators of success? Just like there are many definitions of success, success is measured differently by different people. It is not universally measured. It's all relative. More importantly, flow into the belief that success must be measured by the goal seeker himself and not by others. It must be measured from within not from without. It is the heart that measures success.

The theory of relativity, Newtonian Physics, the Pathagorean theorem, Gauss' statistics and the formulas of Algebra Walamucabula combined cannot completely mathematically calculate or measure success. The Geometric space where success is measured is in the heart and mind of the goal-seeker, the competitor. Competing with the possibility of not succeeding, the competitor often digs deep in the gut to win. So when he does win it is the feeling in this very gut that he carries with him, not just the trophy, honor, or money. The material aspect of success, money and fame comes and goes.

A company has the concept of the bottom line, profit. However, as they teach us in business school, their goal is to create value for the shareholder. Measuring success is more about values than about the accumulation of wealth and prestige or statistical achievements. What do you value? When Barry Sanders scored 37 touchdowns during his final season at Oklahoma State, he celebrated in the end zone only once. The 2,342 yards that he ran for also prompted little celebration. In the pros with the Detroit Lions, he ran for an 80 yard touchdown and did not celebrate.

When the reporter asked him how he feels after a touchdown, he replied, "relieved." Sanders was not just humble, he just did not measure success with touchdowns, yards, and other statistical accomplishments. It was his heart and mind that measured his success. His heart had to enjoy the game and his mind had to know that he was being the best that he could be. It was only with this knowledge that he felt relieved. When his heart stopped loving the game, he shocked the world by retiring premature to breaking Walter Payton's all-time rushing record. Sanders was successful in the minds of fans and peers alike and to many that is enough. However, it was he who measured his own success and enjoying the game and being the best represented his values, at those he was successful.

As Coach John Heisman, the Heisman Trophy, replied, "In the end the heart tells the story." Described by sportswriter David McNab as having the ability to dart through the keyhole, Sanders internal measure of success is the key to helping others stay focused on what's important in their lives. He determined how successful he was and this story reminds me of a famous singer and actress, Pearl Bailey, who once said, "No one can figure out your worth but you."

The spoils of victory, the money, attention, and fame, are incentives and not indicators of success. Value is the ultimate indicator. As Phil Taylor, a Sports Illustrated writer indicated in referring to John Stockton, "It's just that if he could take away all the accolades, all the hoopla, all the nationally televised interviews and just play basketball, he'd be in heaven. John might be the one player who really wouldn't miss it if the fame went away tomorrow and all he was left with was the game." He valued the experience of the game and played until he was nearly 40 years old.

There is a lot of money to be made in sports; Alex Rodriguez had a $100 million contract, Jordan made $20 million for one season,

Randy Moss was paid $17 million just to sign his name, Tyson once earned $21 million in a 91 second fight, jockey Julie Krone raced for 18 years with purses of over $80 million. Redd Foxx once said, "Money can't buy you happiness, but it can be a great down payment." So in a capitalistic society you do require money. However, money is a medium of exchange only and values should be even more of the focus. So there are some key questions to pose. How valuable was the experience? Am I satisfied? Am I excited? Am I content? Did I learn and develop from the experience? These are all very important indicators of success. Equally as important is whether or not you were the best that you could be. This is what psychologist Abraham Maslow called self-actualization or realizing your full potential.

In my life, I have arrived at another concept, the concept of being excited. It is the excitement and exhilaration that an endeavor provides that gives you motivation and strength as well as enjoyment. Nothing ever happens until you are excited. Satisfaction is defined as to supply fully with what is desired, expected, or needed. The properties of success are reviewed below:

1- Success is not finite, it is a continuous process.
2- Success is a cycle or pattern of ups and downs.
3- Success is not the opposite of failure.
4- Success is a mental and practical process.
5- Success involves making necessary transitions.
6- Success is not universally measured.

We have talked about the properties of success, now let's talk briefly about the psychology of success. We have discussed how to get success and how the process works with the conversion of a mental picture to a follow through plan and result. Let us step back for a moment and ask why people want success in the first place. Understanding the *why* helps us understand further the *how*. Property #1 states that success is a continuous process. This tells us the *when* as in when we are successful. The answer is over time. We know the *what* of success from property #6 which focuses on what measures success. The answer is our values. So we have the how, what, and when; the psychology of success tells us *why* people even bother with trying to succeed. From this analysis we can develop a framework which illustrates what successful people have in common. This lays the basis for a discussion of the goal seeker.

Transitively, this knowledge is useful when it is time to make a transition because the goal seeker is reminded of why he wishes to succeed and thus why he needs to mentally and practically transition. Experts say that people want success because of an internal psychological process dictated by the reward of gain and the fear of loss.

It is safe to say that most people prefer winning over losing, progressing over regressing, ups over downs, good news over bad news, profits over losses. The economic principle of marginal utility is that people prefer more over less. Success is desired and failure is often feared. People would rather feel satisfied than disappointed. All these stem from the reward of gain and the fear of loss. I would amend this finding with the inclusion of the fear of invalidity and the 5 IN-motivators of success along with two other frameworks that pinpoint what motivates people to succeed. These frameworks are called the 10 Self's of success and the 4 P's of success.

Psychologist Kruglanski found that one of the two reasons why people wanted to acquire knowledge other than for the knowledge itself was the fear of having invalid knowledge. No kid raises his hand and wants to yell out the wrong answer. So he studies or keeps his hand down. Likewise when people lack success they are susceptible to feeling invalid. Invalid is defined as without force, weight, or cogency; void. Invalidity is a disease that is cancerous to the mind of any goal seeker. They seek passage from that place. The fear mobilizes them to take the necessary matrix of preparation, planning, and action needed to feel invalid.

Valid comes from the Latin word *powerful*. There is power in this type of fear. It moves us. My speed was always better when chased by the neighborhood Doberman Pincher. If a person did not fear invalidity, that would be more cause for concern. The IN-motivators include: incompetence, incomplete, incapable, and insolvent. These are fears that are auxiliary to the fear of invalidity. Take a look below:

The 5 IN-motivators of success:

1. Invalidity- without force, weight, or cogency; void.
2. Incompetence – unable to do what is required.
3. Incapable – lacking power, capacity, or ability.
4. In complete – not complete or finished; lacking in certain parts.
5. Insolvent(for business entities) – unable to meet claim of creditors; bankrupt.

The 8 Self's of Success:

1. Self-determination – the principle of free will.
2. Self-reliance – reliance on one's own abilities, resources, or judgment.
3. Self-confidence – confidence in oneself or in one's unaided powers.
4. Self-esteem – a good or just opinion of oneself.
5. Self-knowledge – knowing oneself; strengths, weaknesses, ambitions, desires, traits, interest, and those objects which are compatible to oneself, etc.
6. Self-efficacy – a feeling of being able to get done what is attempted.
7. Self-respect – a proper respect for oneself, or one's standing, position, etc.
8. Self-respect – a proper respect for oneself, or one's standing, position, etc.
9. Self-preservation – the instinctive drive to protect oneself.
10. Selfishness(self-interest) – pursuing a goal for only one's own gain or interest.

The 4 P's of Success:

1. Pride – a proper sense or feeling of personal dignity and worth.
2. Possession/Privilege – ownership or occupancy/ a special or peculiar benefit, right, or immunity.
3. Principle – a basic truth, law, force, etc. on which others can be found.
4. Pleasure – an agreeable sensation or emotion; enjoyment.

These characteristics are commonly the key motivators of success. People want to succeed not just for the sake of succeeding, but for the actual inner feeling that it offers. It offers a feeling of self-confidence, self-worth, self-efficacy, etc. When I attempt a task such as doing something for charity, I am motivated by helping others and also earn a feeling of self-worth and self-efficacy. People are driven by pride to pursue what they have dreamed up in their mind. Often the rewards of victory are not the only ambition, whereas people often try to succeed for the principle of it. Bill Koch, chief of the U.S. sailing team during America's Cup declared, "I'm dedicated to a principle. And were going to see it through, one way or another." So in addition to motivators such as possessions(houses, cars, assets) and privilege(status, etc.), goal seekers are attached to the principle of succeeding. It often motivates them even more than assets. Below is a list of psychological characteristics that successful people have in common:

DESIRE
ATTITUDE
MOTIVATION
DRIVE
FOCUS
DETERMINATION
WILL
PERSERVERANCE
RESILIENCY

On a statistical Bell curve most people will have moderate levels of each trait. The variance in success is explained by variance in these variables. Most likely the more desire and focus you have the better mentally prepared you are for success. The other traits are similarly important for success to occur as a mental process. On a practical level, successful people come to decisions quickly and solve problems intelligently. On a mental level, they possess the above traits including strong will and determination. They have the motivation from the previously mentioned areas and possess these mental traits needed to follow through with these motivations.

Since the world is in motion, you have to stay in motion. You can not be sedimentary and expect to be successful. Motion is universal law. Success comes to those that move and make moves. If you are standing still, you are not building. If you are stagnant, you are not laying the foundation for success. It's a numbers game, the more presentations you make the more sales you will make. Let's remember the 4 D's of greatness. They are desire, drive, determination, and dedication. First you must desire something, have a goal. Then you must be driven to pursue what it is you desire. There will be obstacles, so it will require determination. You must be determined to meet your goal. Finally, you must have dedication for the goal. This is how success works. It requires effort and energy. Never underestimate the power of a determined soul.

Success is not the opposite of failure. Failure is part of the success process. In fact, remember success may be a product of something you learned when you failed. This is a learning curve that can be very steep. You have to fail forward, learn from your failures. Failure shouldn't be feared and there should be no anxiety about failure. There will be bumps in the road to success, you just have to hold it steady. A ship can't go halfway across the ocean. You must complete your journey.

Success doesn't occur at the end of a goal. Success occurs at the very acquisition of the mindset needed for success to occur. The crystallization of success merely occurs at the end. So if you have the right mindset, you can succeed at a goal even before you begin it. The necessary mindset is that of a mover and shaker with the will to succeed. It is a mindset that you'll do what is needed to obtain your goal. In addition, it is a mindset that will enable you to overcome anything that gets in the way of you succeeding. It is a mindset that will seize every opportunity that comes your way. After all, in this world there is rigorous competition for scarce resources. Finally your mindset must be one in which you are driven to pursue your goals. As relentless as adversity is, is as relentless as you must be. You must be in pursuit of excellence in everything you do. You must have wit.

Success is not an exact science. There are many formulas that may work. You simply add your mental wits precisely to a goal and you follow through. You have to have Herculean effort. The way to succeed is to develop mentally. In the maturation process from adolescent to adult, man's mind develops. If you are not successful then transform your way of thinking as if you were a caterpillar transforming into a monarch butterfly. In this book I project an image of what you can transform your mind into – the way of a champ and king. It teaches not only how to be successful, but how to break from the pack and be great.

Let me break down the success process. You are exposed to achievements of others, you plan to emulate them so you set goals, you develop a plan, you move toward your goal, you face obstacles. From here you either go one way or another, you overcome or you succumb. If you overcome, you get back on track toward your goal.

You follow through mentally and physically. You achieve your goal set. You then set new goals as success is a continuous process and not a finite one. Remember that success requires exploration.

The Success Algorithm or steps to success are the following:

1. Ambitiously setting goals (set timetable to achieve goal and break goal into manageable parts)
2. Understanding what is required
3. Developing a blueprint (map out a plan and strategy)
4. Gathering the resources necessary
5. Energy
6. Work ethic
7. Direction (rely on blueprint)
8. Perseverance and endurance (psychological resources)
9. A gauge to monitor progress (against time)
10. Monitor obstacles: mental and physical (loss of focus or desire, diminished resources, distractions and setbacks, fear)
11. Complete
12. Evaluate Final Project and make necessary adjustments

*My hypothesis is that if you juxtapose hard work with talent, you can reach success in common hours.

It takes pain to make a person want to change. A mal-adjustment causes more pain than what is already causing pain. A successful adjustment elevates you from this pain. Some adjustments are physical and some are mental. In any event adjustments are essential if you want to live. Charles Darwin talked about adaptation in "Natural Selection". He discussed that species that were able to adapt the best would be able to reproduce the most offspring. His work is known as "Survival of the Fittest."

When you adjust yourself you are making a change from a previous condition or state. As a result of the adjustment you have a new condition. The adjustment is the antecedent to the new condition as it would not exist if not for the adjustment. Thus, it is vital that if you are unhappy in life, you make an adjustment in your life. Change offers vicissitudes and these may be positive. The only constant in life is change as a wise man once proclaimed. One major vicissitude is a happier more gratifying life. Stagnation is undesirable at any level.

Let us discuss types of adjustments in life. There is adjustment in mate or spouse if you are unhappy. There is adjustment to career if you want more out of life. Next, there is adjustment in eating habits or diet as many people are unhappy with their body or weight. Additionally, there is adjustment in lifestyle. Nearly every change that a person can make can be thought of as an adjustment. There is adjustment to environment. If it is too hot get out of the kitchen sort of speak. In addition, there is adjustments to bad habits and adjustment to thinking. There is adjustment to ideology or principles of living. Finally, there is adjustment to values and desires. When thinking about success, one must keep in mind that adjustments may have to be made.

Alexander The Great of Macedonia conquered Egypt. He believed in himself and thus was successful. You too must believe in yourself when striving for your goals. When I was a nineteen year old college football player I had to face an all-star defensive player. I had a strong belief in myself and did well against this player in front of 35,000 people. When I was in a PhD program in Marketing, I had to compete against the best and brightest. However, I believed in myself enough to compete with them and I excelled to the top of the class. Belief in self is essential if you are to be successful. Belief itself is a force.

Ask yourself the question, "Am I excited?" If you are not, then seek excitement. Nothing ever happens until you are excited. I am excited about motivating people to be their best self. I am excited about the cosmic process of discovery. Greatness excites me. I am driven toward greatness. After reading this book and acting upon it, greatness will come out of you the way a volcano erupts. A destination is not a place, but a state of mind. What is your state of mind relative to your goals? Do you have the right thoughts? Are you driven? If you are not driven you must first decide on what it is you desire. Then you must think of how badly you want it and what you have to do to get it. Formulate goals and allow your mind to be elevated and fit for the purpose of meeting your goals.

Just to reiterate, success requires the formation of goals. Every mind should engage in the process of forming goals. It's the reiteration of ambition and drive, two antecedents of success. Once a goal has been set up, a person has locked into his future. One of the keys to succeed is for a person to dig deep inside of himself. He will find strength and power from within rather than from the outside. To succeed one must adapt to his environment. Relatively speaking, survival of the fittest is a reasonable proposition. To succeed one must live a principled life. For example, one may be dedicated to the principle of always working hard. Another principle may be to be ethical in all situations. Attitude is everything and ambition is important. If you set out to climb a mountain, set out to climb the highest mountain, Mount Everest at 29,000 feet. In other words, shoot for the stars; be ambitious when you unravel your goals.

Examine the possibilities. Scan your environment for opportunities. Once you have indulged in a goal, get into a zone. For every goal that you set, there will be ten doubters. Don't allow naysayers to discourage you from your goals. Stay with your goals. Be optimistic and positive. Know that there is a pot of gold at the end of the rainbow. Know the ramifications of your actions. Know that your outcomes are a result of such actions. Stand for something. If you don't stand for something, you'll fall for anything. Wait for your time to blossom. Flowers don't bloom overnight. Seek knowledge. One of the prerequisites to long term success is peace of mind. One must also have enthusiasm and effervescence, zeal and fervor.

It is also important to look at why so many fail. A lack of devotion is one such factor in failing. The idea is that if you're not devoted enough to something you will in most likelihood fail at it or not be a champ at it. Russell Simmons couldn't rise to being the CEO of his own corporation if he lacked devotion. Barack Obama couldn't rise to the presidency if he lacked devotion. Another reason for failing is not seeing one's own potential. Here one can sell oneself short. A lack of dedication is another cause for failing at a cause or idea. When a person lacks discipline he is at risk of failing. A lack of hard work and impatience equally contribute to failing at a dream. Finally, when a person gets a few upsets and wants to quit, this can lead to failure and this is not thinking like a champ.

Success has no statute of limitations. You can be great at every stage or phase of your life. Whether you are a youth experimenting with your passions or a grandparent who is endowing your grandchildren with the wisdom of life experiences, you can be great. People will emerge at different times of their journey. You will emerge when you overcome obstacles that are put in your path. Study the lives of Ceasar, Aristotle, Alexander The Great, Imhotep, Roosevelt and others and note at what point of their journeys they emerged to be great. The correlation will be that they emerged at the main obstacles of their lives. You must be as determined as Matthew Henson who climbed through several feet of snow and gusty winds to be the first man to reach the North Pole.

Success is predicated on the way you think and act. In life you have to ask yourself, "Where do I stand?" If you are not where you want to be, then you must do something about it. Becoming successful often means that you have to unravel your potential. You have to unleash your potential. You must manifest your destiny. You must measure up to you own self. In the wake of your goals, you must not let obstacles cause you to stumble. Just stay on the path toward greatness. There's a lot of chemistry that makes up a champ or a king; his knowledge, his wisdom, his effort, the strength of his determination, and his desire. It also takes hard work to achieve one's goals. Tap into the greatness of others. This is called transcendence. Design a plan that is workable for you. Follow through and get a sense of accomplishment. Elevate your thinking and the way in which you act. Know that you must hustle. Know that you have to think out the box. Know that you have to act with grace and nobility.

The mechanism by which a champ becomes a champ is self-confidence. He exudes confidence in everything he does. You have to develop confidence. Move confidently in the direction of your dreams. You can expect success in common hours. Carry the burdens of your dreams no matter how heavy they are. You must focus like a periscope in the water and eliminate distractions.

Getting off your goal can be a distraction. Shifting priorities can be a distraction. Keep the main thing the main thing. Remember man has a yearning.

Your effort for an endeavor has to be superior. What you put into an endeavor is what you will get out of it. The difference between two talented competitors is superior effort. Hone in on putting your best foot forward. Exert enough energy for the task. There's a certain arithmetic that you must do before you pursue success of a goal. You must calculate your chances and the risks involved in the venture. Then you must pursue it with this in mind. Then you will be able to make the necessary adjustments as you go along. Preserve your energy when pursuing your goal. You have to pace yourself. Life is not a sprint, but a long distance race. At the end of your goal you have to have something left in your tank so that you can form and pursue new goals. After all we know that success is a continuous not finite process.

Other formulas for success are as follows: have an understanding of the world and your environment. Have an approach to the game of life. Another formula for success is strength, determination, inspiration, and reflection. Model yourself after other successful people. Take a deep breath and relax. Be poised when pursuing success. A relaxed mind is a clearer mind. Be as productive as you can and let the chips fall as they may. Don't leave anything to chance. Take the bull by the horns.

Learn to prioritize. Put your goals in order of priority. Educate yourself to create possibilities. This is called investing in your human capital. Be multi-faceted. Don't put all your eggs in one basket. Follow your passions. Live a principled life and you will be successful. Always declare a purpose. Then everything you do must be in line with this purpose. Fixate yourself on this purpose and fulfill it. Set standards and don't go below these standards.

If the teacher assigns you ten math problems, do fifteen. In other words, go the extra mile. Study hard. Master the material. Learn. In pursuing your goal, pay close attention to detail. Get into a zone and use the momentum. Break your goal into smaller parts. Accomplish the goal one part at a time. To be successful takes concentration of the mind. To be successful you need to use your imagination. You need to be creative.

It's one thing to strive for success, but you must know what it takes to succeed. Think your way to success. To be successful you have to bring your negative past to an end, to a close. Know that in science for every action, there is an equal positive reaction. So react. Know to be successful in life you have to be economically successful. Thus, you need an economic foundation, especially in a capitalistic society. You need an environment where you can thrive. It's difficult for a fish to be successful out of water. Align yourself with positive people as in Napolean Hill's mastermind principle. Develop highly effective habits. Man is a creature of habit.

Act as if you are successful already. This is the "as-if" concept. If you want to be a champ, act as if you were a champ already. Have a good memory. A good memory comes in handy when pursuing a goal especially when acquiring knowledge and education. The most complicated concept is time. To be successful you must master time. Albert Einstein's theory of relativity tells us that time is relative to how fast you are going. Success requires a spark in the mind of the goal seeker. A spark gets the process started. This spark can be an idea, a concept, an epiphany, an insight, a desire. It requires of you to have courage to succeed. If you are not successful, then transform your mind to be courageous. Success also takes preparedness. You have to be prepared for whatever comes your way.

Bruce Lee said he fears the man who practices one kick 10,000 times. Metaphorically, practice one kick 10,000 times. Practice makes perfect. Everything you do, you do to a rhythm. Move with rhythm, study with rhythm, speak with rhythm. The Greek word for rhythm is *rhythmos*. Listen to your inner voice. Listen to the monologue in your head. It will guide you during your goal. Count on someone. Someone will lead the way to success. The hones is on you to decide what you want to do with your life, but someone else will be put in your path to help you get there.

Love life and you will be successful. Believe in life, believe in broader, fuller life. Never surrender to life no matter how deep it gets. You need firm resolve and tenacity to be successful. You have to look at the big picture – what's the meaning of life? What's the purpose of life? To be successful, you need the ability to reason. The ability to reason is a sign of intelligence. Make sense of the world and work toward its improvement. That will lead to success. Seek and you will find.

In order to succeed you have to get through your struggles. You have to maintain your stride. It also takes stability. Put your heart and soul into your goals. You have to be ready for battle, rain or shine. This means battle the possibility of not meeting your goal. By battling the elements you heat up the mathematical possibility of succeeding. Much of the time success depends on your lifestyle. Your lifestyle may or may not be conducive to success. Conquer your fears. Conquer doubt. Shakespeare said doubt is a traitor.

Withstand the pressure of your goals. Don't let the pressure swallow you up. Don't let it get you off course. After you withstand the pressure, success is eminent. Replace negative thoughts with positive thoughts. This makes you more productive in life. As a man thinketh, so shall he be. Plant your seeds of thought in the world. Live a straight and narrow, law-abiding life. Your freedom is of utmost importance. Break the barriers and limits of life and the authority of success will be yours. Along with success comes authority and power. You can't be afraid to try something for the first time. You have to be a risk taker. You have to be conditioned for success. Your mind has to be programmed for success. If you act like a champ and think like a king, you will succeed. Be focused on the task at hand. Keep everything else on the periphery. Be true to thine self. Be honest with assessing your strengths and weaknesses and what you need to improve on. You have to deal with reality. Reality is your scope.

You have to keep it real. Also don't yield to temptation and deception. Work on your craft one day at a time. Put aside 15 minutes each day to work on your legacy. You need a vision. Vision provides you with a road map to your goal. Always have something to look forward to. This gives you hope and let's you know that there is light at the end of the tunnel. Meditate. Drift off into other worlds. Sometimes for relief and a meditative interlude you have to create a world of your own. Of course, this world is created in your mind. You have to evolve. You have to stay relevant and ahead of the times. Don't be overwhelmed by your own greatness. Take success and greatness in stride.

You have to be moldable and malleable like water. Gather what is good and avoid what is bad. They say if you want to keep a secret, put it in between the pages of a book. Thus, it is evident that you must read to be successful. When times are hard, you must get harder. Be smart. Be clever. Be intelligent. Make wise choices. Know the consequences of your actions. Don't act on impulse. Take care of what's immediately in front of you. Success takes strong will. It takes sound judgment. It takes intuition. You have to be a good observer. You have to be well rounded. You need balance. When you are a far distance from your goal, don't lose sight of it. Nothing succeeds like success.

Telegraph your obstacles. Know when they will occur before they occur and be two steps ahead of them. Sometimes you may feel like you're in a bottom-less pit. You have to climb out of this mentality to be successful. When you think optimistically the possibilities will swell up. In order to succeed you have to be motivated by something. Engage in the process of discovery. Don't leave any stone unturned. The more you discover in life, the better your chances of success. Broaden your horizons. Make good use of your time. Avoid idle time. Take the mystery out of life – figure out life for yourself.

The possibilities are endless. You never know how great you can become. Just know there is a "you" out there that may not exist yet, but it can. There are many domains in which you can find greatness. You just have to put the effort forth to explore the possibility of something. Think long term; don't be myopic. Be yourself. Don't be something that you are not. If you do you might as well be in a hypnotic state.

In science, they say the closest distance between two points is a straight line. Thus, you should go straight at success, go right to your goal. In physics, inertia is defined as an object's resistance to movement. Don't get inert, have movement along the horizontal axis of success. Move. Walk through the valley of life. Endure life's challenges. Don't take detours or turns, go straight at success. Stay on target. This too requires focus and concentration. You must continue to live for your purpose and your goals. Keep unimportant items on the periphery. Maintain your vision. Remember what it says in the Old Testament 29:18, "When there is no vision, the people perish." Have vision and remember the Japanese proverb, "In order to get the cubs, you must go into the lion's den." Keep the main thing, the main thing. Don't spend too much time and energy doing things that don't meet your needs and desires, goals, and ambitions, purpose, and ideals. I know when I was in college, I had to curb my social life a bit to focus on making the Dean's List. So I spent most of my weekends studying. I made the Dean's List.

When talking about going straight at success, one must know how to prioritize. Put the first thing first. What can you do without and what can't you do without? How does each priority meet your goal and purpose? In college my priorities were academics, football, extracurricular activities, and social life. In essence, success is a priority because you require success in health, family, career, and social. You have to determine what in essence is most important to you and this relates to knowledge of self. Once you know yourself you can prioritize the elements of your life.

Another priority for me in life is the intellect and the process of discovery. I don't equate just a good paying job as success. I measure the success of a career by how it arouses and sharpens my intellect and satisfies my thirst for knowledge. I like to explore worlds unexplored and go off in a distance, learning about phenomena unexplained to man. That is a priority. Learning is a major priority for man cannot blossom like a plant until he has learned. Fill your brain cells or neurons with information. Success is the ability to use your brain correctly or effectively. It must process information at the neuron level and store information needed for intuition, decision-making, and creativity. This is part of development. Another priority is to put oneself in an environment that is conducive to one's mental, physical, and spiritual development and development of your brain power.

Although material accumulation is important to some people, one should focus or prioritize learning over acquiring material things. In fact, the more you learn the more likely you are able to acquire material things. We talked earlier about the importance of education, but we must also mention the importance of sophism or wisdom. Everyone should develop their own philosophies on life. This book is my philosophy of success, my technology of success. It provides an algorithm for greatness. It provides an insight for success and greatness. We hone in on the concept of greatness.

When I was in my PhD program at the University of Massachusetts at Amherst, I obtained a great deal of wisdom. I learned the scientific method of research and discovery. I learned philosophy, marketing, consumer behavior, and social psychology. From this wisdom and my life experiences I was able to write my first book *On The Wings Of Perseus: The Life Of The Athlete After Sports*.

This book is a life plan for athletes after their career in sports is over or for any goal seeker making a transition of career and into life.

To be successful you must develop and design a life plan. Come up with a blue print and steps of getting straight to your goal. What do you want and what do you want to do? What do you want to become and what must you do to become this? This underlies your life plan along with your vision, purpose, and passions. What do you enjoy doing? What activities can you undertake? Where would you like to go? What do you want to own? How can you improve your brain? Your body? Your finances? Your social life?

When designing a life plan you should keep in mind that your goal is to achieve an equilibrium, a balance. Your life plan must be well balanced, diversified with vast experiences. You should have a balance of enjoyment and learning. You need a balance of career and family or career and social. The purpose is to be fulfilled and not idle, rather productive and prolific. Grab hold of the wind and live a fulfilled life. Let the sun shine on your life. You can design it and you can determine your destiny. You've heard of the Rock of Gibraltar and Plymouth Rock, so what is your rock? What makes you tick? These are questions you must ask yourself before you embark on your journey. It also helps you go straight at your goal and success. What experiences do you want to have? A bucket list while you are still living is at hand.

For physical health, you must know your body and what it needs to function. It requires protein, nutrients, and energy for everyday functioning. In terms of chemistry, you should avoid too much salt or sugar. Also, it is important not to take illegal drugs and if you are using prescription drugs, you should use only as directed. Also in terms of chemistry, you should use vitamins on a daily basis for vitality. Energy is essential for good health. For mental health, stress should be minimized. I remember when I stopped playing football in college. All of my energy was put for the first time in my life into one area, my academics. I did not have an outlet for my tremendous energy. One needs balance. I ended up ill and my success at college was at risk. Find out what your triggers for stress are.

It is also important what you put in your mind. Too much negativity should not be internalized. Try to keep positive affirmations in your mind. If you be good to your mind, your mind will be good to you. One must learn to relax. There are plenty of relaxation techniques; many involve deep breathing. One thing I like to do daily is meditate. I find that this helps relax my mind. Try not to worry too much. This can wear you down mentally. For mental health, I find it helpful to read regularly. I like to read non-fiction but some enjoy fiction. Try to develop good healthy habits. Bad habits lead to poor health. If you have a job or career that is too stressful then it may be time to consider a career change. Don't compromise your mental health for monetary gain. Have a few hobbies. This can be therapeutic to your mind and is also an outlet for your energy. You only get one mind so take good care of it. You have to remember we are striving for success, we are striving to blossom like a plant, bloom like a flower, and self-actualize.

In terms of mental health, stress can be detrimental, so develop coping mechanisms. You will learn for yourself what helps you cope with stress. For example, another coping mechanism for me is listening to music. This is therapeutic. There is nothing more effective than dealing with your problem directly. For example, if you are in a stressful relationship, it may help to alleviate yourself of that relationship for a while or indefinitely. If you are stressed because of financial problems, then it may be helpful to hire a professional financial advisor. Talking your problems out with someone can be productive and therapeutic. Success comes to those who work. Don't just hope problems and stress will go away, work for their end.

Have balance in your life. A body must have homeostasis and so does your life. Have a balance of activities to keep you from being idle. Have a balance of activities to keep you from being idle. Idle time is not good for our mental health. Your mind as well as your body was designed for activity. Plan activities to keep from being idle. The greatest project that you can undertake is the management of your mental health. Something as easy to overlook as peace and quiet is essential. Noise and confusion is not good for the mind. One must have stability of mind. Whatever you take into your mind, keep in mind, everything in moderation. Remember that even when you do have stress and triggers in your life, you can overcome. You can get back in stride and continue to succeed. Thunder and lightning hit me but I persevered. You must persevere no matter what difficulty you face mentally.

Know your mind, what works for it and what doesn't work for it. Avoid what doesn't work for your mind and experience what works for your mind. Just like your body needs exercise, your mind needs exercising too. That's why reading and hobbies are good for you. I didn't even take an aspirin until I was 21 years old. My health seemed perfect at one time. Keep in mind, poor health can happen to anyone at any time. I experienced a great deal of shock and confusion when my health went awry. What happened to me can happen to anyone. No one is invincible and exempt from setbacks in their mental and physical health.

One must have vitality. This goes for people of all ages whether eight years old or seventy three. It starts with mental health. To be vigorous you must be active. Keep your mind active, actively engaged with the outer world. Surround yourself with people who are good for your mind and be in environments good for your health. Seek therapeutic activities. Seek a therapeutic environment. Be in your element. Poor mental health makes the goals you seek more difficult to obtain. I have been in contact with lots of people who lost everything due to poor mental health and their goal setting process was abbreviated. Not being able to meet goals has an effect on your mental health as well, whether it be stress or frustration or lowered self-esteem. Keep in mind, success is not guaranteed even when you are stable, but it is a requirement to engage the 4 D's of greatness: desire, drive, determination, and dedication.

We stressed earlier the importance of education. Achievement and accumulation of education correlates with financial success. When you obtain a formal education you put yourself in position to have financial independence. Income leads to wealth and wealth leads to financial stability. Of course, entrepreneurship is an alternative to education. The founder of Campbell's Soup had a fourth grade education. So for financial success one can look to start one's own business. Keep in mind the risks – 1 out of every 2 new businesses fail.

You must set short-term, medium-term, and long-term financial goals in order to be financially successful. You want a piece of the

American pie, you want to own resources. Owning a home is the sine quo non of the American Dream. You must live below your means and manage your purchasing power. Investing and saving has to be a part of your financial equation. A capitalist society is all about resources. You must obtain the resources needed for your development and well-being. You have to develop a system of managing money. Invest in your human capital.

At base level in a capitalistic society, your wings will not fly unless you are financially literate. Personal Finance is a topic that must have priority. You must have at least five months of income saved up in case you lose your job and need a transition. You must master the budgeting process. Smart consumption is important to your bottom line. Financial success involves to large degree three items: 1) activity, 2) planning, and 3) productivity. Activity is how busy you are making moves. Planning involves making a plan for your income, your expenses, and your means of multiplying your money. Productivity is how productive you are as a worker or business owner – doing what it is you do to make money as well as investing in your human capital.

Activity can include in addition to work, your investments. There are three basic investments most people make. They are real estate investment, stocks and bonds, and starting your own business. These are ways in a capitalist or free market system of multiplying your money. When you invest in stock, this is a form of equity investment. You are financing a corporation and in return you receive ownership or equity. Bond investing is debt investment. You finance a corporation or government entity for the promise of financial return. Real estate can be a solid investment with some research. It can be lucrative. Despite the risks involved with entrepreneurship, it can be a means of financial success.

There are currently 9 million millionaires in the United States. Thus, there is opportunity in this country to establish financial independence. You must have a plan and be active and productive. Do your research on your financial project. Use computer technology to manage your finances and make investments. Even the federal government makes investments and attempts to save money and balance their budget. You must keep debt down as it can weigh your financial health down. This is also a part of living below your means.

Don't be myopic, think long-term. Everyone's life goes in stages. You must plan ahead for each stage. You have to provide resources for your family. People don't plan to fail, they fail to plan. Make wise financial decisions using available information considering opportunity costs of alternatives. Always be upwardly mobile, looking for a better job, a better investment, a better financial plan. Capitalism can be a beautiful thing when you are winning. It is a game of making deals and decisions. Your wealth depends heavily on the deals and decisions you make. Your net worth is dependent on how smart you are with your money.

Apply your blueprint of success to financial planning. The concepts apply the same way. For example, setting goals now becomes setting financial goals or landmarks. Plan for your future, in terms of retirement or death. You should have the resources necessary for retirement and your family should not be financially burdened by your loss. There are retirement plans and life insurance available for you in this case. Don't leave your family with darkness, leave them with light. In other words, leave them with support and a chance at financial independence.

Finance is about assets, liabilities, and owner's equity. In addition, it is about the equation income minus expenses. Master these equations in your mind and on paper. Ultimately, what you own must exceed what you owe. Prepare for paying taxes like income taxes and property taxes. You must incorporate the fact that you have or want a family in your financial plan. Hire a professional financial planner. This can pay dividends.

Don't just buy things, make investments. Think of the psychological and economic return of your purchases. You know that buying a house can offer great financial return as well as psychological return. If you work then you'll need to purchase an automobile. There are different types of purchases that you can make. Don't make unnecessary purchases. Hone in on continuing to have marketable skills in the kaleidoscopic workforce. The workforce is ever changing and skills must be upgraded and evolving. This can ensure your financial success. Even if it means going back for more education or training, make yourself ready for the job market. Don't forget quality of life. Don't compromise quality of life for money. Keep in mind that stress can be a trigger to mental illness as we have said earlier.

Believe it or not, choosing a mate in life is as important to financial success as the art of business. The art of mating is that you must choose someone who will complement you and help build with you. Like-minded people can build a financial future together.

In addition, the people you surround yourself with can affect your financial success. Do they transcend greatness to you or do they bring you down. Finally, in journeying toward financial independence remember that you must persevere. Perseverance has an economic value to it.

Let's talk about shadow boxing. I love boxing. I even trained as a boxer for a few years. I would shadow box. Shadow boxing is when a fighter works on his punches, his footwork, and his defense on air as if fighting an invisible man. I used to see heavyweight champ Roy Jones, Jr. shadow box; he would work on his jab, hook, cross, and uppercut, his combinations. It was a beauty to watch. In life you too must shadow box. In other words before you step in the ring of life, you must practice. It doesn't matter what you are practicing, it could be academics, music, art, sports, acting or any career, but you must practice. Practicing leads to success.

Bruce Lee said he fears the man who practices the same kick 10,000 times. Practice leads to consistency and consistency leads to mastery. Studying for an exam is a form of practicing. Shadow box your way to an 'A'. Rehearse your vision for you will be auditioning for a role in a play called Life and you must succeed. Success is the only option, it's the outcome you seek and meditate on. You dream it, you visualize it.

Visualization is a technique many top athletes like Michael Jordan have used to prepare for their goals. Chicago bears running back Walter Payton was the all time leading rusher in the NFL. He visualized the cheering of the crowd during the Super Bowl, the game, and even what the championship ring would look like. Visualization is effective in many endeavors. I believe surgeons use visualization prior to surgery. It is an effective way of producing a mental edge. I have used visualization for public speaking, i.e., presentations that I had to give. How closely I performed to my visualization determined how successful I would be. You practice the way you play. You shadow box, you visualize, then you perform it to perfection.

A lawyer shadow boxes before giving his defense in court. He produces his final argument, his cross-examinations, etc. A school teacher shadow boxes as does a beautician. An accountant must shadow box before taking the rigorous CPA exam. Every Saturday game during football season was preceded by a week of shadow boxing. I would visualize playing on the field as well. When it was time to play it would be second nature. To be successful involves shadow boxing, visualization, and another category – imagination. You must use your imagination to set lofty goals, creative goals. Do things that fascinate you, be adventurous, be imaginative. Go off into places far off. Deviate from the norm. Don't just set the goal of getting a job and paying your bills; have an imagination. Imagine all the possibilities. Imagine what you can become what you can accomplishment, imagine what you can own. Theodore Roosevelt was a sickly child, but he had a great imagination. He later became president of the United States. Matthew Henson used his imagination in becoming the first person to reach the North Pole. Hillary Rodham Clinton had a great imagination too. She would become Secretary of State in Barack Obama's cabinet. Imagination leads to creativity. With creativity you make a door where there was no door. The root word of creativity is *create*, you create with your mind, you make something out of nothing.

Shadow boxing also leads to gaining confidence. Although confidence is essential for success, if you don't have a basis for confidence, you won't have confidence. When you shadow box you gain a basis for confidence. A surgeon has done a type of surgery before, he has read all the material, he has shadow boxed. Thus, he has confidence before beginning his surgery. Confident mental attitude is a key characteristic that enables one to persevere and succeed at one's visualization.

We have all seen people do amazing things in life but never acknowledged how confident they must have been to do these things. Dr. Lewis Lattimer discovered the carbon filament that makes the incandescent light work. He had a great deal of confidence in his ability before he helped Edison discover light. Transform your mind to be confident by shadow boxing and through visualization. Your chances of success will be solid as a rock.

We have seen confident people before. We remember Rocky Marciano become heavyweight champion of the world. He retired undefeated. He seemed unbeatable. His belief in himself was un-daunting. His belief in his mental and physical abilities was remarkable. He transcended his greatness and confidence onto those who watched him fight. We live in a competitive, survival of the fittest type world. Thus, you must be armed with confidence as you compete for resources or to meet your physical, psychological, and spiritual needs. Remember what philosopher Henry David Thoreau said about confidence – you can meet success in common hours.

Another mental practice along with shadow boxing, visualization, and being confident is making self-affirmations. Whether it is in the social realm or career area of success, saying positive affirmations to yourself helps transform your mind for success. When you say, "I am a great writer" or "I am beautiful" to yourself, it is registered in your brain and eventually your belief becomes a reality. Look yourself in the mirror and say, "I will be a success no matter what comes my way" or "I am built for success." If you meet a new man that you want say to yourself, "This man will be mine." Whenever I face a difficult task I say to myself, "You can do this!"

You have what it takes within you to succeed. You just have to bring your inner potential to the surface. It is *abintra*, Latin for within you. Live up to your full potential by transforming your mind. You must acquire the right mindset needed for success to occur. You must program yourself for the success of your goals and ambitions, desires, and dreams. Don't forget to shadow box. Throw a jab at adversity and rise. Like Maya Angelou said, "Still I Rise."

So let's summarize this chapter with an overview of success. First, success often requires transformation of the mind. It's mind over matter. You transform your mind by changing the way you think. If you are not successful, 9 times out of 10 you don't have the right thoughts. Think intelligently. Use logic when making conclusions. Come up with creative ideas. Be able to handle situations. Don't think about the negative or how far away your goal seems to be. Appreciate the progress you have made thus far. Stretch your imagination as wide as the river. Ask yourself the right questions. Am I content with my current status? Could I do more? Be better? Own more? Be more complete? Be solution-driven, always thinking of what you must do to get to where you want to be. If you want to climb the Appalachian, do everything you need to do to climb the Appalachian. Take advantage of your talent, tendencies, and skills. Hone in on your passions. Make a financial success out of yourself doing what you enjoy. Master the possibilities. See the light. Realize that progress takes time, that patience is a virtue, and that no empire was built in a day. Adapt. When in Rome do as the Romans do. When in the jungle speak the language of lions and tigers. Lift yourself up.

Make sure in life you turn a deaf ear to negativity. Even lions need encouragement. The measure of success is as important as the strive for success. Chinese philosopher, I Ching said the response is as important as the problem. Respond effectively to problems. Prioritize so that you can use your time wisely. Manage change. Make the necessary adjustments. Make the necessary transitions. Capitalize off your strengths. Communicate effectively to get what you desire. Shoot for the stars. In other words, be ambitious. If you can't get a star at least get a cloud. Remember that success is not finite, but continuous. Thus, effort must be continuous. Keep pushing. Keep hope alive like Jesse Jackson said in his bid for the presidency. Know that you can do it, the unthinkable, the unimaginable. Strive for perfection. In gymnastics, a 10.0 is perfection. So work on your technique. Have a philosophy on life. Make wise decisions and keen judgments. Use your memory as Plato said, "Remembering is learning." Remember Murphy's Law that things may go wrong and they will. So prepare yourself for adversity and setbacks. Continue to make strides. Progress. Don't be sedimentary, keep moving. Move with rhythm. Love life. Do what successful people do. Remember what Thomas Merton said that no man is an island. Surround yourself with positive people. Counteract negative energy. Feed off positive energy. Feed off youth. Lift your spirits. Meet your needs.

Have a method to your madness. Manifest your destiny. Stay attached to the journey like an umbilical cord. Let success be born from this property. Stay strong. Keep pressing on. Keep the faith, having faith in your mind. In an information society, success depends on the amount of information your brain has available to it. If you feel like a success, you will be a success. Make like a champ, make like a king. Move in syncopation with your dreams. You know that success is your destination, so have a culture for success. Make up in your mind to be successful. My basic premise in this book is that you have within you what it takes to succeed, you just have to follow my philosophy for greatness and success. Never give up. Make like Menelik, the former Ethiopian king and be great. Make like Michelangelo and be great. Make like Floyd "Money" Mayweather and be great. Act like Jerry Rice, the great football player or the neurosurgeon, Dr. Ben Carson. Think like the great presidential candidate, Hillary Rodham Clinton. Be successful and make like these great champs. Develop an algorithm in your thinking about success. Become great one success at a time.

Chapter 4:

Act Like a Champ, Think Like a King

◇◇◇◇◇◇◇◇◇

Now that we discussed the back drop for our basic premise, it's time to act like a champ and think like a king. We have described striving for the ultimate, the power of the human spirit, the need for self-esteem like a champ and the state of mediocrity as a nation and as an individual. We have said that mediocrity can be a temporary state. Now let's examine what it means to act like a champ and think like a king.

In Chinese physics, which preceded Galilean physics by 2500 years, waves produce a tide. Tide in Chinese physics represents magnetism. A champ has magnetism. A valedictorian, a president, A PhD, A heavyweight boxer, a king, a CEO all have magnetism. Man is an energy. He gives off energy the way a plant gives off oxygen. You must use your energy to the fullest to achieve what you want in your life. Your energy has to be channeled effectively. Think of a man, in this case a champ, as a wave of energy like a tide.

Focus on "ziji", the Chinese word for self. Everything starts with ziji and ends with ziji. Self-knowledge and self-awareness are keys to finding yourself. The success of your soul depends on this.

Challenge yourself to do more. There is no limit to how far you can go. This is part of the process of becoming great.

Be superior to your former self. Be better today than you were yesterday. A drummer beats a drum for effect. You live your life for an effect. Let people hear the music of your soul. Let them hear you roar.

Like a champ, you have to have consistency, you need persistency. After, you have consistency and persistency, you can have mastery. Once you have mastery, you will eventually have intensity. This is my consistency-persistency-mastery-intensity theory. The process works for any endeavor. Champs undergo this process all the time. You often just drift off, get sidelined from your goals. You have to get back on your mission. Your mind possesses within it, greatness. You have to know the power of your mind; it's mind over matter. Your mind can be transformed into an oasis of excellence. It must be invigorated and often time rejuvenated. The Universe effects the protoplasm of man.

What is the destination of your culture? Your culture must be designed for you to be great. If it isn't you must create a culture on your own conducive to being great. A savvy CEO has a culture for greatness as does a president or PhD. A PhD expands minds. The Greek philosophers Socrates, Plato, and Aristotle were equivalent in those days to PhD's. They had a culture that allowed them to explore the depths of theirs minds. They were champs of philosophy. They brought us "sophism" or wisdom that we still use today. They were thinkers. Your culture has to allow you to think.

Be immersed in the culture of a champ. Not even the moon above is as great as a man who has found himself.

Fill your mind with good information. Store this information for you may need it during your journey. Much like data is input into a computer information can be input into your mind, the neurons in your brain. You have to program that information to work for you. Thus, you can program your mind for the greatness of a champ and king.

A king is a phenomenon like the Cosmos above. Understanding this phenomenon will help you become great and reach your full potential. Approach your goals intelligently like a king. If there is ever a time to use your intelligence, it's when pursuing a goal or attempting to find your mastery and intensity. Make like a sponge and absorb knowledge. You must learn. To be a champ, one must first respond to one's intellectual needs. After all a rose pedal can't live without water drops. Education is as vital as the heart. It pumps knowledge into the minds of goal seekers and broadens their horizons. A person with education looks at the world differently. A person with education approaches life and his goals differently, more effectively. Education takes you to higher heights, higher skies, the exercising of your mind. It transforms you, can help make you into a thinker, can help you think, reason, and understand. It can help make you a better person. After all, isn't that its intent?

The purpose of becoming a champ is self-worth. Claim your right to be great. You were born with a purpose to shed light on this world. Your aura is powerful, your spirit is great. Being great will lead you through the wilderness of life. There's no doubt in my mind that you can find your way. You can reach your peak. Have a dream and live it.

In striving for greatness one must have a "quiet mind". In other words you have to have peace of mind and inner peace. You are in search of something; you have to have peace before, during, and after you find it. Free your mind. Something great can come from a free mind. A champ and king are radiant. Radiance is universal about great people. They have a glow. Their spirits are running free. One goal in life is to exist as a free spirit like a king. A king knows that the sky is the limit.

Man represents a yearning. He yearns for glory. He yearns for success. He wants to be more than he previously was. His mind is on progress. This yearning precipitates the way he acts and the way he thinks. In turn, the way he acts and thinks determines ultimately what he is to become.

A king has substance. You too must have substance. He is about something. He is about the flourishing of his kingdom. Likewise, you have to be about your goal. A king has power. Strive for different forms of power. A king is outspoken. Psychoanalyst, Carl Jung who studied under Sigmund Feud, categorized a person as an introvert and an extrovert. An introvert is quiet and reserved an extrovert is one who is outspoken. You must be like a king and be an extrovert. A closed mouth doesn't get fed.

A king is a thinker. He is an advanced thinker. His thoughts are original and creative. He has insights on life. You have to imagine yourself a king and have productive thoughts. Success requires a breakthrough. You must always be an independent thinker. A king also has intuition the ability to produce knowledge from within. This is a powerful trait. You too be must be intuitive. You have to make sense of the world for yourself. A king processes the situation, then intuitively responds to it. Chinese philosopher, I Ching said, "The response is as important as the problem." Let's not forget that the greatness process starts with desire. You will be great if you desire to be great. A champ, a king-I've never seen it done better. Do you ever dream of greatness? Once you think like this, it will transform your mind. Rise up and live up to the measure of your own design.

In your life you set precedents in how you deal with obstacles. In the future use these precedents to deal with new obstacles. Remember the emotion and logic you used to deal with the past obstacles and apply it again to the future obstacle.

As a person who wants to be great, you must interface with society. As a person who wants to be an overachiever, you must implement your plan. You can't expect greatness to come through osmosis, it will take action on your part. Mimic the greatness of a champ and king. Man is a creature of habit.

Booker T. Washington said, "Cast down your buckets where they are." In other words, work with what you have and make the most of what you have going for you. Use your strengths to your advantage. A king's strength, like a champ, is that he thinks on his feet. Victory goes to the swift. You must be able to think fast under pressure.

A man's mind is broken into three parts according to psychoanalyst Sigmund Freud: the id, the ego, the superego. The id is primitive mind, the ego is the personality and the superego regulates the id. It is the rational mind. You must regulate the id and be a rational thinker. A champ and king are rational thinkers. Driven like a champ, majestic like a king, ascend to the higher heights. Experience Satori. Satori is a word from the Japanese Zen tradition which points to a sudden awakening, the fusing of mind, body, and emotion, the fusing with a higher energy. Experience what I experienced –self-actualization, full bloom like a flower or reaching one's full potential.

Be still and know that you too can become great. Once you become great accept the responsibility of being great. This means you must serve as an example for others to emulate. The difference between the great and mediocre is the example they serve. In addition, as a champ, a king, your word has to be bond.

You must be as vast as the ocean and as deep as the river. You must make like a waterfall and flow. Benjamin Banneker was an astronomer. He wrote the almanac. He designed the blueprint for Washington D.C. He made the first working clock in America. He was indeed a champ in his own right.

Be majestic in the way you walk. Be majestic in the way you talk. Think like a king. A king makes monumental decisions. You too must master life-shaping decisions. A king is responsible for the lives of many. You be responsible for someone other than yourself. A king helps his clergy. He helps his peasants. You too must help someone along the way.

A king like Rameses II or Dsojer was patient. Patience is a virtue. Rome wasn't built in a day. When seeking success and greatness there will be times when you need to be patient. Time is of the essence. Ethics is important to a king. It must be important in your life too. He doesn't compromise morality for success or his prominence. We want you to blast off and beat mediocrity without compromising morality.

A king weathers the storm. A champ weathers the storm. When thunder and lightning come your way, you must weather the storm also. Man has the obligation to try. It has been said that everyone can't be a champ, but man has the obligation to try. A goal seeker, a person who wants to blast off and become a champ must learn from his mistakes. Like a tennis player in a tournament, he must correct his mistakes or there will be consequences. If something doesn't work the first time, he must try another approach the next time. That's how he gets out of his hole or ditch in life. Fail in order to succeed. You learn a lot from failure. Let your mind conceive; greatness will occur. You have to first think it up, then make it happen. I had flashes of greatness throughout my life whether it be academia, athletics or leadership, but what is the key is to sustain greatness. Keeping it up or maintaining is of vital importance because like Janet Jackson said in her song, "What have you done lately?" I had a great football career spanning from the age of 8 to 21 years old. I started off as a precocious hungry little boy who wanted to play with older kids to NCAA football player who won a league championship and a national ranking.

There were many lessons learned throughout my football career and football served as a metaphor for life, the main lesson was to never give up. My academic career was likewise spectacular.

I was an honor roll student throughout high school and college. I received several awards including Highest Achiever, National Honor Society and Mayor's Proclamation, etc. In 1999, I received a Master's in Business Administration from the prestigious Purdue University Krannert School of Management and two years later began a doctorate program in marketing at another leading university.

When one escapes mediocrity and becomes great, the sun will shine on him like never before. People will respond to him like never before. The world will open to him as opportunity will come knocking. The rust of mediocrity in him will be replaced by fire in his belly. He is now fortunate with a great future ahead of him. His time has come.

PhD's who do research that make the world go round inspire me as does the president and his cabinet. Professional, college, even high school and Pop Warner athletes inspire me to the highest. Inspiration can be spark that we talked about. You never know when it's going to come, you just have to be ready to ride the wave. Inspirations is what makes us climb mountains, reach peaks, and see the sky up close for ourselves.

The stars of Hollywood inspire me. They are stellar, the best at what they do. Watching them act like reading William Shakespeare, Alexander Dumas who wrote, "The Three Musketeers", Mark Twain, or Ralph Waldo Emerson.

I'm like a dog on the prowl when it comes to seeking greatness. I want to shock the world. I want to perform like a gymnast receiving a 10.0 in gymnastics. This would be like a breath of fresh air. I am inspired by the challenge and by the quest. If you are to act like a champ and think like a king, you are to have passion for your area. Confucius, the Chinese philosopher said, "Find a job you enjoy and you'll never work a day in your life." If you are a champ you are to train, practice, and prepare like a champ. Talent is important but there is no substitute for hard work and tenacity. To be successful you have to be emotional when it comes to your dream. To be a champ you must be logical. A champ works night and day on his craft. He doesn't give up on his dreams, motivations and fantasies. What kind of love does a champ have for his area? He has to snatch his dream from out of the sky to become great. He must take control of his own body and mind. If you want to be a king you must act as if.

A champ's way is to find solutions to problems. Complex equations are derived, phenomena are unturned, but the key to being champ is find solutions to problems. Problems may arise during your journey. A champ must discover ways around or through such problems. Cover all basis – train, prepare, and educate yourself. Be on higher vibrations not lower vibrations, higher wavelengths, higher ambitions not lower ambitions. Stay true. Look to inspire others by being a champ. You have to have a method, be methodical. Understand life and its intricacies. Master relationship management doing all this, you can be a problem-solver. You can be mighty as a lion.

In order to get out the unwanted state that you are in, you have to identify why you are in that state. You have to be able to identify the sources for that state. Perhaps the source of the state is lack of hard work for instance. When it comes to hard work, there is no compromise. You must work hard to excel in our type of society. Two equally talented goal seekers are separated by hard work. The country wasn't built only on ingenuity, it was also built on hard work.

Blast off from a starting point as in launching, then find your way. The sooner you know where you're going, the better off you are. Be progressive. When you know where you're going the better off you are. Be progressive. You know where you were when you started and marked your progress. Man or nature improving from a lower state to a higher state is progress.

Life is a bumpy ride. It offers an obstacle course that has hindrances and traps. One must be clever not to fall for life's trap and avoid or overcome life's obstacles by being "on point." Being on point means being sharp and able to respond to the stresses that one's environment offers.

Bill Bradley, a United States senator was a standout high school basketball player who had a successful career eventually with the New York Knicks. He won a championship with the Knicks and was named to the NBA Hall of Fame. He accredits his success to practice. He practiced harder than the other players and it paid off as he became a pro basketball player and a champ. To be a champ there's no road you want travel. You have to see greatness. Being great is a special human need, much like love or nurturing from a parent or spouse. It completes a person and alleviates them from the mediocrity. It is such a special need that can separate us by the haves and haves not's. Visualize your greatness. Rehearse the vision as you are auditioning for a part in the play call Life.

Be an inverse paranoid. In other words believe that the world out to do you good. This is a positive belief, it offers an enriching experience. Look for the upside not the downside. Man must have faith in the order of the Universe, that the Universe has something great in store for him. Man must have faith in others. He must believe that other men will come through for him. Deal with your fears. Your fears can block you from reaching the top. If you fear something you must process it in your mind. You must confront it directly and eliminate it or will continue to hold you down. For example, no one can be successful or reach greatness if they fear competition. Competition should be looked at as a stimulus that makes you better. Becoming great is a step toward salvation. Your spirit is invigorated by the feeling it gives. It takes greatness to soothe the savage beast.

If you shoot for the stars you might get a cloud. There is no limit for success of your dreams. You must do just that dream. The bigger the dream, the larger the accomplishment. The more vivid the dream, the larger the accomplishment. The more vivid the dream the more possible the dream.

If you dedicate your life to such a dream and have the drive, desire, and determination required, you will obtain the success of your dreams in common hours. You have obstacles which can cloud your vision at times, but your dreams are so strong that you won't let this hinder you from attaining your goals. The lesson I've learned is that in no shape, form, or fashion should you let obstacles prevent you from going your highest level. In an incandescent light, it's the carbon filament that makes it work. This was the invention of Dr. Lewis Lattimer. The human mind is our carbon filament, it makes us work. Also a carbon filament is information that we take into our brain to be processed. In high school, I had an honors curriculum : Honors math, Honors English, and Honors History. This was the carbon filament that made me work during that time period. It served as a basis for success in college.

A king manifests his destiny. You too must do this. A king succeeds at what he puts his mind to. You must do what Cicero told the children of Rome –emulate this greatness. King Akhenaten was a great king. What are you going to be great at? Act champ-like, think king-like. Open your eyes to a brand new horizon, a greater perspective.

The way a champ acts is the way you should act. The way he moves is the way you should move. The way a king thinks is the way you should think. A king must withstand any thunderstorm. In other words, there will be turbulence and disturbances in his path. He must withstand him. For instance, negative people provide a thunderstorm. You must shield yourself from them mentally. A king instinctively is a leader of men. Make like a king and be a leader.

A king's learning curve has a steep slope. He amasses lesson after lesson until he gets it right. Plato, a Greek philosopher said, "Remembering is learning." King must ultimately remember his lesson in his climb up. This, like success is a process. A king must withstand the storm and be more powerful than a hurricane by remembering his lessons.

A king must have an understanding and view of the Cosmos. He must understand the Universe and Universe Law. He must understand his place in the galaxy. He is no ordinary man. When you go into the jungle you must understand the language of lions and tigers. In other words, like Charles Darwin said in "Natural

Selection" you must adapt. The key to adapting is leveraging one's talent and intellect.

Trace back your greatness. Where did it all start from? It is started with exposure to greatness or the sight of greatness. It's a wonderful sight to see someone dig deep inside of their being amazing - a race car driver like Mario Andretti, a pilot, a surgeon, like Dr. Ben Carson, a teacher, a lawyer like Johnny Cochran, etc.. A flower blooms with time. A boy becomes a man with time. There is power in imagination. Imagine how great you can become. Let this imagination beyour everyday course of thinking. Imagine the Universe is in your mind.

You can also trace back your greatness to being surrounded by great people. Michael Jordan was surrounded by greatness: Scottie Pippen, Horace Grant, and Jim Paxson. They won six championships together. General George Washington was surrounded by great commanding officers during the American Revolution. They went on to win at Valley Fo rge and the war. Put yourself in position to being great by being around great people. A CEO has certain people around him on daily basis on his executive board. He can only be as good as the people around him. The flower in a field must be surrounded by other beautiful flowers and not weeds to flourish. This is called transcendence. You can trace your greatness back to an initial excitement. Being excited leads to greatness. Nothing happens until you are excited. It's a spark, a charge, cosmic energy, a chemical process. You are not complete until you have achieved. To achieve you have to believe in yourself to a great extent. Acting like a champ is being bold and courageous. It's thinking big, beyond the sky. Acting like a champ is practicing one's art preserving in difficult and trying times. If you could be great, what would you be great at?

To make it takes perseverance. One must persevere and stay the course. Perseverance made Ali the undisputed heavyweight champ of the world. Perseverance is what led explorer Leif Erickson to his discoveries. Perseverance helped Thomas Edison overcome 10,000 failures before inventing the light bulb. When it comes to your dreams, persevere to the end. Endure life's long distance race for life is not a sprint.

What do we admire about a champ? In addition to champ's perseverance, we admire him for the "mental high" that he gives us. I remember the mental high I got from watching Mike Tyson fight in the ring. His performance was flawless and he seemed invincible. He was intense and the intensity transcended to those who watched. The other thing we admire about this champ is his strive. Finally we admire both his endurance and his struggle and sacrifice.

A king strives to further expand his intellect. His creative in his thinking. Repeat the self-affirmation. "I am a king (or queen)", " I am a champ". A king is optimistic. He sees light at the end of the tunnel. He also instills hope in other people. In 3100 B.C., King Menes gave Egypt hope that it could cradle civilization. A king has a mountain of hope. In your endeavor to be great, you need hope. You have to think on a high level like a king. He is above anything petty. His mind goes to dimensions untraveled to by the average man. He explores the unexplored. He leaves no stone unturned. Imagine yourself a kingdom. Imagine having the mind of a king. A king stretches his imagination. His reach goes beyond any geography. His mind is limitless. His mind flows like a river.

A king's mind is like gold, malleable. He is a critical thinker and fiery. He bases his decision on reality. He deals with directly what is in front of him. Seek a breakthrough, an idea whose time has come, an idea that will break the sound barrier. Lift yourself up. When the dust clears you have to be standing. When the storm is over you have to be on point.

A musical composition offers a key lesson about life; it has to be steady. In life you have to keep it steady. You aim for a goal, you must keep it steady as well. General Napolean Bonaparte was a great general because he was informed. A king becomes a great king when he is highly informed. In life you must be informed. This helps you make decisions.

In Greek Mythology, Zeus, the god of lightning and thunder is the protector of the people. A king is also a protector. In life you must protect those you love, your interests, and your mission. A champ must protect his mission.

In life we are looking for something. We must continue searching and striving until we find what we are looking for. King Dsojer had wit and a mental edge. Keeping your mind strong will give you a mental edge. A mental edge is key in our competitive capitalistic society. A king exemplifies character. He has strength and will and is determined to succeed. When you act like a champ and think like a king you will find yourself.

In a dark world the king has light. Greatness as in a king can bring you to life. A king illuminates the atmosphere. A king has spirit. He is the life of the kingdom.

The greatness process has two ghosts - doubt and fear. Doubt and fear are juxtaposed in stymieng the process.

The greatest of heavyweight champs was Muhammad Ali. He was the glory of the black race. Boxers to follow modeled themselves after him. As a goal seeker you may find it helpful to model yourself after someone who preceded you and was great. I model myself after Socrates and Imhotep. You are your own king, your own champ. Thus, you have to perform like one. You have to act like a champ and think like a king. When a task is un-daunting, dig deep inside your being and fulfill it. You are intrinsic, everything in your quest for greatness is inside or within. Martin Luther King Jr. was a PhD. Thus, he was a champ. He pioneered a struggle for equal rights in America and received the Nobel Prize. He was amazing.

You are priority number one. Focus. Examine the possibility of your greatness. Blast off like a rocket ship. Remember the cosmic energy of man has to be used to better himself. Alleviate the burdensome oblivion that leaves you in a state of confusion. In other words, don't be confused by your quest for greatness. Mediocrity is not an option. Imagine the magnitude of how great you can become and the perimeter of your greatness. It's your destiny. It's your will. Look in the mirror and say to yourself, "I am king, I am champ." And do it. You have to phase into the mentality that you can be as great as Osiris, Isis and Ra. This is indeed reaching for the stars.

Like a king, you have to unravel your greatness. You cannot let it go dormant. You have the potential, you just have to tap it. Recognize the fortune you have in the challenge to be great. The climb up the mountain is as much an adventure as reaching the peak.

You have to be able to handle the pressure of your dreams. Put in the work necessary to make your dreams come true. You have to build. That means constructing or making something out of nothing.

A king is very noble, very just, understanding, and fair. You too have to reach a level of nobility. Be just and understanding as well. In dealing with other people, you should be fair like a king. The striving for excellence requires for you also to be persuasive.

With a champ and a king you know there is a certain threshold of greatness. With a champ and king there is massive greatness. So to achieve greatness, you have to have a minimum level standard of excellence.

You have to attach yourself to a cause of some type. It may be the cause of greatness or the cause of helping others. With fervor commit yourself to a cause. Most people act according to what they don't want. This refers to unwanted conditions or circumstances. An unwanted state can drive you to do something great.

A champ is someone who has played the game of life intelligently. A king has mastered the system. Exchange your vices for characteristics of greatness. Trade in your bad habits for progressive action. Serious efforts culminates into great results. A river flows in one direction. You must go with the flow of your ambition. Find that thing you want and go after it. Serious effort determines your trajectory towards greatness. Your greatness will come into existence.

The PhD is trained in the scientific method. He develops a hypothesis to explain the phenomenon. A hypothesis is a conjecture. Once his hypothesis is confirmed he develops theory. You must develop theories on life to be successful.

Bring your bad habits to a halt. We are creatures of habit. Develop good habits and traits. Timing is everything. Wait for your time to shine. Then emerge. Rain or shine you have to be a participant in your own journey. Remember there are no excuses or alibis. Even when your journey looks difficult, you have to be willing to take it on. Visualize greatness. If you can see it, you can do it. Many of the great ones, Michael Jordan and Walter Payton used visualization techniques to achieve greatness. Olympians use visualization techniques. In addition to visualization, there is power in fantasy. Dr. Albert Einstein talked about the power of fantasy.

A king is a visionary. He sees it in his mind. You have to see in your mind where you want to be ten years from now. A king is confident in his own circumference. A king has a mathematical mind. He is constantly calculating risks and chances and making postulates and estimations. Does it seem like the stars have to be lined up correctly for you to be successful. The elements have to be lined up. The chemistry of success is on one which your make-up, i.e., mental and physical, must be in sync with the external world, your environment, Thus you must respond to your environment correctly. For every action, there is an equal positive reaction. A king has consciousness. Consciousness is awareness of things around you. For example, one must be conscious that one's environment may be indifferent to one's survival.

To be successful you must revel in your strengths. You are your own destiny maker. Whatever you do affects your destiny. Ascend to your highest. Greatness is no illusion; it can happen. Where you end up is usually a reflection of the decisions you made. Your decisions are a reflection of the way you think. Be a keen decision maker like a king. Be progressive minded like a king. A king is always trying to do better for his kingdom. Thus, he look for ways to do things. He is emotive. We remember the Trojan War.

Always be up to the task. Face your daunting challenge head on. Know that greatness requires superior effort. It often takes Herculean effort. When things get difficult to you, turn to nature. Take a look at the trees, listen to the birds chirping as if they're talking to you, and the wind blowing. The formation of clouds is much like the formation of your dreams. The blue sky, the cosmic bodies at night. Then raise up like a brand new day.

A king is also insightful. He has insights as to what it takes for his kingdom to flourish. As you grow from a boy to a man your insights of the world grow as well. Then you must think like a king ruling the kingdom. Once you do this the world will open up to you as if you had a kingdom of your own.

The climb of life is steep, but if you are motivated you can reach the top. If you have drive, no mountain is too high for you to scale. You can reach greatness in common hours with sheer determination. If your life is not going the way you want it to, then turn around. Brace yourself for catastrophe will come. How great you are in life depends on how well you deal with catastrophe. It's a matter of the moment. In dealing with catastrophe, always be intelligent and apply the strategies you applied when dealing with lesser obstacles. Apply a 360 degree circle. In other words cover all basis for the solution.

In the blink of an eye anything can happen to your journey. You must be able to overcome the adversity. For this it takes flexibility and resilience. Man has progressed through time due to these two characteristics. A champ, a king has these characteristics. The mind is a powerful instrument. It also possesses diligence. It allows you to overcome the most catastrophic states and conditions. It allows man to have one of the greatest journeys.

It takes discipline and fortitude to be a champ. It takes courage. You must elevate your mind and have psychological awareness and the ability to change your thoughts. We can get more people to be champs by looking inside of themselves and by encouraging them to look positively at things.

King Seti, Ramses II's father ran his kingdom with discipline and fortitude. He looked inside of himself and was positive. Much like an athlete, a champ has to struggle and sacrifice. Frederick Douglas, an abolitionist, said "If there is to be progress, there must first be struggle." A doctor embarks on a rigorous journey for a lengthy period of time to become a doctor. Thus, he knows struggle and sacrifice. A lawyer has to go to law school, pass the bar exam, and interview with firms after graduating. He too knows it takes time, effort, struggle and sacrifice. Anyone wishing to blast off must have the mindset that they will have struggle and sacrifice.

Communication skills is key. In the journey of life and competition it will be essential to be able communicate effectively. When you go into the jungle you have to speak effectively the language of the lions and tigers. A CEO is a master communication as is a PhD and president. A king has to communicate to his clergy effectively.

We have mentioned previously that desire is a key ingredient to reaching one's full potential, but hope is also essential along the way as one will face pitfalls in life and career. An ounce of hope goes a long way. A lack of hope is costly. There must be hope for a better self, better state and better life. A champ know your state and what you can do about it. He grabs hold of the wind and clings onto hope. Wash away mediocrity the way a dishwasher washes away grease.

A chance to shine like gold, a chance to move crowds, an intellectual can move crowds as much as a basketball player can. He must first see the power in it, the glory in it. There is glory in being a king, a president and CEO, valedictorian and heavyweight champ, and PhD. These people reach great heights. People look up to them accordingly. A king has glory the way an astronomer has planets. The perimeter of his glory is as wide as his audience.

A king can succeed amidst chaos. He makes something out of nothing. The closest distance between two points is a straight line, so a king goes right at his goal. A champ's mind is a force. This force is more powerful than any hurricane. The key to a king's mind is to feel free. Look to the Universe. The earth is but one planet, the many planets preoccupy but one galaxy, the Universe is made up of billions of galaxies. So as big as the Universe is, your mind must be. One thing, one common denominator of champs is that they are intense. In life it's a race and victory goes to swift. 9 times out of 10 with focus, the hare can beat the tortoise. Consciousness of your abilities is part of knowing thyself. This is knowing what you can do and what you cannot do, but also knowing your potential.

In a tumultuous world the greatest asset one can have is peace of mind. It is the ultimate end. You engage in battles on a daily basis. Your mindset must be of peace. You must have peace amidst chaos. Everything flows from peace. Peace makes the world go round. The mind faces great adversity. It must adjust.

In life it is as if everyone starts off with a clean slate. It is up to you to build, to make knowledge, just what we acquire. We are presented an environment to live and strive in. We must facilitate energy from our surroundings in order to survive. We must fit ourselves to survive. The biological clock is ticking. We are seriously in contact with our species and this contact produces conflict. Survival is predicated or one's ability to adapt.

In 1963, Dr. Martin Luther King led a march on Washington, D.C. Hundreds of thousands of people in attendance to hear this leader of the Civil Rights movement speak. His speech was entitled "I Have a Dream" and it captured the imagination of all who heard it. It inspired millions as it talked about getting to the Promised Land. Getting to the Promise Land as a people is equivalent to blasting off as people. King has charisma. A champ has charisma.

You need understanding - understanding of your environment, understanding of your needs, understanding of nuances of being a champ, and understanding of man's relation to the Universe. You must also keen judgment. The difference between man and animal is judgment. Also, move to the rhythm; don't be flat. Your brain works to a rhythm, your body moves to a rhythm. A boxer, a dancer, a president candidate during a speech, a valedictorian studying for an exam all do it to a rhythm. A writer must write to a rhythm with every stroke of the pen.

Often a goal seeker gets pixilated or confused, he must eliminate the confusion in his quest. He has to control his instincts. Also, he must "run-a-muck" or do whatever it takes. The stratosphere is not the limit. You have to have the right mindset. You have to have exclusive commitment and be capable of conscious conversion, the conversion of mind to action. Gratitude is required and you need the ability to evaluate your progress. Separate your needs from your wants, having un-daunting confidence and courage.

Leverage your skills. "Lever" means put into action. A champ is like a steamship. A steamship produces energy and power from steam. He is also like a windmill, producing power from wind. In other words, a champ produces power from natural elements and from within. You have to know the idiosyncrasies of a champ. He is competitive, instinctive, witty, resilient, and supple. Without a shadow of doubt, champs are purposeful people. They have a purpose and they set to carry it out. A man without a purpose is a ship without a rudder.

You have got to want the world and be willing to take possession of it. A champ revives the spirit of the world. A champ gets a vision. When he sees everything in his mind he sets out to take action. A champ, when he acts and thinks like a champ and king, is dedicated to a principle. This principle is being the best you can be and never settling for mediocrity. A champ has his eyes on the prize, his eyes on the world. My barber made it perfectly clear to me that the difference between a barber and a "master barber." My barber is a master barber who acts like a champ and thinks like a king. He wants to maximize his potential. He, like a champ, wants to be his best.

A champ has to know his strength and weakness. He has to know what he can do well and actually what he needs improvement on. He must then train to get the improvement. A Japanese proverbs states that the biggest room in the house is the room for improvement. Improvement leads to glory. There is glory in being great. When President Barack Obama gave his inaugural address it was a glorious day. When Lennox Lewis became undisputed heavyweight champ of the world, it was a glorious time. When Sue Cobb climbed Mt. Everest it was glorious. When Bill Gates founded Microsoft and was the richest man in America, it was glorious. One must work toward the crystallization of one's dream. He must effectuate action in the heat of the moment. Also, one must use his instincts and stick with his goals. He must use the strong tides of momentum to do well. If you have urge to be a winner, then act on it. In other words, if you're feeling froggy then leap. A champ must not get distracted from his goal.

My mind has been configured to achieve. You must get your mind configured to achieve. You have to program your instincts to achieve. LeBron James is the best basketball player in the world; he has his mind configured to be best. He uses visualization. He leverages his mind, that mental edge. Cassius Clay transformed into Muhammad Ali. You must transform from who you are to what you can become. Become your greater, self-actualized self. Lew Alexander became Kareem Abdul-Jabar. He found himself. You too must find yourself. That is essential to reaching the peak of Himalayas, the Rocky Mountain, the Appalachians, Mt. Everest and Alleghenies of Pennsylvania.

Change the course of history. Take your time and you will succeed. Imagine yourself on top of mountain, you can clearly see sky. Become the person you imagined. Take no shorts. There is a scarcity of economics in society. To be a champ with the times bring reality into its own. Base your life on life realism, be steadfast, read, listen, and act according to what you're sure about and not confused about. Be just like a king. Be yourself, break down barriers, have self-control and discipline, challenge yourself, brace yourself, bring and embrace change. This is what makes the great great.

A plant's chlorophyll absorbs sunlight in a process called photosynthesis. This is how it grows. A champ's mind is like chlorophyll it absorbs the energy of its environment to grow as well. A champ has to have wisdom. He gains wisdom from experience as a champ whether he be a president, CEO, a heavyweight champ, PhD, valedictorian, or king. Be wise like Solomon who wrote Proverbs. There are a lot of wise men and women in the world today. They solve the mysteries of the unknown world. What separates them is the way they think. A champ likewise must have vision. He has too see himself doing glorious things in the future. He has to rehearse this vision in his mind over and over again, then make it a reality.

What's important to a champ is intelligence. Intelligence is defined as the ability to think reason, and understand. A rare commodity, intelligence must guide society and mirror society. A champ has to have ability to lift himself up. He has to be capable of being inspired by himself and others and see the stars for what they are or see life for what it is intelligently. He has to be able to look at his own work and be excited.

A champ has to have a certain psychology. He must be able to identify obstacles. He must evaluate his environment. It is the utmost importance that he determines if his current environment is conducive to his development. Can it sustain him? Like Hercules in Greek Mythology, in life a champ will have to pass a series of tests. Obstacles in his environment represent a test that he must successfully pass.

The old mantra, "No pain, no gain," is operative in the life of a champ. He must train to be the best. A valedictorian must read and read between the lines. It's like a champ to work his muscles to build them up. This involves pain. The best way to nurture your dreams is by having the right attitude. Attitude is everything. You must replace limited beliefs with solid facts. The whole truth is that you can be what you want as your dreams dictate.

Chapter 5:
Profiles of Some Champs

◇◇◇◇◇◇◇◇◇◇

Kings:

King Menes reigned in Egypt. His reign was treated as the dawn of Egyptian civilization by experts. In earlier Egyptian lore he was called Ohe and Mena, "The Fighter" and was also referred to as "The Established". King Menes is remembered as the conqueror who first united Egypt under one rule. In other words, he united Upper and Lower Egypt and established the famous capital of Memphis, the seat of Egyptian unparalled cultural achievements during the reign of the Pharaohs.

King Dsojer or Zoser reigned in Egypt from 2668 to 2649 B.C. during the Old Kingdom. This was the Third Egyptian Dynasty. His father was Sanakhte and mother was Nimaethap. King Dsojer was a great military commander, a warrior king who waged war successfully against the inhabitants of the Sinai Peninsula. He increased the wealth of Egypt by the mining of Turquoise and other precious gems and metals. King Dsojer is mostly known as the king who commissioned Imhotep to build the Step Pyramid at Saqqara. This pyramid reaches the height of 60 meters.

King Ramses II also spelled Rameses or also known as Ramses The Great reigned as the third king of the 19th dynasty of ancient

Egypt from 1279 to 1213 BCE. It was the second longest reign in Egyptian history. He had wars with the Hittites and Libyans. Ramses II was the son of King Seti I. He set on restoring Egyptian power in Asia. This king was known for his extensive building programs and for the many colossal statues of him found all over Egypt. Ramses II lived to over 100 years old and was married to Queen Nefertarri.

King Akhenaton was also called Amenhotep IV. He was king during the 18th dynasty in Egypt and reigned from 1353 to 1336 BCE. He was married to the famous queen, Queen Nefertiti. Akhenaton introduced major changes in the spheres of religion, architecture, and art. He established a new religion dedicated to the aton, the sun's disk. Hence he assumed the name Akhenaton meaning "beneficial to Aton".

King Tut or Tutankhamun was a minor king in Egypt. He was one of the most famous Egyptian kings. He was a boy king dying at the age of nineteen mysteriously. He reigned in what was called The Golden Age of the Pharaohs. The discovery of King Tutankhanmun's tomb and its wealth is what made him so famous. His wife was called Ankhesenpaaten.

Heavyweight Champs:

Joe Louis was born Joseph Louis Barrow on May 13, 1914 in Lafayette, Alabama. Nicknamed the Brown Bomber, Joe Louis was heavyweight champion from 1937 to 1949. He was considered one of the greatest heavyweights of all time. His championship reign lasted 140 consecutive months during which he participated in 26 championship fights. He was victorious in 25 title defenses, a record for any division. In 2005, Louis was ranked as the #1 heavyweight of all-time by the International Boxing Research Organization. Louis was known as a hero in America during his reign. He was instrumental in integrating the game of golf, breaking the sport's color barrier in America by appearing under a sponsor's exemption in a PGA event in 1952. He was known as a modest, clean-living person and poised in the ring.

Muhammad Ali was born Cassius Marcellus Clay, Jr. on January 17, 1942 in Louisville, Kentucky. By the age of 22, Ali won the world heavyweight championship from Sonny Liston in 1964. Nicknamed "The Greatest", Ali was a controversial and polarizing figure during his early career. He is best regarded for his skills in the ring. He is one of the most recognizable figures in sports history and was named "Sportsman of the Century" by Sports Illustrated. Ali remains the only three-time lineal World Heavyweight Champion; he won the title in 1964, 1974, and 1978. Ali also won a gold medal in the 1960 Olympics in Rome.

Evander Holyfield was born October 19, 1962 in Atmore, Alabama. He is the former Undisputed World champion in the cruiserweight and heavyweight divisions. He earned the nickname "The Real Deal" Holyfield is the only four-time World Heavyweight Champion winning the WBA, WBC, and IBF titles in 1990, the WBA and IBF titles in 1993, and the WBA title in 1996 and 2000. He won the bronze medal in the Light Heavyweight division at the 1984 Summer Olympics.

Valedictorian:

Paul Robeson was born April 9, 1898 in Princeton, New Jersey. A graduate of Somerville High School in Somerville, New Jersey, Robeson won an academic scholarship to Rutgers College where he became a football All-American and class valedictorian in 1919. He received a total of fifteen varsity letters at Rutgers in football, basketball, baseball, and track. At Rutgers, Robeson was a debating champion and an orator. He was inducted into Cap and Skull Honor Society, one of only four students to do so. He was a member of the Glee Club as well.

Robeson received a law degree from Columbia Law School, while playing in the National Football League. At Columbia, he sang and acted in off-campus productions and after graduating, he became a participant in the Harlem Renaissance with performances in *The Emperor Jones* and *All God's Chillun Got Wings*. He next appeared as Othello at the Savoy theatre before becoming an international cinema star through roles in *Show Boat* and *Sanders of the River*.

President:

John Fitzgerald Kennedy was born on May 29, 1917 at Brookline, Massachusetts. Kennedy studied at Harvard University and after he had finished, he also served in the war. He was lieutenant of the PT 109 and when he was shipwrecked he survived and saved the lives of his crew. In 1952 he became senator of Massachusetts. In November of 1960, he was elected president after defeating Richard Nixon. At 43, he became the youngest person ever elected to the White House in American history 'till then. There was a crisis in 1962 when intermediate range missiles were placed in Cuba by the Russians. The world was close to a nuclear war in October, 1962 as Kennedy's military consultants recommended immediate air strikes. Kennedy instituted a naval blockade against Russian ships and demanded removal of the missiles. The Russians agreed to remove the missiles. Kennedy also put forth a lot of plans for equal rights for Americans during his administration.

Barack Obama was born August 4, 1961 in Honolulu, Hawaii. He graduated from Harvard University with a law degree. His wife, Michelle, also received a law degree from Harvard. Obama taught Constitutional Law at Harvard for a number of years. He also was a community organizer involved in many leadership activities. After being elected as a United States senator from Illinois, Obama served one term successfully. Then he ran for president of the United States and won. During his administration, Obama kept the government from shutting down and also initiated the ObamaCare Health Insurance program. He has been very active in foreign affairs as well and he removed American troops out of Iraq.

PhD:

Dr. Cornel West was born June 2, 1953 in Tulsa, Oklahoma. He is an American philosopher, scholar of African-American studies, and political activist. West was influenced by leaders of the local Baptist church in Sacramento, California where he grew up. He was also introduced to the writings of Karl Marx and the importance of political activism by the Black Panther Party. In 1970, at the age of 17, West entered Harvard University on a scholarship. In three years, he graduated magna cum laude with a bachelor's degree in Middle Eastern languages and literature. He attended graduate school in philosophy at Princeton University and was influenced by the American pragmatist philosopher Richard Potty. After receiving his doctoral degree in 1980, West taught philosophy, religion, and African-American studies at several colleges and universities including Union Theological Seminary, Yale university, the University of Paris, Princeton University and Harvard University. West book *Race Matters*(1993) critically examined the crisis of black leadership and was a best seller.

Dr. Neil deGrasse Tyson was born on October 5, 1958 in Manhattan, New York City. He is an American astrophysicist, cosmologist, author, and science communicator. Tyson received his B.A. from Harvard University, his masters from the University of Texas at Austin, and his Ph.D. from Columbia University. He is the Frederick P. Rose Director of the Hayden Planetarium at the Rose Center for Earth and Space in
New York City. He also founded the Department of Astrophysics in 1997 at the American Museum of Natural History and he has been a research associate there since 2003. Tyson is also a professor of astrophysics at Princeton University.

CEOs:

Bill Gates was born on October 28, 1955 in Seattle, Washington. Gates was founder of Microsoft and one of the most influential and richest people in the world. Currently Gates is working on his charitable foundation "The Bill and Melinda Gates Foundation." He founded Microsoft in 1976 when he formed a contract with Micro Instrumentation and Telemetry Systems (MITTS) to develop a basic operating system for their new computers. In the early days of Microsoft, Gates was very involved in several aspects of operations. In 1980, IBM approached Microsoft for a new BASIC operating system for its new computers. Microsoft was able to gain a dominant position in software manufacture as the personal computer market started to boom. In terms of his philanthropic activities, Forbes magazine estimated that Gates has given over $24 billion dollars in the four years from 2000 to 2004.

Oprah Winfrey was born on January 29, 1954 in Mississippi. Learning to read at two and a half years old, Oprah continued her excellence as an adult becoming America's first lady of talk shows. She surpassed the competition to become the most watched daytime show host on television as she was host of the Oprah Winfrey Show. This show earned her wide popularity as well as her own production company, Harpo, Inc.. Oprah was host of the Oprah Winfrey Show for over two decades. She is also an actress who has starred in a number of movies. In addition to being a talk show host and actress, Oprah is a businesswoman who owns her own television network known as Oprah Winfrey Network (OWN) and an editor of her own magazine, O Magazine, which is widely successful.

Chapter 6:
The Power Of Life

◇◇◇◇◇◇◇◇◇◇

The configuration of life is one in which you must live it to the fullest. You must self-actualize or live up to your fullest potential. One thing for certain you only get one life. In a matter of thinking one is sufficient. Use your imagination to direct your life and pave the way to a great fulfilling life. Like a flower blooms, man must bloom. Like a caterpillar metamorphoses, man must metamorphose. He must develop into an animal of power. Appreciate life for what it is worth. It can see you maximize yourself or minimize yourself.

The Universe has in store for you great things. You created yourself in your own image. Nothing is more powerful than life. It can be a man, a plant, an insect, a reptile. It is phenomenal. There is light. Life is light. You can look a man in the eyes and see life. The power of life is cause and effect. What effect does your life have(your life being the cause)? What impact does your life have on the ecosystem. An insect flapping his wings has an effect on objects thousands of miles away.

The foundation of life is action and reaction. For every action there is an equal positive reaction. This is science. Life produces motion much like the Universe. Motion is Universal Law. The more motion a life has the more powerful the life. In physics inertia is defined as an object's resistance to motion. Avoid inertia. Stay

transient. Life began in the ocean with an electrical storm acting upon a single celled organism. Hence, life began as man is a multi-celled organism. In fact, man has 200 million cells in his body.
In life man must elevate his action and reaction. He must adapt to his environment. When he adapts life elevates. He must adapt his mind and his body to deal with the chemistry of his environment. He must use the electric charges in his brain and his neurotransmitters to adapt to his situation. Much like the weather changes, man's life changes. He must be ready for changes. His readiness allows him to adapt and change.

Life is full of hardship, but through this hardship man has power. Of course, it depends on his reaction. Much like in psychology you have stimulus and response, in life you have hardship and reaction. How does one react to danger? You react with motion, positive motion. Self-preservation of life depends on motion. Sedimentary beings do not elevate, they do not progress. When man self-actualizes it is a reflection of motion, reaction, and progress. And of course it is a reflection of hardship. The power of life is increased with positive reaction to hardship. The mind is strengthened.

Much like the constellations have a place in the sky, man's life has a place in the Universe. Powered by his imagination he is a gem in the Universe. Although the Universe and his life is an accident, he is here for effect on the ecosystem, the Universe, and life. At every stage of life, man must upgrade. He must advance. Early civilizations of Persia, Babylonia, and Egypt were advancements or upgrades of mankind. The configuration of life took shape. Mesopotamia, another early civilization was a reflection of the upgrade of thinking. Man's power is his thinking. Thoughts are the seeds of life. With action, these thoughts produce the root of an eventual upgrade.

How does man metamorphose? He must transform his thinking in an upward direction; more action within his thoughts, more advancement. Life is powerful when thinking reflects powerful thoughts. Powerful thoughts can get you in motion and get you out of inertia. So having metamorphosed, man can fly. This adds credence to the fact that man like life is powerful.

When will life have power? When you align yourself with the power of the Universe. What gives a planet the power to remain in orbit? Being aligned with the arrangement of the Universe. What keeps man with life? Being aligned with action and reaction. Man is only as powerful as his reaction.

A man's reaction is only as powerful as his thoughts. If his thoughts are, "I am great" and "I am powerful", then he will be powerful. If his thoughts are, "I am less than" and "I can not do it", then he will lack power. His life will lack effect, lack power. He will be less than powerful reactions to hardship. Thus, he will not upgrade his life. He will have little transcendent impact on the life of others.

Thinking of life as light, a lack of light is darkness. Lifelessness is an ocean without fish. Light itself is power. Light is an upgrade from darkness. Light is a reaction to darkness. With every breath there is power in life. There is power from birth to death. You are born with an infinite mind; there are endless possibilities what you can conceive with it. You think with this infinite mind. Your mind is the power source. You are made powerful by what your mind can see. It has the capacity to reflect. Thus, you can reflect on your life, your actions and reactions, and you can upgrade yourself or make better actions and reactions. The mind has evolved into the most important organ of man in his life. Once simple, it is now complex. Once not able to do much, it can now do very much. The mind is a transistor of the Universe. It gets its power from the Universe.

With the mind, man can react or overcome obstacles that are in his path to fulfillment and reaching his full potential. Man uses his mind to battle the hardships that he faces in his life. He sees in his mind what position he wants to be in and moves toward getting in that position. His mind is capable of details and blueprints. Man mind is more powerful than any hurricane.

It is mind over matter. In life man must have mental edge. Usually in the field of battle, it is the man with mental edge that will be the victor. This is true in sports, business, and in life. The one who adapts mentally will prevail. Survival of the fittest pervades and you must rely on your mind, your psychological edge. Think your way to survival. Think your way out of a problem, a disadvantageous position. Think your way to better reactions. If your environment is not conducive to your mental development, react. Don't be a fish out of water. Be in an environment where your mind can flourish. One of your life's needs is self-actualization. This requires the proper environment and position with respect to your actions and reactions. Self-actualization is the full blooming of man – reaching his full potential. It is a god-like feeling, intense to the highest degree. Self-actualization makes life even more powerful. Experiencing the emotion, love is another power of life. Progress or going from a lower position or state to a higher one is another power of life.

There is nothing more chemically powerful, i.e., inspiring than human progress. Progress like a man who could not walk to a man who can walk is an uplift, an upgrade. It can be sudden or it can be gradual. Man's progress is the composite of all his actions and reactions. His capacity to react to hardship leads to progress. Man is powerful because of the fact that he has life. Man spreads his wings and flies over the clouds of life. He advances to a greater civilization, greater medicine, greater science, greater understanding of the Cosmos. He has discovered the undiscovered and seen the hidden. Nothing is more powerful than a man with life. Man has nothing more powerful than his life.

Along with life must come salvation. Man's reaction to his circumstances and the variables of his environment determines his salvation. It is errant to think that some celestial being is going to swoop in from the sky and provide 6.5 billion people with their salvation. That's not prophecy, that's man made ideology and myth. *You* must react. *You* must take action. Use your life force itself as a means of salvation. The striving of greatness and success is a reaction in itself and an installment on salvation. We cannot possibly be waiting on a man who lived 2,000 years ago to somehow come back and give us salvation. That is illogical and unscientific. Our minds are more powerful than that, besides we have been waiting patiently for so long and calamities still affect us daily. The scientific approach is to provide salvation for yourself by flourishing in the physical and mental as well as spiritual, intellectual, and emotional.

Man's reaction is his thinking. His infinite mind must be used for salvation from hardship, pain and suffering. Thoughts must be pure and far reaching. Thoughts are the greatest technology that man possesses. Mediocrity is no correct reaction to man's environment. A still mind with inner peace is what he strives for, a positive reaction. What lies in man is the great self-responsibility of his own salvation – the salvation of humanity. We must advance the collective psyche in order to react effectively to the hardships evolving in the world. We must react intelligently to the ills of life as intelligence is our greatest power of life.

There have been those who have exemplified great reactions to their environments. Kings have reacted with wisdom and knowledge. King Menes united Upper and Lower Egypt founding civilization. King Ramses II went to war for his kingdom and he reigned longer than any Pharaoh except one. Akhenaton's reaction to the collective psyche of his dynasty in Egypt was to change the thinking of the people. The salvation of the people of this world may require a change in thinking. We must let the great ones lead the way and harness the power of life. The power of life is about chances. We have been given chances to react. We must make the most of our chances. Our salvation, our greatness depends on how we use our chances. We must emulate those who used their chances wisely and effectively.

The power of life is the power of the human spirit. Our reaction to hardship affects our spirit. You can observe how powerful a man's spirit is. When you react by striving for greatness you are maneuvering for the salvation of your spirit. When you succeed at a goal, your dream you are positioning yourself to salvage your spirit. Acting like a champ is positioning yourself for the salvation of your spirit and mind. Your mind must survive as well. You must be fully alive. You must be fully free. Along with the power of life comes the endowment of an imagination. Your imagination comes up with action and reaction to situations. Your imagination must be wide. You must imagine yourself a champ, a king, a successful person, a great one. Imagine all that your body, mind, and spirit can accomplish. Look to others for inspiration and ideas.

An example of action and reaction toward salvation was Dr. Martin Luther King, Jr.'s reaction to injustice in the United States. First he was exposed to the reaction of India's Gandhi, namely nonviolent protest and civil disobedience. He then emulated the great Gandhi. He led a bus boycott in Montgomery, Alabama that was a successful reaction and it catapulted him into the leading civil rights leader of the time. King thought of the salvation of humanity as he led his movement with vigor and energy. He led a march on Washington that was historical. Hundreds of thousands listened to him speak about equality and the power of life. His imagination was wide as he dreamed of a new nation that judged people by the content of their character not the color of their skin. This was King's reaction to hardship. Reaction must be a reflex, an equal positive reaction. Man must master his circumstances together by being great collectively and individually.

The power of life is our challenges. Our inner desires produce challenges for us all. We want this and that. We want trinkets. So we blaze the saddle in search for our desires. This provides a spark within us. In addition to our desires, the architecture of our own salvation provides us with a spark. The strive for greatness is in essence a strive for salvation as we psychologically depend on this greatness. So we take our chances. The strive for greatness helps us maintain our sanity. We cannot be aloof, we must be focused on our reaction for our desires and salvation. We must save ourselves and we must meet our own desires. Man helping man is the way to do this. Technology is a better way of doing something. A better way of reacting to the environment is acting like a champ and thinking like a king. This is the blueprint for success and greatness and even salvation of the spirit, mind, and body.

One must have faith in the Universe to know that we were designed with the ability to survive. Man's brain is made of protoplasm. It contains billions of neurons that carry information related to survival and reaction. It is the most complex computer that exists, more complicated than any microcomputer with its bits and bytes. A mind is a terrible thing to waste. The mind is the apparatus that has to be operationalized in order to react to life's many variables and conflicts. Man must be a problem solver and a decision maker. He has choices in life. He is charged with making the right choice given many alternatives. The brain and the mind are two powers of life that define man's chances and circumstances. We are still evolving; we will only get greater and greater over time.

Another power that man has is the ability to metamorphose. His mind may crawl for a period of time in his youth and early adulthood, but by the time that he has made many reactions and choices and experienced life, he will be able to fly. This is development. You must take action when there is something in the way of your development. Call on all of your supports. Call on the Universe for guidance as your reaction determines your fate. In life, you will drift toward what you were supposed to become. However, to get to your destiny you must respond to obstacles, adversity, hardship, and conditions that impede your progress. Life has power, you can't waste it away by drifting off into a spell. Movement is recommended. Forceful action must replace complacency and hopelessness. You cannot be inactive and expect to be successful or afforded the greatest possible chance of salvation and survival.

This book tells you the maximum way to react to your environment. You must react the way the great ones have reacted. How do you react after reading this book? You apply the philosophy of this book to your powerful life force. Your life force has the potential to convert dreams into reality. It has the ability to carry you to a better place, a better state of being, a better existence. React to your environment by being a free spirit. Having a life is just half the battle, you are expected to do something with it. This has been a philosophical chapter about action and reaction to hardship; you must take it a step further by challenging yourself to become a champ possessing the power of life.

Chapter 7:
COVID 19, We Must Not Surrender

◇◇◇◇◇◇◇◇◇

Frederick Douglass said if there is to be progress, there must first be struggle. Life can be a struggle because life has adversity. Adversity can block you from becoming great, becoming a champ, or becoming successful. Obstacles will come your way like storms. You must weather the storm in order to achieve your best. As far as you go down is as far as you can go up. You have to use adversity to your advantage. Let it make you stronger, wiser, more complete and knowing that you can overcome. Crisis can leave your life disjointed. You can progress. You can get back to life once the storm is over. Man is more powerful than any thunder and lightning. Man has it in him built-in an ability to overcome the most difficult adversity.

Adversity can come in the form of situations or people. This is called personified adversity, when people are the obstacle that is in your way of reaching greatness. For example, you may tell people that you want to be CEO of a corporation. For every one person that encourages you, there will be ten that will dissuade you or discourage you. I have been around difficult people before and I know that they come in between you and your goals. I just try my best to circumvent them as much as possible and keep my eyes on the goal.

You can't be encumbered by adversity. Don't be intimidated by it. Approach it the way a young Serena Williams approached a tennis match with Steffi Graf. She knew her own ability so she wasn't intimidated. Approach it the way David approached Goliath, the way the tortoise approached a race with the hare. You must know your ability and be confident. You must commit yourself to overcoming the adversity. Life will present you a series of obstacles, but keep in mind it will also present a series of opportunities. Don't judge the glass as being half empty, judge it as being half full.

For every goal there is a negative pull or force going against that goal. However, for every action there is an equal positive reaction. So you must react to the negative force called adversity by adjusting. For example, we live in an information society. There is a clutter of information that makes your vision cloudy. Thus, you must tease out the important information and base your actions on the important relevant information. We live in a competitive capitalistic society with many people vying for the same scarce resources. You may be competing for a job, a mate, or other goal. Have a plan and follow through. Expect obstacles. Just be ready for them. Be ready to swing one way or the other. This means you have to be flexible.

Adversity comes in many shapes, forms, or fashions. You just have to first recognize them when they come, then have a plan to overcome them and be even better off after them. Just know that the task is not impossible. Hercules had to overcome a series of obstacles beginning with his birth in order to progress. Moses had to overcome great obstacles in his journey. They are not impossible rather possible. You just have to believe in yourself and know that where there is a will there is a way.

Murphy's Law states that things may go wrong and they will. Adversity is reality. It affects everyone at different points of their lives. There can be loss of a loved one, financial loss, setbacks in one's career, failure of one's health, etc. It can be a myriad of things that may go wrong. You must incorporate this law in your thinking by preparing for whatever comes your way. Adversity can affect you mentally and/or physically. You have to be strong. You have to be resilient. Don't let adversity prevent you from reaching your ultimate goals.

In quantum physics, quanta represents uncertainty. In life we have to deal with uncertainty. In mathematics, X represents the unknown. Not knowing and having uncertainty equates into adversity. We have to make decisions in the context of uncertainty. We have to choose among options with unknown variables. Uncertainty makes decisions more difficult and life more challenging. All you can do with this is make the best decision you can possibly make with the information you have available.

The only constant in life is change. Change can serve as adversity. You have to be able to manage change and realize that change can be good. It can create a different situation for you or lead to new experiences. You have to embrace change. It can offer some key vicissitudes, many that are positive. People face a change in spouse, a change in career or geography, a change in lifestyle, etc.. Things may be different at first, but you learn to make adjustments. You adapt. You have to understand what the change is about and how it affects you. If it is an undesired change, you must brace yourself then make decisions to work around the change. Going from high school to college was a change for me. I embraced change and prepared for it by studying at a college library while still in high school to acclimate myself to that new environment. Thus, change and the adversity that comes along with it requires a transition. This transition must be mental and physical. When you face a change, perhaps something about you must change too. You may have to change your way of thinking or your strategy.

Adversity is borne from the conditions around you. It is relentless. Thus, you too must be relentless. Your perseverance must be relentless. Survival goes to those who persevere and adapt to such adversity. Society has faced depressions, natural disasters, war, poverty, and other adversity. However, we produced the proper thought that catapulted us out of these crises time and time again. You must have the right thoughts when you face adversity and you cannot give up at the first sight of the adversity. Many of the great thinkers of our time faced adversity before becoming great. Albert Einstein had a learning disability. This did not prevent him from becoming a Nobel Prize Laureate in Physics. He discovered the theory of relativity. Abraham Lincoln faced depression throughout his lifetime. This did not prevent him from becoming the sixteenth president of the United States and preserve the union. Jackie Joyner-Kersey had serious asthma that often impaired her from breathing. This adversity did not prevent her from winning a gold medal in the Olympics. Stevie Wonder was born blind. That did not prevent this musician from reaching stardom and winning several Grammy Awards.

It's how you react to the adversity that matters. If you fail to react then it will swallow you up. However, if you resist it you will have a chance to resume your progress. It takes resistance, readiness, and resilience. You must resist the effects of the adversity. You must be ready for it at all times as it can surface at any time. Furthermore, you must have a high level of resilience to this powerful force. Without these characteristics, you will be set back by adversity and you will not capitalize off the adversity the way Einstein, Lincoln, and Joyner-Kersey did.

A champ or a king doesn't rise to the top without adversity. They face it as well. Mike Tyson did not have any of his natural parents in his childhood. He faced this adversity early on. This did not prevent him from becoming the youngest heavyweight champ ever at 21 years of age. Facing adversity is a psychological thing. When you face it, you cannot let it break you down. You can't fall apart, you must keep your mind intact. When you face adversity this isn't the time to try less, it is a time to try more. It is pivotal that you don't falter. You can fall down, but you must get right up. After everything is said and done, after the dust clears, you have to still be standing. It takes a focused and strong mind to deal with certain adversity. Some people fall by the waist side, but a champ, a king will get stronger because of it.

Imagine yourself losing everything you own. In other words when it rains, it pours. Are you strong enough to deal with this? Will you crumble? Or will you prepare to build once again brick by brick? You must stay hopeful and think optimistically under this pressure. You have to dig yourself out of this hole some way. Don't fall apart. This is the time to get stronger. Don't let it affect your neurological system negatively. Calm yourself and move quickly, but intelligently. Realize how you got in that situation, so you can figure out how to get out of the situation. Employ the ideas and input of others. Adversity can be life-shaping and life-altering. It can shake you where you stand. You have to remain determined. The possibility of progressing should drive you to push harder.

Remember that as far as you can go down is as far as you can go up. Be relentless and work hard despite adversity. A king faces adversity in his kingdom all the time. From his throne he quickly reacts to the adversity wasting no time to mobilize his clergy. Your life is your kingdom, you must react to the adversity and mobilize your thinking.

With adversity comes circumstance. Your life is made up of circumstances, some wanted and some unwanted. You often have to live with circumstances. However, if circumstances are within your control, make adjustments to change them. Adversity has a spirit of its own. Man's life has adversity the way a garden has weeds. The weeds have to be removed. Circumstances must be removed as well as conditions. Adversity puts you in an unwanted and undesirable state. This, you know, is where you don't want to be, so you are driven to do what you have to, to get out of this state. So you are driven not only by what you want, but by what you don't want.

Adversity is like a storm. There's thunder and lightning and a gusty wind. You have to weather the storm in order to get beyond your circumstances and get to your goal or destination. It's not always easy, it's often difficult, but that's what a champ does – deal with the difficult storms. Once you go through one storm, it prepares you for upcoming storms. Adversity is the same way. Be prepared for obstacles. This will make it more feasible to handle it. You have to telegraph obstacles. In other words, you have to see them coming before they come. Expect the unexpected. Man is more powerful than any storm. Man can and has overcome difficult storms. However, the key is to have adversity make you stronger. Only the strong survive. The elements will challenge your survival so you must battle them to the fullest. You beat the elements by being focused and having a clear mind. Clarity of purpose is also important to overcome adversity. A king knows his purpose above anything else. A champ wouldn't be a champ had he no clarity of purpose.

Adversity distracts and can disturb the mind. You may have momentum toward a goal, then a setback occurs. This can disrupt your mental focus and your confidence, your hope, and your drive. Adversity can be counterproductive to all the effort you put into a task. It should be thought of as a challenge – a challenge to your mind and body. The key is to remain focused. Reinvigorate your Herculean efforts. Resume your hard work and determination. Don't fall down at the first sight of adversity, stand up and progress forward. Converge on your dreams. Crisis can come at any time, you have to be ready. Make adjustments when you can. Don't let anything hold you down. Master your environment, be a product of your environment not a victim of it.

Don't let setbacks or adversity impede you from having peace of mind. The best thing to do is overcome it directly, but where that is not possible, overcome them indirectly. In other words, mentally overcome it. The mind is that powerful if you use it powerfully. You have everything you need innately in most cases to deal with adversity, crisis, and setbacks. Don't let obstacles change who you are and what you want or want to become in life. Don't let it be darkness for you, let it be light. Adversity is feedback according to some experts. Take it as feedback on your efforts. The Chinese have two meanings for the word crisis; one is problem and the other is opportunity. Think of adversity as an opportunity to make an even steeper climb of Mt. Olympus. Remember if you want to climb Mt. Olympus, do everything you need to do to climb Mt. Olympus. To overcome adversity, do everything you need to do to overcome adversity.

In some cases adversity can make you need to switch ships or switch paths, change goals. This means change and a new focus. That's why it is helpful to be multi-faceted. If one avenue is taken away, you can make another avenue. There are many types of changes people make in life – change in college major, change in spouse, change in career or geography, i.e., environment, change in lifestyle, etc. These changes require adjustments and transitions to be made. The adjustments must be made intelligently. The concept is called change management.

Adjacent to change is failure. Failure of one's goal may serve as a major obstacle. It's not over. You have to regroup and know that failure is a part of the success process. The author of *Chicken Soup For The Soul* series talked about how his book failed to be published for a long time before it became a best seller. He persevered and believed. The results were astonishing. The author of *Harry Potter* spoke about how she lived in poverty before coming up with the breakthrough book and made millions. The glass is not half empty, it's half full. You can be a champ in your own right.

When facing adversity think of what someone great would do to overcome it. You emulated the great to become great, when you face adversity you have to continue to emulate them. They obviously have a formula for success. More than likely they have a formula for overcoming obstacles. Most importantly they have the mindset needed to overcome adversity. It comes a time when you just have to say to yourself, "it's time to do things right."

Don't settle for less. If you want to be a movie star, do everything that movie stars have done to become movie stars. If you want to be a surgeon, do everything that surgeons have done to become surgeons. If you want to be an astronaut, blast off and do what they do. If you want to be rich, do what rich people do. Overcome the obstacles that they had to overcome to reach your plateau. In addition to mindset, it takes strategy and an approach. Come up with the concept in your mind that adversity can make you that much better, an opportunity like the Chinese believe.

The soul of man can be offset by adversity if he allows it to. His soul is everything that makes him *him* - his brain, his mind, his body. Adversity threatens the well-being of man and at the same times gives him a chance to grow and develop. He can turn a bad situation into a good one. The measure of man, how great he can become depends on how well he adjusts to adversity. What else explains how a deaf man can become a great composer of music? You have to first have in mind that it is possible to overcome obstacles. Be a possibilitarian. Overcome un-daunting challenges that make up your life.

You have to maintain calm when facing crisis or adversity of some kind. Remember that adversity is a force and a champ is one who overcomes a force of some kind. So be a champ. You need to have poise when facing obstacles. Do not let it break you down to pieces or fragments of yourself. Solve the riddle. Your goal is what's at stake, all of your effort. Fierce battles are ahead. You have to be calm and poised in these fierce battles, it helps you mentally and physically. Don't defer your dreams because of adversity and crisis. Michael Jordan remained calm when his father was killed and went into minor league baseball leaving the NBA. He remained poised and excelled at a sport he had not played since he was a teenager. He returned to the NBA eventually and won a championship despite the loss of his father. One has to be poised for success. A king is known for always remaining poised when his kingdom faces crisis. He calmly comes up with the solution to the problem. Your mind works better when you are calm and poised under pressure.

King Menes united Upper and Lower Egypt developing the first civilization in 3100 B.C.. He was enterprising. Often to have the mindset to overcome obstacles requires you to think like King Menes and be enterprising. He faced the obstacle of change when uniting Upper and Lower Egypt, but having an enterprising spirit, he succeeded. The world has been afforded mathematics, architecture, navigation, accounting, science, and medicine ever since the birth of his civilization. These Egyptians made something out of nothing. You too must be enterprising enough to make something out of nothing. Nearly 500 years later the Egyptians built the first pyramid with King Dsojer. They were enterprising and inventive. You have to think outside of the box also. The Chinese came up with physics 2500 years before Galilean Physics. They too were enterprising. This study of physics helped them overcome many obstacles. They discovered that waves had cosmic energy, that tides had magnetism. Satori, a sudden awakening and the momentary fusing with a higher energy was discovered in Eastern philosophy, i.e., the martial arts. It is helpful to experience Satori when facing adversity. Your intellect works better. Your mind becomes more powerful.

When you self-actualize you can overcome adversity that you could not prior to self-actualizing. You are at your best self, your highest self and you can handle adversity with calm and poise. When you self-actualize it's like you're suspended in air. What's happening internally in your mind rarely happens to anyone. It is the ultimate greatness. If you had a life of adversity that you powerfully overcame and you became more powerful after it, you can self-actualize. Man only uses about 5% of his brain, when you self-actualize this must increase dramatically. Being a champ, you put yourself in position to self-actualize. It's a complicated concept, but I have experienced both self-actualization and Satori. My mind had been taken to the limit, I adapted, and thus was able to reach my highest. It was amazing. Not everyone will self-actualize, but many of us can be great. Not everyone will experience Satori, but many will experience different levels of energy.

Adversity can clip your wings. Prior to adversity, you were soaring high in the sky, but adversity can come in at any time and distract your flight. Figuratively, man can fly. I am not talking about the Wright brothers. I am talking about spiritually and psychologically flying. You can lift from the ground of mediocrity and become great at something. You just can't let anything hold you down to the ground. Spread your wings and take off, hover over the clouds and under the sun. In order to fly you must have transformed your mind for greatness. You must have transformed your mind for success. For Satori. For self-actualization. Blossom like a plant, bloom like a flower. Like a flower that receives pollen, receive energy from your life and others and your mindset, desire, and drive. Let what you don't want push you to action. You don't want mediocrity. Calmly navigate the rigid terrain and the bumps in the road. Take charge of your life.

There are two things you need to know when trying to overcome adversity. You must know yourself and you must know your environment. You must know when you are a fish out of water or when your environment is not alright with you. It may be counterproductive or contrary to your survival or your goal. How successful can a lion be in a cage? He must be in the jungle where he can roam. Man is the same way, he must be in an environment where he can flourish. In some environments adversity will be prevalent, whereas it might not be prevalent in other more suitable environments. You have to determine what is the right surrounding for you, knowing yourself.

Do not ever give up on yourself no matter how difficult an obstacle may be. Maintain your belief in yourself no matter what you face. This is important because you are the person that you mostly rely on to overcome the adversity. Your mind must remain confident and intact. Know that there is light at the end of the tunnel and that the sun will shine on you again.

Being ambitious helps you overcome adversity. When you shoot for the stars, you don't let anything get in your way of getting there. Set high goals, goals sprung forth from your imagination - goals that others wouldn't dare to set. Think big like a king. Think positive like a champ. Have an adventurous spirit. Be a supplanter which means "one who overcomes by force" – the force of your ambition.

In reading this book, one can see that life is about competing forces in the world. Adversity is a force, but your mind is a force as well. It can be a powerful force if you program it like a champ and king. These are powerful entities. Whether in contemporary society or historically, a king, a valedictorian, a CEO, a PhD, a president, and a heavyweight champ have been a force and they overcome other forces. Power concedes nothing without force. In physics, there is the concept of centripetal force. The drive for success is a force in itself. The world revolves around forces. Even in space, there is adversity. Cosmic bodies hit up against one another. Asteroids exist. What are the asteroids in your life?

The first step to overcoming adversity as a force is awareness. You must be aware of the adversity that threatens your goal. If you are not aware of it, you cannot battle it. You become aware of obstacles that may come your way by learning from others who pursued the same goal or path. Once you are aware of the adversity, you can rise above it.

Chapter 8:
Persevere the Pandemic and Strive for Greatness

◇◇◇◇◇◇◇◇◇

Prime Minister of Great Britain, Winston Churchill was asked to make a speech at Harvard University. Churchill stood up said, "Never ever give up!" That was his entire speech. Obstacles will come your way. You may have a goal, an ambition, and a dream. You must be relentless. Your effort must be Herculean. In Greek mythology, Hercules faced a series of obstacles. Hercules was not crumbled by obstacles, he persevered and survived the test. I was told by an expert that I would not graduate college. I stayed the course and persevered and graduated with an honor award and two bachelor degrees.

I had configured in my mind that you will obtain your goal and nothing would stop you from getting it. Thus, perseverance is a psychological characteristic. It takes a certain mindset to keep going or like Churchill said, "To never ever give up in the face of adversity."

Thunder and lightning will come inevitably. You must protect yourself from it by preparing. Preparation is a common denominator for those who obtain their goal. Don't be encumbered or intimidated by obstacles. David was not intimidated by the giant Goliath and wad thus able to defeat him. He preserved over the odds as he had his mind fixed on winning. When the tortoise raced the hare knew the hare was much faster than him. However, the tortoise persevered and won the race. They told Ossie Smith he was too small to play major league baseball. Smith could have encumbered by the negative feedback, but he responded by preserving and the rest is history. He not only made the major leagues but was inducted into baseball's Hall of Fame after his stellar career. These are examples of having that mental edge, the ability to persevere to the end.

Michael Jordan was not a starter on his high school basketball team, but he persevered any way. He eventually starred for the University of North Carolina and later won six championship and several scoring titles in the NBA. He had the mindset that if fail, you try again. Thomas Edison failed 10,000 times before successfully inventing the bulb. In my case there was the catastrophic failure of my health in college at age 21. I struggle through the storm and I preserved. Now I'm an author of multiple books and my health is stable. I want to obtain master's degree in Business from a top 25 Business School. I was prepared and I overcame.

It is the spirit of perseverance that makes a man great. It is survival of the fittest as Charles Darwin says in his treaties, "Natural Selection." The man most fit is the man with the ability to persevere that amidst obstacles. Perseverance is the way of adjusting and adapting to circumstances or conditions. Once you are in circumstances that you do not want, you must persevere out of it. If you have an unwanted condition much like a fatal illness in my case, you must adjust and adapt this you must persevere.

Patience is a virtue. In addition, patience is a psychological characteristics that works complements perseverance. As they say

Rome wasn't built in a day. Nor was Egypt, the Ottoman Empire, or the empires of Songhai, Mali, or Ghana in West Africa. These great civilizations preserved strife in the elements, but each developed over time with patience. Jordan had to wait before his time to his shine came. Edison was very patient and his trials and tribulation and brought light to all of us. Beyoncé Knowles wasn't a megastar overnight. She patiently waited for the process of success to take place. Now she is one of the most famous singers in the world. Albert Einstein had a learning disability. This he preserved with patience and became a Nobel Prize winning physicist as he came up with the Theory of Relativity, $E=mc2$. The great Pharaohs of Egypt endured many dynasties and discoveries before they could build the Pyramids and the Sphinx. Their civilization begin in 3100 B.C. while the first pyramid wasn't built until nearly 500 years later.

Time is of the essence. If you master time, you begin to master perseverance. It takes time for flower. Man is similar, he blooms over time. A caterpillar larvae must wait until he completes metamorphosis before he can fly as a beautiful butterfly. Barack Obama honed his craft by teaching Constitutional Law at Harvard. He then went on to community organizer and senator. He underwent a process of patience and perseverance and became president of the United States of America. Elizabeth Taylor went through a mutual process of patience and perseverance to become the leading actress in Hollywood. My fellow Purdue alumnus, Drew Brees spent a great deal of time playing football before he won a Super Bowl for the New Orleans Saints. He was patient and he persevered the elements of adversity.

Hold fast to your dreams. You dream of making something of yourself so you can feel proud and have a sense of self-worth. The best thing comes to those who wait. And the best thing comes when you have perseverance. You must endure. If you want to climb Mt. Olympus, do everything you need to do to climb Mt. Olympus. There will be challenges, the climb might be steep, but you must persevere. If you want to be a champion golfer, you must be patient and get enough reps. You must persevere and one day you can become Tiger Woods. If you want to be a leading astrophysicist, be patient and one day you will become Neil deGrasse Tyson. If you want to be a leading brain surgeon, just be patient and persevere and you can become Dr. Ben Carsen.

The process starts with a goal. You must set a goal. There are many approaches to setting goals, but for the most part begin with something you want or want to become. Be unsatisfied with your present circumstances or conditions and strive for more. The key is to not get complacent and the key is to not settle for mediocrity. No great man ever settled for mediocrity. When he was young, Muhammad Ali told Joe Louis that he too would be heavyweight champion of the world. He didn't settle for mediocrity, he strived for the highest peak and became heavyweight champion at the age of 22. Ali persevered. Mediocrity doesn't measure up to greatness. If you want to be great you must first set the goal of becoming great.

It is easier to set a goal when you know your purpose. Your goal must directly satisfy your purpose. If your purpose is to help others, then perhaps your goal may be to become a brain surgeon. Know your passions, what you enjoy doing and what you're good at. I had a passion for football growing up, so I climbed Mt. Olympus. I got in my reps in Pop Warner Football and high school. This made it possible for me to meet my goal of becoming a college football player. I had to persevere season after season to get to my destination. I got there.

So you must have patience, purpose, and passion in order to persevere. You can control your own destiny. You can control the elements and outcomes. There is no excuse. You must strive. Never give up. Endure. Life is not a sprint, but a long distance race.

Dr. Maya Angelou, author of the poem, "Still I Rise" was passionate about writing. She knew her purpose and she patiently honed her craft. After the process of perseverance, Maya won a Nobel Prize. She reached the pinnacle of greatness because she wanted to be great. You have got to want to be great. You can never fuse with higher energy unless you want to be great. This fusing with a higher energy is called Satori.

You must persevere to meet your needs – physiological, psychological, and spiritual. You can never self-actualize or live up to your full potential until you persevere and become great. I have self-actualized in my life. It took many battles and obstacles to make this proliferate. It feels God-like, powerful, intense, and incredible. Even after you self-actualize, I have found, you must persevere. I want to be the best writer that I can become, to disseminate information to my reader that will help them persevere the hard times and storms. Man is more powerful than any hurricane and his ability to persevere makes this a reality. You can make your own way and carve out a niche in this world.
Lay to rest all the excuses and don't procrastinate. Have courage.

Another antecedent to perseverance or ingredient necessary is to think positive. Philosopher, James Allen reiterated the saying, "As a man thinketh, so shall he be." You must be in a positive mindset to be in position to persevere. Plato, born 426 B.C., thought positive as he attended The Academy. He was Socrates' student and he thought positively about philosophy. He persevered opposition to become Western civilization's greatest philosopher. Paul Robeson was an all-american football who became a singer, actor, linguist, lawyer, and activist. He was a positive thinker and he persevered grave opposition to become a modern day multi-faceted, multi-talented genius. When I went down with a fatal illness, I didn't stop thinking positive. I thought what can I still become and what can I learn from this experience. Consequently, I fought hard and it is not known whether I would have self-actualized if I didn't think positive about my fatal illness.

There are 4 D's to success. They are desire, drive, determination, and dedication. As we said earlier you must set a goal or desire something. Then you must have the antecedent drive or motivation to strive for and go toward the desired thing. The sun doesn't shine until you have determination. Finally, you must make a commitment. This is dedication. In addition, the sun's rays doesn't burn without a focus. You need focus in addition to the 4 D's of success. You must make like a submarine's periscope and focus your sights on a target or in this case, a goal. Focus can make all your dreams come true. Winning is preferred over losing. Persevering is preferred over quitting. There will be setbacks and life can be a roller coaster, but you have to maintain your Herculean effort. You have to maintain your persistence. You must complete what you start. If you want to be an astronaut, you must start from the beginning and work toward mastering this science. If you want to be a mathematician, you must work on mathematical equations and persevere the subject matter. I was once an accountant. This is a complicated field, but I persevered until I became good at it.

Sport is a metaphor for life. In sports much like in life, you must have stamina to win. Stamina is the ability to maintain your effort and performance. Life goes in stages. You must persevere at each stage. Like an essay has a beginning, middle, and end, life has a beginning, middle, and end. Thus, you must persevere in the beginning, middle, and end in order to complete your journey and win. One thing you don't want is obsolete goals, goals that you set and never persevere to obtain.

In order to persevere, you must work hard. Many of life's most successful people are those that worked hard. It is the Protestant work ethic. When I was an All-State football player at the high school level I got by mostly on talent, but when I played at the collegiate level everyone else was talented so to distinguish myself, I had to work hard.

Perseverance is a spiritual characteristic and not just a psychological one. One must have enthusiasm and spirit to persevere difficult times. The power of the human spirit is that it can lead you to overcome whatever comes your way. When you persevere you will have progress. There is nothing more powerful than human progress. I remember I had to take heavy medication to the point where I couldn't hardly walk. My wife took me to a park with a pond full of geese. We would walk around this pond every day for weeks until I got my limbs working again. Before you knew it I was playing basketball at the park. Progress is a beautiful thing – baby steps. I progressed one day at a time and one step at a time.

When you persevere, hard work comes to fruition. It pays off. It is a magnificent day when your hard work pays off and you have crystallized your goals.

It will storm on your sunny day. You must hold fast. Keep your destination or the end in mind. Know that there is a pot of gold at the end of the rainbow and that the sky is the limit. Keep your dreams upstream. Learn from the stories of other people who persevered and reached their goal. If they could do it, you can too. If they can gather the psychological and spiritual resources necessary to hold fast and meet their goals, so should you. There are lessons in life. You must remember the lessons given to you by your parents, your teachers, your leaders, and your contemporaries. Napolean Hill, success writer, interviewed rich businessmen and wrote "Think and Grow Rich", a success formula. What he was provided from Rockefeller, Ford, Carnegie, and others were lessons of perseverance and the concept of perseverance itself as it helps you survive life and meet your goals. Once you persevere your difficulties, you will roar like a mountain lion.

There is something from the Universe that allows man to persevere and persist. Man is connected to the Universe and has the Universe inside of himself. Thus, man experiences Universal Law. One Universal Law is motion. Man has to accomplish his goals and meet his ambitions. Of course, when it comes to ambition, man must shoot for the stars.

The Universe is in order. Thus, you should pattern your life to be in order like the Universe. Everything you do should fit your purpose and maintain such order. This takes patience and discipline. You have order in your life when you live by certain principles. These will vary but overall you should have principles and virtues. Your goal should not surrender your principles. When I went down with a fatal illness, I didn't get desperate or undisciplined; I focused and honed in even more to my principles.

Man is powerful. He has been on Earth for 200,000 years and has evolved into a powerful entity. Man invented flight, electricity, the computer, medicine, art, and philosophy. He has the power to give life. He controls his own destiny from the time he comes out of the womb until the time he dies. His brain is the most complicated and powerful organ that exists. With his brain processing his outer world, he overcomes obstacles and solves problems for his fellow man. Modern medicine and science are examples of this. Man is like Imhotep, the physician who discovered the circulation of blood in the veins or Cesar, who discovered the cure for rattlesnake bite, or Dr. Daniel Hale Williams who performed the first open heart surgery. The process of discovery enthralls man. Man is always progressing. The overall life expectancy of man in some countries exceeds eighty years. Man has persevered tuberculosis and cancer. Guided by the Universe, he persists and never gives up. Guided by the luminescent stars, man continues to fly beyond the horizons.

Chapter 9:
Hope

◇◇◇◇◇◇◇◇◇

Hope comes in many forms. In the midst of a storm, there is hope. At the end of the rainbow, there is hope. When love is lost, there is hope for a new love. Death is replaced by life. Darkness is replaced by light. Disease is replaced by ease and pain is replaced by relief. When life is at a disjunction, there is hope to get back on path. Life itself is hope and hope is life. When you have lost the battle and lost the war, there is hope. There is still life left in you. Reach for the stars and look to the heavens. Grab hold of the wind and cling onto hope. Hope will lift you. Above all else, hope for a new day, a new beginning, a new chance in life, in the battle, in the war. Win the battle, win the war.

Life is hope and hope is life. If you have hope, you will live well. If you have a mountain of hope, you will climb to the top. The hopeful go beyond the norm and those who have hope go beyond the mediocre. If your goal is to be a doctor or an astrophysicist, then hope that you can get over the obstacles you face to become these professions. An ounce of hope can go a long way. A lot of hope strengthens the soul. Hope helps keep the soul at ease. Hope cures illness. Hope lifts spirits. When times are difficult, people must have hope. When things go awry, realize there is light at the end of the tunnel. When you are stuck in a hole in life, have hope. Hope can break the shackles that we have around us. Once enslaved, we are now free. This is due to hope.

We hope to meet our ambitious goals and we do so. New goals arise as does new hope. Along with this are new challenges. We hope to fulfill our own demands for a good life. We hope to meet our standards of excellence. We must ebb out a landscape of hope for the future. We must create doctrines of hope to live by. As a navigator of life, we need to gather all the pieces of the puzzle of life together. If we can't find all the pieces, we must hope to find them all.

It is the kingdom of love that we find ourselves. Love magnifies our lives. It completes us, our beings. Love lifts our spirits, it makes us dance, it makes us run. On the throne, the king knows the importance of love. So he has a queen to share his life with. A loss of love can be unbearable. Thus, it is hope that we find ourselves turning to. While love magnifies life, hope preserves it. Hope allows you to return to where you began. It gives you reassurance and consolidation. Hope is knowing that you will get there. Hope is knowing that the great day will come. Hope is knowing that love will conquer all and that all your problems will be solved. Hope is as wide as the ocean. It encompasses good feelings toward good outcomes – optimism.

Borne out of positive thoughts, hope is the seed planted in our head that keeps us abound. Hope transforms the soul of man. The personification of greatness is through hope. Hope is the great driver of civilization. Disasters have come our way, but hope has kept us afloat. Even when we only had a little bit of hope, it catapulted us to salvation. Hope gives us perseverance and perseverance is important in our journey. If you desire something, you must persevere to get it. This process starts with hope.

We can hope for a brighter day. Things can get better. A cancer patient must cling onto hope; he must cling onto love. He must persevere. When things seem dismal, one must look up and hope will come. When man has his back up against the wall, he must have some form of hope. Hope can alleviate us from anxiety and stress. Stress comes from one's outside environment and can weigh a person down. Anxiety can hinder a person from performing their best at something. The great athletes of the Olympics today and thousands of years ago performed well because they hoped to perform well. Their hope and dreams guided their movement through air and space. They hoped to win gold and this was the reason they trained so hard to get it. Their stories are amazing.

No man is an island according to Thomas Merton. When you have man, you have hope. They say you are the company you keep and you must surround yourself with positive people. The positivity of the people around you transcends onto you. If the people around you have hope, you will have hope. If the people around you lack hope, you will correspond with a lack of hope.

When the weather of life is torrid, we follow with hope. The hurricane of life comes our way, we follow with hope. A topsy-turvy society with displaced values must be followed with hope. When a tornado of problems surface, we must grab hold of hope. I cannot think of a better place for hope than in our lives. I cannot imagine a world without hope.

In order to have a clear understanding of the Cosmos, we need hope. This is a complicated event that requires discovery and judgment. Philosophy is man's relation to the Universe. We have to hope to have productive philosophies on life like Confucius in order to have productive minds. The yin and yang of our existence is hope. It is our North Star, our Big Dipper, our constellation of stars. It is our galaxy, our Universe, our sun, our center. We won't let hope run out; we will replenish it at every turn. We will let hope run its course in our lives, setting us free. This is freeing us from worry, trouble, and strife. Opportunity will come knocking at our door and we will seize it. We hope for more arising opportunities.

Hope puts us in position to maximize our opportunities. Hope for a better position in life, in career, in family, in health, etc.. Wars have been fought due to lack of hope. Nations have fallen due to a lack of hope as have empires. Lands have been conquered due to a lack of hope. We need hope for our salvation. Nothing from above is responsible for our salvation, so we must engineer it ourselves. Much like we have to seize our own destinies, we have to seize our own salvation. Our lives offer us a lot of pain and suffering, we need salvation. It starts with hope. We must hope to be lifted from pain and suffering and discomfort. We can have speculation and beliefs that vary, but our common denominator must be hope.

Education is a catalyst for hope; it is a spark. A broadened horizon gives one the ability to hope for a better tomorrow. It is such a spark that carries man into the future with a chance to succeed at his dreams. And it is with this hope that man brings forth a powerful next generation. As we educate others previously uneducated we give them hope for a better life. This is occurring all over the world. When one has purpose and follows it, it fastens hope. There is nothing more powerful than a hope that won't waiver no matter what. An ounce of hope goes a long way. A lot of hope can be the building block of a new world. Keep in mind that some people do, for some time, lose hope and their plight is not great. However, there is hope in the air.

Our basic premise is that hope is the antecedent to good living. It lays the foundation for great things to occur. It is the basis for good health. Being positive and optimistic creates a good outcome for man, as man is the product of his thoughts. You are your own captain of your ship. You are your own leader. You must be guided by your inner hope. You can achieve peace through hope and vice-versa. An avalanche of problems can come tumbling down on you, you must hold onto the solid foundation of hope to stay on your feet.

Adversity comes in many forms. It can handicap you to the fullest. You must not allow it to do so. You must hold onto a seed of hope and be prepared for the rainy days. A cold winter storm cannot even stop a man with basic hope. A man with hope can fly over the cloud of adversity that hovers above us all. Even the wind is not too much for a man with hope.

Hope begins the process of believing or faith. We must have faith that we will survive the elements and we must have faith in others. This process does not work without hope. Hope can be instilled in us by our parents, our siblings, our teachers, etc. We hope for the best and prepare for the worse. We must believe or have faith in the process of life, in the process of discovery, in the process of health. Faith empowers man, but it too does not occur without the installation of hope and this may start at an early age. We must have faith in love, love of humanity, and world peace. We must have faith that our problems will be dealt with intelligently.

We must allow intelligence to rule our world. Intelligent decisions must be made and we must come up with intelligent strategies for coping with society's ills. This is our hope. We can hope for this to take place. Rational thinking is preferred over irrational thought. Logical positions must be taken on issues that affect us all. We hope this will happen. We must not define intelligence as being able to place a square peg into a round hole, but as the ability to think, reason, and understand and solve effectively society's ills.

We know that no empire was built in a day. So no matter how hopeful we are, it will take time to cure society's ills. Time is of the essence. Time is a complicated construct that millions try to master but fail. Hope along with the proper management of time can get us to our destination. There is a great deal of gravity in hope; it keeps us grounded. Hopelessness itself is a disease. Armed with hope, man can meet his goals in common hours as Henry David Thoreau said. Without hope we will just float over the circumstances of life. With hope we will have the will to win. With hope we will be able to adjust to the different terrains of life. A life without hope is a catastrophe, a devastation.

With hope, the sky is the limit. If you conceive greatness, you can achieve greatness. This requires hope. In my game whether it be the game of football or the game of life, there will be turning points. You have to have hope when things are not so well. In any event, you can reach high stakes if you are equipped with hope. Hope leads to courage. Courage leads to courageous acts. Through courage, man can accomplish many things. He can withstand adversity and succeed against odds. Man can measure up to his own design through courage. All champions in life in many walks of life have had courage and hope. Joe Louis was one of the greatest of all time in the boxing arena. He had courage and hope as well as perseverance. Dr. Martin Luther King, Jr. put his life on the line for a cause. His courage was apparent.

A lion in the jungle gives birth to cubs. Even the cubs have to have hope to one day grow up as mighty and ferocious as their mother. So they learn from their other how to hunt and make it in the jungle. Man is not unlike the lions. People have to one day be great and meet expectations. So man trains, educates himself, practices, and prepares for his future. He too can become mighty.

Hope is something that occurs inside a man. It is embedded in his soul, his being, his inner self. Hope is a spirit in of itself. When a man is ill all these facets come into play. He digs deep inside for whatever strength his soul has left. Hope lifts him by giving him the feeling that he can make it through. There is nothing more inspiring than watching cubs progress or in this case, man.

Human progress is hope. One step at a time, we progress. We gather a little bit of hope at a time and move forward. Every day we face events that jeopardize our progress as human beings. The force that we have to combat this is hope. Hope is just that, a force. A master is someone who has perfected a skill. It can be martial arts, Economics, science, or basketball, or in this case, hope. A hope master is a master who can use a little bit of hope to get a long way. He can get out of a difficult predicament with an ounce of hope. He can withstand the torrid weather with just an ion of hope. He can use hope to the best of his ability. Even if he is ill, hope can begin to make him well.

Everyone hopes for something. The extent of one's desires determines the extent of their hope. People hope for people, places, and things. They want to own and experience things that better their lives. A hope master makes these things happen using hope – various levels of hope. A hope master, by nature, desires greatness. This is a thing. Thus, he holds onto hope until and even after he achieves greatness. A champ by nature is a hope master. He clings onto hope in good times and bad. His greatness can not occur without hope. A champ must meet many challenges in order to be a champ.

I was thirteen years old living in New Brunswick, New Jersey. I was a straight A student and an outstanding Pop Warner Football player. I played for the New Brunswick Raiders football team. For my excellence I was honored as a Pop Warner National Scholar, one of only two in the state of New Jersey and thirty-five in the country. I entered New Brunswick High School during the fall of 1987 with high expectations of achievement. I continued my path of excellence over the next three years making the honor roll and playing varsity football. I also ran track and played basketball. All of my efforts culminated into an award winning senior year in which I was voted "Mr. NBHS" and Highest Achiever. In football I was awarded Most Valuable Player and named to the All-County and All-State teams. I graduated at the top of my class in 1991.

This took me to the next level, an academic and athletic scholarship to Lafayette College in Easton, Pennsylvania. Lafayette was a member of the Old Ivy League, a very elite college with just 2,000 students. My first two semesters at Lafayette, I made the Dean's List and won a NCAA silver medal for academic and athletic achievement. I wrote for four college newspapers and edited another and was a peer counselor. My second year I studied at the University College London in London, England. Here I studied Economics and Mathematics. I had a chance to travel to the Csech Republic, Poland, Romania, Latvia, Lithuania, Estonia, Russia, Ukraine, Austria, Bulgaria, France, Amsterdam, and other countries during my travels. I experienced the culture of various different countries.

After returning to the states I presumed my workouts for football and continued my classes. Then there was a tragic turn of events. I had just returned from the trip of a lifetime, I was in a zone, and my mind was filled with power. I was a top student at the university and among the best and brightest in the country. Only, now I was diagnosed with a tragic illness by a doctor. In fact, I was diagnosed with an illness in which 1 out of every 4 persons with it dies.

I had to leave college for the rest of the semester and a doctor told me that because of my fatal illness I would in most likelihood not be able to graduate college and graduating college meant the world to me. I returned to New Jersey to regroup. To keep my spirits up having had my health fail, I would go to my eleven year old brother's baseball games three days a week. His youthful spirit picked me up and I had hope. I had hope that I would one day be able to return to college and fulfill my destiny.

Staying positive, I defied the predictions of that doctor and returned to college that next semester. I knew I had a year and a half to go and my body was filled with medicine. I wanted it though and I had hope that I could overcome the shocking tragedy. Even though I had to struggle through the material and work twice as hard to master the courses, I beat the odds and graduated with two degrees and a scholastic award. If it were not for me having hope, I would not have graduated and I don't know what my fortune would have been. I worked for two Fortune 500 corporations and taught for a brief period of time before embarking on another journey. I matriculated into Purdue University's Krannert School of Management where I would pursue a Masters of Business Administration.

Still with the fatal illness and the dream of becoming a master, I entered the school with optimism and a strong drive. The curriculum was rigorous at this top 20 business school and it was very competitive. Fighting through all the medication, I studied hard and I graduated from Purdue in two years. I had the opportunity to teach as an instructor for a year as well at Purdue. Once again, hope allowed me to excel and beat the odds, go against the grain, and prove them wrong. After a brief career as a sales consultant for another Fortune 500 corporation, I was accepted into a PhD program in Marketing at the University of Massachusetts in Amherst, Massachusetts. I had a rare and fatal illness and yet I still excelled to the highest possible level of education.

I stayed in the PhD program for three years amassing a 3.8 grade point average, going off to conferences, and excelling in Social Psychology as well. Then my illness nearly took my life this time. I didn't finish my promising career as a doctor, but I managed to hold onto to hope for my life. After making through the difficulties, I pursued writing. I wrote my first book and I also trained as a boxer in the boxing gym. I trained as a boxer for five years and embarked on a career as a writer. I wrote this book for the people and my goal was to become one of the world's greatest writers. Now I can reflect on my life and share my lessons of hope with the world.

At times hope was very little in supply. I had a major illness and dreams of greatness juxtaposed with it. There was suffering and pain and despair. There was anguish and discouragement. I had my doubts at times, but glimpses of hope came in and rescued me from mediocrity. Hope is that last breath that you may have left. Hope is a bright light in a dark situation. It is that fire in your belly. It keeps your spirit working. It saved my life and saved me from becoming just another man who had a chance to reach his full potential. I had trials and tribulations since becoming a successful writer that go beyond the scope of this book and are the subject for the next book and my mind has been stretched to the limit. However, I have seen a lot in my journey and I have self-actualized or reached my full potential. It happened in June of 2014 and I will never forget the powerful feeling. This further gives me hope that I will reach my plateau again as I form new goals in life.

I have a fatal illness, but that didn't stop me from making like a bald eagle, the greatest of birds, and soar high above the clouds. I blazed the saddle and mastered the material. Hope permeated my sick body and what emerged was a powerful spirit settling for nothing less than greatness. When you are down and out, hold onto hope, onto light, onto anticipation and see things through. See things all the way through. See how far you can take this life - this great, broad, and full life. Dig deep inside your being and pierce your way through the mist of despair. Then you can see clearly how great you can become.

Chapter 10:
The Physical, Mental, and Spiritual

◇◇◇◇◇◇◇◇◇◇

So the greatest is the physical, mental, and emotional. Act like a PhD. A PhD approaches his problems like he is doing research - very scientific in his thinking. Life and greatness require strategy. A champ is always strategic in his thinking. In Greek strategy is strategos meaning ingenious plan.

In this time and place, greatness is made in mental space. The mind is the initiator of greatness. The body must be conditioned for greatness also. Love your own heart, be fascinated by your own mind. In a storm of adversity, the idea is to stay. In Chinese, "stay" is doului. You must resonate greatness.

A champ must have integrity in not just his professional life, that which he is known as a champ, but also in his personal life, that which he is known as a man. Ethics and morality, knowing what is right versus what is wrong should not be overlooked in his journey to the top.

A champ must elevate his game to match the circumstances in his environment. His circumstances eventually have to be lifted. A champ is not unlike anyone else in that in life we have to deal with uncertainties. So he must make decisions amidst uncertainty with his mind. A champ blazes the saddle. He blazing. You can feel the aura of the champ. There is a certain magnetism about them. When you are in presence of a champ, you feel the greatness. You feel the energy. Rome wasn't built in a day. It takes time and patience to become a champ. It doesn't surface overnight. A valedictorian goes to school from kindergarten to 12th grade. A heavyweight champ trains for years before getting his big chance, a president like a CEO has a hierarchy of positions before becoming president, a king usually has to wait his turn to take the throne like Ramses II, Pharaoh of Egypt. A PhD must build his skills and knowledge over time. Patience is a virtue.

When at Lafayette College, my undergraduate institution, I had to wait patiently to get to the football field. By my sophomore year I was on the field making a contribution to the team's success. We were Patriot League Champs that year. So I know how it feels to be a champ. It takes time and patience. Furthermore, to be champs, we had to act like a champs.

No matter what type of champ you are, you have to involve yourself in the process of discovery. There are mysteries in life that must be uncovered. Who will discover the next truths? Veritas is truth in Latin. Who will explain the next phenomenon? There is knowledge out there to be obtained. The mind of a king is powerful. He has a positive self-image. He has wit and spunk and he is majestic. He configures his thinking strategically. He thinks positively. He is worldly and he is passionate. You must think like a king when you strive for greatness. Think like a king when facing competition and think like a king when you pursue your goals. Imagine yourself a kingdom. You have to rule over your own kingdom. After all a king meets the criteria of greatness.

A king will be with you in your darkest hour. A king will exhaust all avenues of opportunity for the betterment of his kingdom. He will explore as exploration is the first phase of success. He will emulate the greatness of those who came before him. He will succeed against the odds. He will challenge himself to be a better thinker. A king is a champ in his own right.

A king is ambitious; he dreams big. His horizon is broad, he shoots for the stars. He formulates a plan and crystallizes on his plan. He is mover and shaker. He reaches his full potential. You too must strive to meet your full potential. In other words, measure up to your own design.

In a tumultuous climate and chaotic world, a champ must learn to be calm. In the face of any adversity, you must be calm and poised. A boxer is poised as he faces flurry punches from his opponent. A president is poised like John F. Kennedy when on a brink of war. The world is shrinking. There is a need for new champs all over. Together they can make it a brighter world for all of us. Champs bring a great deal of zeal and energy into our society. Whether it be president making a policy or a CEO bringing new products into the world, there is a lot of energy being brought to society.

Michael Jackson was a champ of people. He wasn't any of the categories discussed in the book, but his album, "Thriller," made him the best of all time and we mentioned champ is a metaphor in life of being the best or blasting off. Actor Samuel L. Jackson is a champ of movies. He made more movies than other actor. Ralph Ellison was a literary champ. His book, "Invisible Man," won a Pulitzer Prize. A champ can indeed conquer the world.

A champ has to prepare for perils that will surely come in life. A champ doesn't have it easy. His life is a challenging and rigorous. He must be up to such a challenge. He must change this challenge into an adventure. A champ has to be able to deal with crisis. The world is not seamless; it has its dysfunctions. A champ must stay. You have to get rid of the prison that's in your mind.

Be explicit when designing self-affirmations: "I am a winner, I am a king, I can do this, today will be a great day, there is nothing I cannot do." "I am beautiful, I was born to fly." When you face an obstacle use self-affirmations. When you face an obstacle, you must switch it in your mind and make an adjustment. You must remain on course. Your thinking will not just sway you toward greatness, it will get you there.
The Universe is connected to my thoughts. The time has come asunder when I must lay it all on the line. With unlimited thoughts and an infinite mind I scheme on the goals that I set. My intelligence has been tested. With Herculean effort I embark on my journey. The world is mine for the taking. In economics there is principle of marginal utility- the utility one gets from using one more of something. What's the marginal utility of one more step toward your goal?

Intertwined with your goal is everything you must do to get the goal. If you want to climb Mt. Olympus, know what you have to do to climb Mt. Olympus. If you want to be a doctor, do everything it takes to be a doctor. If you want to be a mathematician, do everything you must do to be that. You must discover the requirements for success in life. Ask any man what caused him to be wealthy. He will tell you he found out what it took to become wealthy. It's that blatantly simple.

With the determination of a mountain climber, you must be focused. When I was faced with unsurmountable adversity, a wise woman told me to stay focused. She told me if you love freedom, stay focused. I remained focused and overcame the adversity to stay focused. Find something to shoot for and stay focused on it. Even if you shoot for the stars, stay focused.

Pitfalls, downfalls, rainstorms, and setbacks are a part of the process of success. It is at these times that you have to try harder not less. Don't give up psychologically just because the road gets bumpy. You have got to get to the point where you expect rainstorms. The key is that you are able to adjust. On the frontier of life is the presence of personified adversity or difficult people. You have to adjust accordingly. Don't let difficult people in your mind. Be the bigger person. Be a champ.

When I was thinking of ambition, our theme for this book, I think of my 9 year old niece, Jayla. She is the best and brightest in her class, especially in math and science. She received a letter from the president for her academic achievements. She is champ. What I am most inspired about her is her ambitious mind. With ambition you can raise the roof. You can move mountains. You can be an example of excellence for people to follow. Jayla is like the pyramids of Egypt; she's amazing.

Act, think, and walk like a champ. Circuitous routes may be taken but you must be a champ at all times. The heights you reach will astound you. The plateau is for you to reach. With the certainty of tides, hope will be springing high. The shadow of greatness will be seen by others, so make it happen. You can be a maker of history. An African proverb states that "until the lion gets his own historian, history will always glorify the hunter." You will be lionized. The world will hear you roar. Start from the bottom and reach the top. Cover all the basis. The glory of greatness is in the balance. Don't let anything abbreviate your dreams. Stand erect. It's not lonely at the top. Be the crème of the crop. Let your inner light shine brightly. Only the sun, moon, and stars can be as great. I fantasized my way to the top. Einstein said, "There's nothing more powerful than fantasy. It was my ambition to make fantasy reality." First, you must acquire perception that you can be great. Let your imagination protrude the perimeter of possibility. Let your mind go beyond the boundaries of thinking.

A Japanese proverb states, "In order to get the cubs, you have to go in the lion den." In other words, you must make like a champ and king and be courageous. Greatness will come out like a bird hatching from a nest. Find your greatness. With one success after another you are building something. Remember you are in search of something. Break from your former self-improvement. Like the sunlight shines on plants, greatness will shine on you. You'll gravitate to what you're supposed to be. Greatness is eminent. As a champ you must prevail. A valedictorian prevails. As does the other champs mentioned in this book. As a champ you often have to have a personal Renaissance or rebirth. You may have to adapt to new situations and redefine yourself in light of new circumstances.

Lift yourself up. When you stumble and fall literally you have to lift yourself up. Likewise, when you fall figuratively you must lift yourself up. You must overcome obstacles. Adversity must not dull your glow. You must remain bright. You have to get back to your feet and stand tall. You must engage your mind with thoughts of progress. Watching a man progress is inspiring. Plant the seeds of possibility into your mind. Cast no shadow of doubt into your process. Just keep constant in your mind that you will live to see that day when you are great.

In life one has to be swift. To be swift one must bypass the illusions of other people. One has to bypass the disbelief of other people. Many will say that you cannot do it, so you have to believe you can. When someone is negative toward you, stand up tall, look them in the face and say, "I am somebody."

There is no scientific device that can measure the heart of a champ. The sky is the limit. He can go as far as his mind and body will take him. To become great means you have had a breakthrough. It can be an idea or ability of yours, but you must push it to the top.
A preordained destiny is not possible. You must form your own destiny as it is your own hands. When you work hard, you will find yourself light years ahead when you didn't work hard. It's simple mathematics, the more effort you put into something, the more you will get out of it.

A CEO is the most responsible for calculating the dreams of his corporation. He makes this dream a reality and for that he is a champ. A king is a protector of his clergy much like Zeus, God of lightning and thunder, was protector of people. A valedictorian polishes up his or her mind to be the best graduate in the class. A president makes the journey with his electorate. A PhD does the research needed to push this world closer to intelligence. A heavyweight champ is the pulse of us all as he excites us to the fullest.

A champ is psychological being. He has gotten there with his mind. Know that you have to have certain intimacy with your journey. Obstacles will be lurking. You need to balance yourself and deal with them.

You should seek to become a champion. You only live once. A philosopher who wrestles with the deeper meanings of life can be as much of a champ as a heavyweight boxer. A champ is somewhat a celestial being from the sky, a giant of Herculean stature. A champ has physicality and intellect; the two not only co-exist, they complement one another. You must tap into emotions that makes you a champ, the passions, desires and ambitions. You must know what pushes him to greatness. The winds of success will blow right by unless you get these.

The requirements needed to be a champ is not an Alfred Hitchcock murder mystery, it takes hard work and determination, skill and talent, circumstances and conditions. You need the right temperament and you have to be whole. In the mind of a champ, you'll find adventure.

Whether it be a president or a heavyweight champion of the world, to be a champ requires you to be hard, a certain level of hardness. To get out of an unwanted state or set of conditions often requires a certain level of hardness. As a champ you have to bring on the power - a magnitude of energy and ability. A champ is powerful. He has gifts. He has ability to make things happen. He is a mover and shaker.

When your life is at disjunction and you're in an unwanted state, you are half not whole. To get out of predicament and blast off, become a champ, you must hone in on becoming mentally, physically, and emotionally whole. A champ has strength and goals. Sometimes you got to grab hold of wind and go for the ride. Greatness is back where you belong. You were once great, now you should be great again. Make like a Fortune 500 Corporation. They differentiate themselves from the rest and are large enough to sustain large profits. They have strategies plans, goals and methodologies to accomplish such goals. You too must have a Master Plan.

Be aggressive like the Baltimore Ravens linebacker Ray Lewis or the San Francisco 49ers, Jerry Rice. Take self-initiative and be proactive. Your environment can bring out the best in us or worse in us. It can be conducive to blasting off. A fish does not flourish out of water.

A champ has to have certain mode of thought. He must act in accordance with his thoughts. His greatness will be eminent when he acts upon positive thoughts. While the thoughts helps form the intention, he must implement the intention, or act on his thoughts much like the brain send messages to act to the body.

When one acts upon a thought he wants success to occur as a result. When one embarks on any type of career, one wants to be successful at it or climb to the highest level. The result may be worthy of his effort and his effort must be great. The thought precedes the action, so in order for the act to be successful the thought must also be successful.

To become a champ you must almost have to become a machine with a fine tuned engine. You must become a machine that can repeat tasks effectively. Through repetition or practice with intensity you gain consistency and mastery. A champ is master of his art.

A lot of people don't know success, but more people know failure. May people have failed thousands of times before successfully completing their goals. There are many formulas for success. However, there is one main reason for failure - people get a few upsets and want to quit. They fall and instead of getting up they stay down.

Another area that keeps man from blasting off is man failing to see his full potential. This is part of knowing the self and one's own potentialities. This includes knowing one's strengths and weakness, challenges, and opportunities for growth. You can't reach the highest point until you believe you can.

The science of striving is consistent with the fact that what people admire is a champ's strive. It's the way which they strive for their goals, dreams, and fantasies. A CEO strives for his corporation to be a fortune 500 company. A heavyweight boxing champs strives to be undefeated and undisputed. A president strives for a strong economy and a valedictorian strives for academic excellence. Finally, a king strives for a powerful and protected kingdom that reigns forever. A champ must do away with doubts as Shakespeare said, "Doubt is our biggest traitor." It's as if all champs were called upon to do a job. It's up to them to answer the call. Just like any endeavor, a person seeking a goal must have a push. What's your push?

When you shoot for the stars, if you can't get a star, perhaps you can get a cloud. Remember to be ambitious in this world; you must have an ambitious spirit. Everything is there for your taking. The world is your oyster. The term "champ" is a metaphor for life. It means being the best. The most commonly known champ for instance is the heavyweight champ in boxing. In addition to the heavyweight champ in this book we have discussed other champs such as the king, the CEO, the president, the valedictorian, and the PhD. However, you can strive to be a champ at whatever you do as long you strive to be best at it.

A champ is casted in the role of leader. Once he becomes a champ, he assumes a role of leadership in our world. A champ is a role model as well. He must lead by example and conduct himself as a champ of the people. A valedictorian as much as heavyweight champ is a champ of the people. A lot of young people in school look up to a valedictorian. People look up to presidents, CEO's, kings, and PhD's as well.

The feeling of evading mediocrity is irreplaceable. The experience of becoming a champ and blasting off is unforgettable. The gain one gets in the blasting off from the norm is large. You gain mentally, physically, and usually financially as well. There is a strong correlation between blasting off and satisfaction in life. Becoming a champ offers you balance too.

Whatever is sleeping inside a person is awakened when one blasts off and acts like a champ. In order to do that he must first have the proper mode of thought for being a champ. Most importantly, he must think larger than life with large actions and standards for excellence. He must seek greatness to the fullest. When I got to the college football level, I realized that my natural talent alone couldn't catapult me to the top; I had to practice. This is true in many if not all areas. As competition and challenges get steeper a goal seeker has to rely on not just talent, but practice. It is one of the keys to success.

Man must do some soul searching. He must find himself. After this happens, watching him is like a beautiful symphony orchestra playing at the Russian Bolshoiy Theatre. It's like watching Madame Butterfly on Broadway or Shakespeare. It's like watching an Alvin Ailey dancer perform a dance routine. Watching a champ who has found himself is like a beautiful oasis to see with your own eyes or listening to the sound of music.

Make your goal the center of your life, the center of your Universe. Master your plight. Don't be dominated by others. Remember the lessons of your ancestors. Take action where necessary. Be virtuous. Unravel your problems or break them down - see them clearly for what they are. Size up the problem, then commit yourself to doing away with it. Clear your mind. I can't enough stress the importance of a clear mind. A clear mind is important whether learning physics or competing for a heavyweight boxing title. Finally, have a swiftness about yourself and be a fast study. Remember that life is a puzzle. To be successful you have to put all the pieces of your life together.

To blast off may require you to be different from the norm. We remember in the past the norm believed the world was flat, but Leif Erickson, Eric the Red, The Vikings and Christopher Columbus were different. As a result they made major discoveries for the rest of the world and they did so confidently.

In terms of confidence and assurance, my past history as a Pop Warner football star gave me confidence and assurance so that my senior year in high school despite injuries I made All-Star and All-State at running back. This confidence and assurance carried forward to college as I made the traveling team as a freshman and was playing in varsity games as a sophomore. I had the basis or grounds for confidence my past successes. It's one thing to know the theory about success and blasting off, skyrocketing above the competition and actually having the basis for the confidence to do something about it. Superman was the manifestation of Clark Kent blasting off. This took confidence.

In physics, inertia is defined as an object's resistance to motion. When trying to progress, we often times face inertia in the process. People emerge at different points or stages in their life. They avoid inertia. Emergence is the appearance of a better self - coming into your own. Man has to make connection to the world. He must touch the very soul of the world. He has to keep on reaching to the top, reaching his life capacity in the process. Notwithstanding the heat and passion of a champ is the anguish he feels when not being his best possible self.

Take your ambitions to the moon. The basis of strength is mind. You must get into the mind of a champ. He has a mental process unmatched and unyielding to any challenge. The mind lights up when a new challenge or idea presents itself. The mind also lights up with the extinguishing of any obstacle in the way of progress forward in any journey albeit big or small, mental or physical. Take a stand so strong that even horrific weather cannot move you from your position.

A champ is phenomenal in every sense of the word. He has mastered his environment, taken on his challenges, and blasted off into orbit. He is one of a kind. His pathway to greatness began at an early age and he stayed on path until he reached his plateau. There is an internal combustion that occurs when a heavyweight champ is competing. The same mental process occurs for the other types of champs or anyone breaking through to become great at something. The way of the world is that you have to break through the soil to reach the sunlight. You have to absorb the sunlight or whatever rays of energy your surroundings have to offer you. You have to have strength to carry out your goals. You have to search high and low for your calling in life. In other words, you are connected to and called upon by the Universe to fulfill a task of some magnitude. Become a champ at such a calling. It often takes acculturation or adjusting to a culture on the part of a goal seeker to become a champ.

Society depends on magnanimous individuals. A champ behaves in such a manner much like a president or king. A champ whether heavyweight boxer or PhD longs for intellectual stimulation. When you see yourself at the bottom, you must dedicate to climbing to the top the way you climb the Himalayas or Mt. Everest, the tallest mountain in the world at 29,000 feet. Remember the ultimate goal is to be a champ. Stay in the mind of a champ, respond the way he responds. Like a bird flying over clouds, you must ascend over your goals.

A champ has to be a forerunner. He cannot fade into the background. It is center stage for him. A champ has to negate all the negative and capitalize off of the positive. He has to mobilize the positive. A champ has to keep dreaming and not get complacent with his accomplishment. Tiger Woods accomplished a great deal in golf at an early age, but in his later years he still dreamed and strived to be the best golfer in the world, many years after he first blazed the saddle.

A champ has to have love and the ecstasy of love. He must share his triumphs with someone else to realize the full experience of it. Psychoanalyst Sigmund Freud said, "Love is the center of civilization." Monk Thomas Merton said, "No man is an island." Thus, a champ must have a better half in order to be complete.

A champ must stay inspired. He must be able to extract inspiration from experiences and life, his own abilities, and from the abilities of others. When you believe in something so much higher than yourself, you limit how powerful your belief in yourself can become. You'll never know how powerful you can become and your own worth. Thus, it would be difficult to have the make-up of a champ.

No phraseology can describe the essence of a champ, you must experience a champ's greatness for yourself. The ultimate champ is one who succeeds amidst chaos. A champ rises like a sun. He must shine like the sun's rays upon the surface. You must veer from the orthodox and avoid the axis of narrow thinking and offer deeper analysis of life. We have to challenge ourselves to be better thinkers, better mediums. We must strive for perfection. It is a great thing to strive for. We have to move forward with a will power too earnest that nothing can get in our way. Revamp your efforts. In basketball when a player loses a one-on-one game. He says, "Run it back", meaning play again. In life if you fail, you must run it back. Get a rematch, and try your chances. An elimination in life is giving up without a fight. We must not give up until it is obviously beneficial to do so and this takes judgment on your part.

Man must find his equilibrium. He must have equilibrium on a daily basis in order to function and operate. Your body must be at a homeostasis or equilibrium to be alright. When you are out of equilibrium you have to be able to realize it and make the necessary adjustments. As an athlete competing with my body and a sport I always had to be in equilibrium.

Speaking of athletics, even a scholar must engage in as transformation of the body is as important as transformation of the mind. Abraham Lincoln, the nation's sixteenth president preserved the union as he applied principles of vision, determined priority, and focus. Franklin Delano Roosevelt got us through the Big Depression with Keynesian Revolution and was champ in his own right. Not to be outdone was President John F. Kennedy, who resolved the Cuban Missile Crisis and offered many civil rights landmarks. He was a champ. President Ronald Regan met with Gorbachev at the White House in Russia to end the Cold War. He too was a champ.

A champ has to have an international or world frame of mind. After all, a president must be capable of foreign affairs, and heavyweight champ is a champ of entire world, a CEO must market products and services to international markets, and a PhD must have an international perspective to do proper research and teach international students.

As a champ you will face plenty of outside criticism. This will help you improve yourself as your journey goes on. This also allows you to correct mistakes and embrace your chances of success and greatness must be honed. A PhD is a doctor of philosophy. He explores unexplained phenomena and seeks to explain them through scientific empirical research. He then disseminates his knowledge or teaching others what he has discovered. Only 1% of the US population obtains a PhD.

Education is an instrument of achievement. It tests your intelligence. Be engrossed in a climate of discovery, man elevating his thinking and bringing it to a new level. He now faces his environment for an oasis of opportunity and progress. He is a better individual, more capable of reaching for stars, more capable of climaxing his thoughts. The champ is educated in his field of endeavor as well.

It is believed by the author of this book that the mind has transverse powers. It's mind over matter. The man allows man to adapt to his environment. The mind can be transformed into a tool for greatness. You must make the transition from thinking unsystematically to thinking like champ and king. The rational mind is a powerful entity. You must use your mind to the fullest. Think the proper thoughts and you will succeed. This increases the mathematical possibility of greatness.

Use your mind to weather the storm. Know that it is a swift wind that makes a bald eagle soar high. No ship can sail without a gusty wind. No muscle can be built without a friction. No great man has ever gone without adversity.

In Greek, "pneuma" means air. We must get off the ground and into the air to succeed. We must carry our burdens and face the terrain of life. Life is about pluses and minuses. We must maximize the pluses and minimize the minuses. We must react to our surroundings. Modern man has been here 200,000 years. It is time for him to reach greatness.

Consciousness is the awareness of the self and one's surroundings. A sheep must be aware of his own frailty and vulnerability to the attacks of the fox. He must know the whereabouts of the fox and how he attacks. Every prey must know himself and his predators in order to survive. If you go into the jungle you must know everything about lions and tigers. So know yourself and your surroundings.

Mathematics is an exact science. Apply mathematics to your life. Every goal, every dream, every pursuit allows for the application of mathematics. In business, psychology, and personal, mathematics is important. Always in mathematics there is a set of instructions or an algorithm. In life there's a set of instructions as well. Life can be a mystery, but with mathematics this mystery is solved. Gauss was a mathematician. He used math to map out the Universe. Statistics are used in our lives to help us make decisions.

Like a volcano erupts, greatness will come out of you once you transform your mind. It is a process much like success is a process. Train your mind the way boxer trains his body. Develop strategies for excellence. Come up with an ingenious plan for goals. You will swell up with enthusiasm once your idea is fixed in your head. Enthusiasm makes the difference as a philosopher Norman Vincent Peale said, "One must apply the mental laws." They are the law of practice, the law of mental equivalency (your thoughts) the law of reciprocity, and the law of habit. These laws are immutable in reaching one's full potential.

A man has instinct to give up. Rather than give up go with the current of the river. Stay afloat and don't go under. Maintain your composure and stay poised. Let progress unfold. Have hope that you will get through the difficulties. Let yourself get through the cataclysm.

A sedimentary man never progress. Michelangelo would've never progressed as a sculptor had he been sedimentary. Mark Twain would not have become a classic writer had he been sedimentary. Plato would not have been a great Western philosopher. The nomads would have never survived had they been sedimentary.

We need to stop treating greatness as if it's the isolation of a gene. Greatness is not always genetic, it can be taught. If you program your mind in a certain way, you can reach high plateaus and achieve what you desire. In economics we talk about supply and demand, but for success it's a supply of strategies for attainment.

Spread your wings and soar. Ascend to your highest, don't settle for mediocrity, and seek greatness. See it in your mind and do it. Make the most of innate abilities. Let no obstacle prevail over you. Prevail over your circumstances. Be greater than the mightiest of storms.

Chapter 11:
The Call of the Universe

◇◇◇◇◇◇◇◇◇

Think like a duchess, act like a duchess, talk like a duchess, and one day you will be a duchess.

-George Bernard Shaw

The concept of a calling is a metaphor for man taking flight or soaring high in career and life. The Wright brothers answered the call of the Universe. Now the goal of this book is for man to answer the call of the Universe despite the pandemic. We have a call to end COVID 19. My career as a professor was my calling. My battle with a brain disorder caused a lot of pain but I strove for reaching my full potential anyway. Quintessential examples of other men and women will be utilized as well.

Life is about succeeding by any means necessary. If you want to climb Mt. Olympus, you have to do everything you need to do to climb Mt. Olympus. If you want to be a star, you have to make the necessary steps in order to achieve this level. Success renders one important, a valued member of society. Human flight means taking it to the next level. When I played college football, I took my high school game to the next level. When I received my masters degree from a prestigious university, I took my undergraduate experience to the next level.

There's nothing more powerful than the human spirit. Let your human spirit drive you to your highest ascension. The effervescence of the human spirit will move you to greatness in your lifetime. It also provides you with vitality. A champ answers the call of the Universe. The Universe calls on him to be great. He accepts this calling. He feels it inside. He wants to become powerful like the Universe. We know the Universe is made of billions of galaxies. Man's brain is made of billions of brain cells. The Universe is governed by various laws called Universal Laws. Man has inherent in him various laws of success and principles of life. There is a connection between man and the Universe. You must understand this.

Be a realist. Base your plans on operating in the real world. Don't expect some celestial being to fly in from the sky to produce your success for you. You have to do your own push-ups to build your muscle. Absolutely the faith that a savior will deliver you can give you comfort, but at the end of the day you get more comfort from being prepared for life's battles in which you take your own action. That's reality – the metaphysical.

Many will argue that perfection is not possible. They forget that in gymnastics a 10.0 is perfect, that in school a 100% on an exam is perfection. Whether you believe in perfection philosophically or not, it is important for you to strive for perfection. Great things come as a result of this striving. With determination you can strive for perfection. You can control your outcomes. Remember that in order to get the cubs, you have to go into the lion's den.

A Japanese proverbs states that the biggest room in the house is the room for improvement. As long as you keep improving, your journey toward greatness and reaching your full potential will be realistic. Improve your mind, improve your body, improve your spirit. Then make the connection between your improvement and your success. I remember watching the improvement of Lebron James in the NBA. This former high school star made the transition from high school to the pros by constantly improving. He inevitably became a champ. One of the most successful basketball players in the world today, Lebron is always prepared to play at the highest level. Every champ, every king leaves a legacy. A legacy is what you are remembered for and what you leave the world. It usually measures up to your greatest accomplishment.

A valedictorian, like a PhD will tell you that knowledge is power. You must fill your mind up with valuable information. Challenge yourself to know more. With this you are powerful. Having power can spark greatness. With the composite of greatness achieved by individuals, civilization is advanced. This is why we have advancement in medicine today. No matter how talented you are at what you do, you must be successful in managing relationships. No man is an island and your goals don't exist in a vacuum.

The way of the world is that you have to be superior to your obstacles, your circumstances, your conditions. You cannot surrender to these states. You have to leave the past behind. You can't dwell on negative thoughts. Whenever you face crisis, whenever you face adversity, cling unto hope. A mustard seed of hope goes a long way. Hope helps you rise up. You have to rise up over the ashes. When the dust clears, you have to have hope. When you have hope your greatness is eminent. Without hope you have darkness; with hope you have light. Also remember that bad habits are perpendicular to your goals. You must develop good habits.

You are not alone. There are others you can call on. Your ancestors can hear your call. They were great. You can be great as well. Ring loud and clear. Since you are attacking your goal, it should come into fruition. Since you approach your goal as a mountain, you should be ready to climb, however steep it is.

Life is an open door. You will have the chance to make something of yourself if you walk through it with the grace of a champ and the dignity of a king. If only you knew how great you are. This is precipitated by self-knowledge and self-awareness. You have to control your own destiny, it is in your hands. Be a mover and shaker, have substance. There will be struggle in life, there will be progress. You must remain intact despite catastrophe and turmoil. Like King Perseus overcame Medusa in Greek Mythology, you can overcome adversity. Rescue your efforts by following through on your goals. It's mind over matter. Cherish the journey. You only get one life, if you live it right, once is enough. In life you are in search of something. You will find it.

A king has wisdom. He is a wise man. You too must be wise as you strive for your goals and aspirations. Be among the chosen few. Without a shadow of doubt, you can go from rags to riches like a Horatio Alger story. The Universe is yours for the taking. It's time. A king loves his kingdom. You have to love humanity. If you give love, you will receive love – a mother to her child, a man to his wife, a brother to a sister. Love permeates the fiber of our being. The combination of the two is stronger than the two parts if left separate.

Love precipitates the conscious mind. It soothes the savage beast. No man is an island. We all need love. It heals wounds that would otherwise not heal. Psychoanalyst, Sigmund Freud said love is the center of civilization. So to be centered requires love. Love is a powerful creature like a bird that can fly over the clouds. Every man needs a woman for himself and every woman needs a man for herself. Love must come pouring down like rain. This is what is meant when we say, "Rain on me!" A champ needs love during his journey as a spark. He doesn't want to blast off alone. Love is the spirit that ignites man. He is motivated by it and driven by it. It encapsulates him to the fullest. It helps him move; even helps him wake up every morning. It is his direct channel to the Universe. All the emotions that make up man are captured by love.

This book urges one to be multi-faceted. So if one avenue is closed, you can open up another avenue. Have multiple passions like Paul Robeson. Robeson was the ultimate champ. He was valedictorian, an all-american football player, a lawyer, a singer, an actor, a linguist, and an activist. He has the record for most appearances in Shakespeare's Othello at 298. He won an Emmy for his acting. He spoke twenty languages including teaching himself Chinese. He graduated from Columbia Law School and passed the bar exam. His song "Ole Man River" is one of the most popular songs of all time. There was a mountain in Russia named after him – Mt. Robeson. He received a U.S. postage stamp honoring him. He was a great one.

In life it is intensity-in-intensity-out. This means if you put intensity in something, you will get intensity out of the experience. A champ has been intense, a king is intense. You must be intense. This book has uncovered the secrets of life. A king is by nature a mentor. He guides others on their path within his kingdom. Once you become successful, you can take on proteges as well. This is the system of giving back to the ecosystem. Our ultimate goal is tranquility.

Asia, Babylon, Persia, Mesopotamia, Egypt, Ethiopia (Kush), Meroe, Axum. Songhai, Mali, and Ghana were great ancient civilizations. To be great it helps to learn about these great civilizations, the people, the societies. How did they live? What made them great? My emphasis and preoccupation with kings began in graduate school when I made a trip to Egypt, a civilization than began in 3100 B.C.. I had the remarkable experience of seeing the pyramids and the Sphinx. I saw the Tower of Kings and many other amazing monuments left by the kings of Egypt known as the Pharaohs. The Pharaohs were majestic, great rulers, wise men. The most impressive of these kings was King Ramses II, son of Seti. He left great monuments in Egypt and had a successful rule of Egypt. Ever since then it dawned on me that I should think like a king to be successful, to be great.

My emphasis on thinking and acting like a champ stemmed from my admiration of heavyweight champ, Mike Tyson. That was my era. His devastating presence in the ring, his greatness. Then I thought of others like Roy Jones, Jr., Lennox Lewis, Evander Holyfield, and earlier fighters like Joe Louis, Rocky Marciano, and Muhammad Ali. Then when I thought of the mentality needed to break from the pack I considered the same greatness in other types of champs, i.e., kings, valedictorians, presidents, CEOs, and PhDs. Hence, I came up with the philosophy of "Act like a champ, think like a king". Keep climbing the mountain of life.

There is drama in greatness. If you want to understand the people, you have to understand the drama of the people. If you want to understand a champ and a king, you have to understand their drama. Then unravel your own greatness and you too will be producing drama. What drives you to do the things you do. This is a fundamental question you need to ask yourself. The goal of man is to get to the highest heights; to get to the top of the mountain. To self-actualize. The shadow of man is his success. The forefront of man is his greatness.

Your goal is an extension of you. Your passion is an extension of you. Many of us have mental gifts. We have to work these gifts to the fullest. Your mental wits can lead you to become a champ. You can be great in many categories. Make like the Pharaohs of Egypt and be great. You may be a boxer that needs just one more blow or a poet that needs one more verse or a painter that needs one more stroke of the brush.

You have to strive to ascend to your highest. Life is short, you have to maximize yourself while you have life. Ascension is the goal of a king, a champ. Your head can be way up in the clouds. Your greatness resonates differently in different surroundings. You can flourish in some environments more than others. So choose your environment wisely.

A king is a bit of a philosopher. He develops a philosophy of life. He rules with his philosophy in mind. He makes decisions accordingly. He develops views on the cosmos, the Universe, mankind, and life. He is a deep thinker. Albeit a king is your majesty, he listens to the people. To be successful you have to be a good listener. A king is honest. He is moral. He is dignified. He bases his life on principles and virtues. His thoughts are with you as you attempt to succeed in this thing called life.

A king has mastered adversity. He strives on it. He begins to persevere. A champ is tough, a king is wise. The combination of both will make you great. Michael Jordan isn't just a champ; he is a king. His mindset is one conducive to greatness. He beat mediocrity. He overcame a force of some kind. He mastered adversity. He blasted off like a rocket ship. You too must make like a champ, a king, and blast off.

Make the most of your situation. Use your ability to the fullest. This is the art of survival. In the end it's about survival. In the game of survival of the fittest, being great makes it possible to survive. The purpose of life is to live it to the fullest. The meaning of life is to be great. This takes acting and thinking in a certain way. A champ acts powerfully. A king thinks wisely. Life is a puzzle; it's up to you to put the pieces together to complete the puzzle. Many have preceded us in being successful and great. We must emulate them. Our time has come. This process is as deep as the deepest sea, but this book has philosophized about how to be great given your innate abilities and amidst adversity.

This has been my philosophy on greatness, my philosophy on success. Attach it to your mind and be fruitful. Assert your genius. Move with a rhythm in your soul, a music in your ear, a dream in your head. Greatness is universal. It rings loud from America to England to the Carribean and Asia, through Russia and the Baltics to Africa and all over the world. Great ones inspire us all to be great. Master the elements, those things that comprise life. The characteristics of a champ and a king make it possible to master the elements. It is with this power that you take on life and its many challenges.

Always in life, have a mountain of hope. Whenever a mountain of hope is not available, gather whatever hope you can and proceed. Hope is necessary for the spirit. You have to be high spirited. Mediocrity is not a curse from the gods; it is not irrevocable. It can be eliminated. This requires that you change your thinking, your thoughts. The gods call on you to be great, to be powerful in your thinking, to overcome the fiercest of obstacles. They call on you to eliminate anything in your path that may hold you down. When you hear a lion roar, it is the yearning to be great. Remember to always persevere like the tortoise that beat the hare in a race to the finish line.

Expand yourself. How much you learn and what you become depends on your breadth of experience. After a breadth of experience your mind is expanded. You have to cover all the basis. You need a breakthrough idea. Set sail. Determine your course. Reach your destination. Excellence is within your reach. Being a champ is possible. Remember that being great is a chemical process. Your brain is made of chemicals like serotonin and dopamine. It's an electrical organ that allows you to be great when you use it right. Our brains have evolved to be powerful, processing millions of messages daily. You obtain greatness from brain power.

Where you end up is often a reflection of how hard you have worked. Hard work is the simplest formula for success and reaching the threshold of greatness. A great deal happens to your mind when you work hard, so be industrious. There are 168 hours in a week; be productive with this time.

When you reach greatness, you will have discovered a brand new world. You will see things and feel things you never knew existed.

You will be at the top of the world and you will be intense. It will mean that you have mastered your environment and mastered yourself. The journey of life can be beautiful. You have to believe in life.

A champ has to evolve – evolution of the mind, body, and emotion. A champ must be a body-mind master. Dan Millman, Olympian, wrote the book, "Body Mind Master," explaining this phenomenon. The phenomenon of body-mind mastery propels a lot of people to excel in sport and life.

Knowledge is power and power is what keeps us in motion. According to Newton, a body in motion stays in motion unless acted upon by an external force. A champ stays in motion. He must constantly be moving. He must learn faster. A baby has a steeper learning curve than an adult. A champ must go back to when he was a baby.

There's nothing like the spirit of a champ. I was a champion college football player; my mind was in a zone. When I was a champion scholar, I was equally in a zone. Martial artists are champs. They have mastered the art of movement, much like I was mastering the art of movement when I played running back and wide receiver for the football team. It takes rhythm, coordination, and flexibility. These are also needed in life, especially a champ.

A valedictorian is a luminous star, bright as anyone. Shining to the eye, intelligent and studious, a valedictorian progresses one step at a time. In life most people go by the results that are numerical or quantitative; a champ focuses on quality.

So we want Cornel West to philosophize for us and raise the stakes for PhDs. We want Bill Clinton to show us the way to be president. We want Mike Tyson, the youngest heavyweight champ ever to lift us up with his powerful fists. We want Paul Robeson to show us the valedictorian mind and Oprah Winfrey to show us how to excel. King Dsojer will show us how to be majestic. We are champs. A champ will devastate the world. A CEO will bring business into light. A president will make policy that will change the atmosphere. A heavyweight champ will inspire us to be great. A valedictorian will mesmerize us with her brain. A king will look after his kingdom and a PhD will discover the unknown phenomenon.

Superhuman power is possible. Man is that great, capable of miracles. His greatness stretches across the four corners of the Earth. He is amazing grace. Nothing can stop him, the power lies in his hands. The power is manifested in a champ. Your mind goes through a lot in life. You have to resurrect your mind and get back to the path. You must be in range of possibilities. Once the possibilities come, you must blast off.

The magic of being a champ arises from the people you affect. It has a major place in time and space. The reality of it is that you are all the people have. They look to you for inspiration and leadership. The injection of yourself into any lifestyle takes consideration. You must think about it thoroughly as it affects the path you end up on. Take nothing for granted. Appreciate everything you get and use it to the fullest. Make the most of your moments. Experience life. Rise up.

A champ must focus on self-preservation. He must deliver the goods. He has to make the world go round. His greatness can be felt in every layer of the Earth. Man makes mistakes. The key is to correct these mistakes. A champion tennis player must not continue to double-fault. A boxer cannot continue to get knocked out. They must be aware of their mistakes, then correct them. You have to pay close attention to detail. Napolean Bonaparte was a great general because he paid close attention to the details of the battle. Magic Johnson was a great point guard in the NBA because he paid close attention to detail.

Ralph Ellison was a champ of novels. His book, "Invisible Man", won a Pulitzer Prize. Ellison's character, they refused to see. Thus, he was invisible. A champ is the opposite of that, he is very visible, especially a heavyweight champ, president, or king. Refuse to be invisible. Dr. W.E.B. Dubois was talking about the "Talented Tenth". The Harvard scholar was talking about champs. He proposed that our nation be led by this elite.
Watching a champ work is like a beautiful symphony. The melody of his movement is like a butterfly spreading pollen onto flowers on a sunny day. A champ is the link to the world. He links the people to the cosmos. He is a star, luminous in the dark sky. He amazes us every day. He baffles us, perplexes our minds. He is a winner.

Bruce Lee was a warrior. He was the quintessential champ. He acted like a champ and thought like a king. Wilt Chamberlain was basketball royalty. He was the leading scorer in the league and the definitive champ. Lennox Lewis, the undisputed heavyweight champ at 6'5", 245 pounds was the grandest of modern champs. This British champ was the last heavyweight to unify the heavyweight titles. He acted like a champ. A champ is greater than not less than. He is greater than thou. He follows the leads of those who came before him, the Bruce Lee's, The Michael Jordan's, the Carl

Lewises, the Usain Bolt's, the Eric Dickerson's. He is a king. He is a god.

Much like the sun stands out among the planets in the galaxy, a champ must stand out among other people. He must have a great quality about himself that stands out. This attracts people to him as he reigns supreme. Tyson stood out, Lennox, and Evander stood out and Vladimir Klitko is beginning to stand out as heavyweight champ of the world. Know that the possibility is limitless. The greatness is infinite. This is the space in which you can achieve great things. Much like the sun has a place up in the sky, you have a place in society.

So be great like Beethoven and his music, DaVinci and his painting, Jordan and his basketball, Angelou and her verses, Denzel Washington and his acting, Usain Bolt and his blazing feet, and Bill Gates and his computers. Be great like the River Jordan, like the Niagara Falls, the heightening Alleghenies of Pennsylvania, like the pyramids of Egypt.

At the dawn of day, succeed against the odds. At the dawn of day, be better than mediocre. Trust your instinct, climb with intention, and with intensity. Flourish like never before. Flourish like a fish out of water who has just been returned to water. Reach the Promise Land. You may not have been there yet, but you will know when you get there.

As the world turns, we must turn with it. We must turn an opportunity into a victory. We must turn a disadvantage into strength. We must turn our heads on negativity. We must know right from wrong as morality is the character of man. In essence, what we are talking about is mind power. It is the use of the mind to effectuate change to a better state. It is the use of the imagination to become great. It is the tapping of the secrets valleys of the mind. Endurance is an idiosyncracy that you must possess. Only the strong survive. Life is not a sprint, but a long distance run. Every time you go out there you must endure to the end. The tortoise endured to the finish line to defeat the faster hare. David endured Goliath, slaying him in the end. Ali endured the bigger Foreman and became champ. You have to have it within your psychology to endure. The course is long, but you have what it takes.

Even Zeus, with his thunder and lightning cannot overshadow your greatness once you act like a champ and think like a king. Your transformation is complete. You are ready to strike a chord of excellence onto this world. You are ready to make amends. The magnetism of your spirit, the effervescence of your soul, and the brightness of your mind will lift you to glory. A breakthrough idea has lifted you to a pinnacle, to a point of no return. In the process of becoming great, you have found yourself. There is no time to surrender. Surrender is "mattai" in judo. Never mattai.

Rise up! You can keep thinking about the things that keep you down or you can just rise up. Rise up above the sometimes chaos in life. Rise up above the powers of despair and discouragement. Rise up above the flames of hopelessness. As far as you went down is as far as you can go up. Rise up above impossibility. If you think you can't rise, then think again.

You are a beam of light brighter than any other light. You shed light onto the world that we live in. Because of you, we can see the struggle for what it is. We can adjust. We can proliferate with greatness. Whether you are a champ of some type or not, you have to have self-control. You can exercise self-control majority of the moments of your life, but it takes just that one moment when you lose self-control that can jeopardize your freedom. We know that freedom is a prerequisite of success in this world. Freedom is the dawn of a new day. No one can fully exist without freedom.

The man who understands is the man who wins. Proverb 22 states, "He who understands shall speak the truth to the seven churches of the world." There is power in understanding; it is an aspect of intelligence which is defined as the ability to think, reason, and understand. You must understand the process of transforming the way you think and act. Iterate this process through philosophies that will put you in the mind of a champ and king.

You have to escape elements of complacency. Don't be satisfied with "almost good enough." In life's long distance race, always strive for your personal best. A man has his day in the limelight. You will have your day to shine. The galaxy will respond to your efforts. You will achieve beyond the monotony of everyday life. You will make souls clamor. The world will be your oyster. All of the elements will line up and the stars will be aligned correctly. Your life will correspond with your desires and aspirations. Take this life to the limit. Demand a lot out of life. Unequivocally, you can only have one life to live. This will be enough if you live it to the fullest. Faith in yourself is the greatest faith you can have. You'll need it for your journey.

You need to be able to see through the veil of the world. You have to see the world for what it is. When striving for a thing in life, it is important to take care of your health, both mind and body. You have to imagine greatness. Stretch your imagination as wide as the ocean to realize how great you can become. Flat out true is that often to be a champ, you must be ingenius. Apply the same ingenuity that the Egyptians applied in starting mathematics, science, navigation, and architecture. Apply the same ingenuity that Mike Tyson applied in becoming the heavyweight champ by the age of 21.

Along the journey there will be temptation. As a champ or someone developing into a champ, you have to be unphased by this temptation and keep your eyes on the prize. The hope is that from reading this book someone will rise above the ashes of oblivion and make their presence known. They would make the statement to never sleep on potential. So look to your mind to deliver you, salvation and all. Look to courage and imagination and with the boldness of a champ, progress one step at a time. Acquire ions of knowledge along the way and with the wisdom of a king, share with the world.

Be great like General Hannibal of Carthage, who with his soldiers and elephants crossed the Swiss Alps to surprise and defeat the Italians. You must cross the Alps and succeed. Learn your history. Make like the Greek historian, Herodotus and learn history. As you learn from the people of the past you will learn from their mistakes as well as their achievements.

Make like a crutch and lean on my words. Be still and know you're great. Make like Apollo. Make like Atlas. Make like Poseidon. Make like thunder and lightning. You know that you exist, you have molecules. However, you must do more than exist, you must live. As Dr. Cornel West said you don't have to be free to struggle for freedom.

Your destiny is not preordained, you can act, think, and react to what you face. Your mind has the power over your circumstances. Your fate is not sealed at birth, it is your actions that determine what you are to become. Your brain is a microcosm of the Universe. The Universe is made up of billions of galaxies, your brain is made of billions of brain cells. Both your brain and the Universe are governed by laws. The Universe is governed by Universal Laws and the brain is governed by mental laws. The roar of lions is a call to the Universe.

Throughout history man has been called upon to be great. Moses had to become great to lead the Jews out of bondage in Egypt. Winston Churchill had to become great to save Great Britain from the Germans. Economist John Maynard Keynes had to be great to help America get out of the Big Depression. Often man has had to become great for the sake of mankind.

A kingdom is a metaphor for life. You have the people and in life you have leaders. To a kingdom you have potential threats. In life there are various threats to your wellbeing. You are a player in this life much like a king is a player in his kingdom. So we can relate to the thinking of a king to life as you know it. He is the master of his destiny. You must be the same in your journey.

You cannot expect a Shangri-La or Utopia, but this doesn't mean that a vast number of people cannot be great at what they do. Religious leaders will promise you paradise if you get on your knees, but the only paradise you can reach is individual greatness. They say look to the heavens; I say do your bit on Earth because you know the Earth exists. You only live once. My assertion is that if you live it right then once is enough.

You have to refuse to be invisible. Ask for more out of life. Life is beautiful. Project yourself forcefully into this one. Make like a tall tree and have a presence. Be poised. Take flight. I say to you unequivocally, make like a king. Make like the waves in the ocean. Close the chapter on mediocrity. Maybe you've felt the heat of oppression. Perhaps you've been discriminated against.

This is when you act like a champ especially. What would a valedictorian do? What would a president do? What would a PhD do? It's all about your response to these ills. Embrace humanity and go forward. Don't give up on man and don't give up on your ambitions. Henceforth, you will make it. Poverty discourages the greatest of men. Know that you can have the riches of life as the streets are paved with gold with the right mindset. You just have to find your niche of greatness and you have to find yourself. Listen to the words of Nobel Prize Laureate, Maya Angelou who said, "Still I Rise."

We remember Malcolm Little who later became Malcolm X. His schoolteacher told him that he was too ambitious wanting to become a lawyer and that he should strive to become a carpenter. Malcolm became world famous. Never let anyone sell you short; you can never be too ambitious.

Your mind has to be made up to prosper and not struggle all of your life. Prosperity comes to those who think prosperity. A wise mind will prosper as he knows how life works and sees through the veil of society. Bill Gates did not amass $81billion thinking like a peasant. He used his imagination in the process of discovery. He leveraged his ability and executed his idea. Greatness is analogous to financial independence.

Life can be a fierce battle. You must liken yourself to a soldier. It is the soldier that protects the kingdom. That's why we included boxers as our champs among intellectuals. With so much emphasis placed on the mental, it is also important to emphasize the importance of physical prowess. Your physicality is essential in life's battles. Patience is a virtue. Rome wasn't built in a day. A lack of patience in striving for a thing leads to anxiety. Remember to enjoy the journey and not get too anxious. Mt. Everest is over 29,000 feet; you have to climb it one step at a time. Live in the present with an eye to the future.

You need to desire to be great to be great or else it won't happen. Desire is the spark that gets the process started. Two ghosts haunt the success process: fear and doubt.

It is within my population of knowledge that in order to be great you must maximize your strengths and minimize your weaknesses. Do what you do best. In other words, revel in your strengths. Coordinate a plan in which you can use your strengths. You should not have a sense of entitlement. This means you feel as though something is owed to you. Instead you must earn and work for everything you get. This is fundamental in your struggle for your goals.

I worked for three Fortune 500 corporations in my life. They manufacture a product and sell it to the consumer at an advantage. As a goal seeker, you must provide something that the public wants and do it better than anyone else can. Your talent, your skill, your idea can be what you proposition to the public. Do what you must. Tackle any challenge. Be at your best. Solve the puzzle of life. Don't surrender your will. Persevere. Outlast the elements. You have to decide to be great in order to be great. Lift yourself up every brand new day with the intention of being better than the previous day. As your mind transforms, greatness is created.

In the present and in the future, tap into the emotions and psychology that you had in the past when you were great for it is the mindset that delivers the punch. Use the same reasoning, the same thought pattern, the same disposition. The situation may be different but if you reproduce the characteristics when you were successful, you can reproduce the same results. Remember man is capable of miracles.

Achieve something where you can say, "I can't believe it!" One of the purposes in life is self-expression. Find ways to express yourself upon this world. Express your personality, your thoughts, your mind. Manifest your destiny. Become what it is in your heart to become. Move with the heat of the times, the 21st century.

Being a champ is not an exact science. A champ has to do what he has to do to separate himself from the pack. A champ is always going to be in search of the truth. He is in search of "veritas", Latin for truth. This is tantamount to one of his goals in life. The truth shall set you free. I was driven by the truth as a young college student and this was invigorated when I started writing. I wanted to know "why". A champ can't be afraid to dream. He must also be able to dream big.

I can imagine that any champ has a lot of pride in himself. This is reflected in the way they act. The advice here is that no matter what profession you're in you should have pride in yourself and such pride will be reflected in your work. Michael Jordan prided himself as a basketball player and the result was six championships and several scoring titles. Serena Williams, a very proud tennis star was the oldest number one ranked tennis player ever at 31. Gabrielle Douglass, a young and proud gymnast won gold in the Olympics.

One thing I learned in college was that you had to master the material. You had to master the literature and the other assignments in order to make the grade. Being a champ is no different. You must master the elements. It depends on your area, but mastery is essential. Success follows mastery. Proficiency follows success.

King Dsojer built the first pyramid, King Ramses II built several monuments and had a peaceful kingdom, King Solomon solved problems for his clergy with his wisdom. These kings like others had successes and failures, but what they had in common was they each had the mindset of a champ. The ingredients of the thinking of a great heavyweight champ like Lennox Lewis or Evander Holyfield is similar to that of kings. They think grand, big, massive, beyond the norm, beyond the stars, beyond the stratosphere.

An astrological observation says that when the stars line up, champs are born. There are currently 400,000 NCAA athletes, thousands of pro athletes, thousands of Olympiads, and a plethora of actors and singers in Hollywood. The common denominator is that they pursue life as if they were champs. That's the way you should pursue life – like you were a champ. This is the as-if principle.

Don't get it twisted, a champ has flaws. He is not unlike any other human being. He just reached a certain level of greatness, avoided mediocrity, and separated himself from the pack. However, he makes mistakes along the way. It's how he deals with his mistakes that matters. When one look back at his or her life the one thing they want to know is whether they had impact on the lives of others. Tyson inspired generations of boxers to be champs, Barack Obama inspired a race of people and gave them an example that they could accomplish what they wanted, Robeson inspired millions to be great athletes, scholars, singers, and actors.

The greatness of champs is for the eyes to see; others must be exposed to the exploits of champs so that one day they may want to emulate them. This is how a kingdom becomes powerful. When in Rome, do as the Romans do. A champ has to climb the highest of mountains. Victory goes to the swift. A king has to reign over his kingdom, a president has his nation, a valedictorian must outdistance all the other students, a CEO must bring his corporation into the light, a PhD must discover, and a heavyweight champ must knock out his opponents. They must all blast off like a rocket ship.

A king by nature is a renaissance man. By nature a king is a visionary. King Dsojer was innovative in bringing us the first pyramid, the Step Pyramid at Saquarra. Like him, be innovative. Be majestic like Tut. King Solomon wrote Proverbs. Like him be wise. Our journey into the mind of a champ and king has been philosophical, it has been pedagogical, it has been insightful.

It has transcended the mind of a king, a heavyweight champ, a president, a valedictorian, a PhD, and a CEO. We have been on the wavelength of learning, an algorithm of lessons, and a view of greatness and living up to one's full potential.

You can only stand as tall as your ambition. If you shoot for the stars, you might get a cloud. Think big. Ambition is the glue that holds the whole greatness process together. Greatness is a process. Greatness comes to those who first have ambition, to those who think greatness, to those who envision reaching their highest potential, to those who want to win, to those who won't let anything get in the way of their reaching their peak.

What's makes the great great? Ambition. Ambition separates the mediocre from the good and the good from the great. It can be taught, it has to be acquired or something within a person. Like greatness, ambition is a process. When a person is exposed to greatness, he can acquire ambition. Likewise, when a person is tired of being in an unwanted state or condition, he can acquire ambition. Man has arisen, he has come asunder. He had left his state, his condition. He has launched from the launch pad and gotten into space.

The greatest accomplishment of man is man's transformation. He has gone from mediocre to great. He has succeeded. He has blasted off. His transformation from mediocre to great is much like caterpillar larvae to butterfly. He now flies. He now acts like a champ, he now thinks like a king.

When I was 19, I had traveled, as part of an expedition, to Russia. The country had just opened up to the West and my travel partners and I were a part of the first wave of travelers to enter Russia since the collapse of the USSR. In Moscow, we went to the Kremlin, Russia's equivalent to our White House. Lenin's body was on display there and Stalin's grave was outside the Kremlin. The White House, at least their version, was shown to us. This is where Reagan and Gorbechev met during his administration to end the Cold War. We also traveled to St. Petersburg, Russia. Here we visited the world's second ranked museum, the Hermitage Museum. We accessed this museum and saw all that it had to offer including its Egyptian monuments. The trip to Russia was fascinating and it broadened my horizons. If one is to blast off, reach their full potential, they must have their horizons broadened. Traveling is a great way to do that.

Each person must map out a Master Plan for life to be successful and to realize their full potential. It must be well thought out and premeditated. It must incorporate all your desires and all possible obstacles. The juxtaposition of a champ and king is your greatest ally in this conquest you call life. Your goal is a quest. Your commitment to a goal is a pact. Make a pact in your life. We remember those three men who grew up in the tough city of Newark, New Jersey and made a pact to become doctors. They succeeded in doing so. A champ, a king are on a quest; they make a pact.

You can reach the sky. You just have to believe. Believe in yourself and your ability, your chances. You can break the sound barrier. Float over the laws of nature. Take the mystery out of life. Be free. Press on. Fulfill your destiny. React to life. Know that he who leaves the battlefield first, loses. Appreciate your fortunes. If you are fortunate enough to succeed at something, appreciate this. Your hard work paid off. Your vision came to. Your imagination led you to greatness. Now it's time to appreciate yourself. Use the self-affirmation, "I am great!"

There are some budding successes that blazed the world worth recognition. In athletics there was Jim Thorpe, Jesse Owens, and

Rocky Marciano. There is singer Brandy, and the late Michael Jackson, economist John Maynard Keynes who helped us get out of the Big Depression, philosophers Adam Smith, Neitchze, and Karl Marx, psychanalyst Sigmund Freud, explorer Marco Polo, Rhodes Scholar Alaine Locke, leaders Franklin Delano Roosevelt, and Winston Churchill, writers Ralph Ellison and Ralph Waldo Emerson, historian and scholar W.E.B. Dubois, minister Malcom X, leader Marcus Garvey, the blazing Frederick Douglass, the Nobel Prize in Physics Laureate, Albert Einstein, and Sir Isaac Newton, discoverer of gravity.

We have told you to rise up, to illuminate your mind, to act like a champ and think like a king, to be inspired, to be great, to beat mediocrity, to overcome whatever force opposes you. We've told you that knowledge is power, to tap the secret valleys of your mind, to embrace adversity, to work hard, and to persevere. We've told you to be superior to your former self and be superior to your circumstances. Finally, we've told you to make like a champ and king by being bold and confident and pursuing greatness with intelligence. We hope that this will help you transform your mind for greatness like King Dsojer, King Ramses II, Barack Obama, Muhammad Ali, Dr. Cornel West, Oprah Winfrey, and many others who inspire us all and lift our spirits. Take this philosophy and apply it to your endeavors.

What we are talking about here is the soul of a champ, the soul of a king their many dimensions, their dispositions, their idiosyncracies, their auras, their effervescence. They serve as our angels, our guides to a dimension of our own, a dimension of greatness. What I wanted to accomplish between the pages of this book is to show you how to master your journey and capture the essence of the struggle. The goal was to make what seemed impossible possible. It's your world. You can move mountains.

Life is a mountain; the steeper the climb, the greater the triumph. You will be a champ. When I was a champ in NCAA football, the climb was triumphant. It brought harmony to my soul and light to my mind. I experienced greatness as an athlete, scholar, and writer, and as a man and I diffuse my knowledge to you in hope that you posit yourself as a star in the dark distant sky leading the way for others to follow and be inspired to overcome various forces in your life and live up to your full potential. Remember to blast off into orbit like a rocket ship.

You are a maker of history. You make history every time you read a magnificent book and impact the lives of others. I wrote this book with you in mind. I wrote it for those with goals and ambitions, dreams, and aspirations. I wrote it to let you know there are others who are waiting for you to take hold of your destiny. Walk with me. Apply the philosophies of this book to your life and endeavors and the day will come. Acquire the mentality needed for success. You deserve the best. You desire greatness and the psychological feeling that comes with it.

Walk a mile in your greatness. Walk the way Akhenaton walked. Walk the way Ramses II walked and the way King Dsojer walked. Walk a mile in greatness like the great Theodore Roosevelt and the great John F. Kennedy. Walk the way of the great Cornel West. And still yet walk the way of Martin Luther King, Jr. Walk the way of the great television host and actress, Oprah Winfrey. You have the presence of greatness. Walk like the great heavyweight champs, Muhammad Ali and Joe Louis. Especially walk like my mentor and hero, Paul Robeson. Walk the way my 9 year old niece and straight 'A' student, Jayla walks. This book is my walk and it is dedicated to her and Beyonce. It is for them to have when I am no longer here to tell them to be great. And when I am gone tell them to walk a mile in my shoes and see what I have seen.

Chapter 12:
Blast Off

◇◇◇◇◇◇◇◇◇◇

In blasting off, one must know the difference between the mind and the brain. The two are distinct from one another. They perform different tasks. Your brain is made up of protoplasm and contains neurons, receptors, neurotransmitters, synapses, dendrites, axons, white matter, 100,000 miles of fiber, genes, and protein. It has a cerebellum, frontal cortex, and a brain stem. There are electrical charges in the brain. The brain is a processor of information and it is where your memory takes place. It must be programmed. The ancient Greeks called the brain, "animal spirits". Philosopher Aristotle likened it to a refrigerator. The brain is a part of the neurological system.

Your mind, on the other hand, is everything else – what makes you *you*. It includes your upbringing. You think and reflect with your mind. While the frontal cortex of the brain determines your personality, the mind makes you who you are. It is with your brain that you remember; it is with your mind that you ascend to a higher level. Ascension is a function of how well you nurture your mind. While your brain is made of billions of brain cells, your mind is made up of your experiences.

Blasting off is a mental process. It's mind over matter. We saw through jockey Julie Krone that even a race horse can blast off and separate herself from the pack. The 5 octave vocals of Mariah Carey separate her from the pack. To blast off you must possess a powerful inner feeling. David blasted off to beat Goliath. The tortoise blasted off to beat the hare. They possessed properties of greatness. Blast off like a mighty mountain: the Himalayas, the Appalachian, the Rocky Mountains, or Mount Everest in excess of 29,000 feet. Blast off like General Hannibal of Carthage, the military genius who fought in battle with one eye and took elephants over the Swiss Alps to surprise the Italians. Blast off like the Tuskegee Airman who fought during the world war. Or blast off like the great Pharaohs of Egypt or the great astronauts Dr. Ronald McNair and Dr. Mae Jemison.

The quest to blast off is, in essence, the expression of self and a quest for freedom. It starts off with a burning desire to be great and then you get into a zone. You become mighty like a mountain, like a king, like a god in Greek Mythology. As a man thinketh, so shall he be. Blast off of your launching pad like a rocket ship and get into space. Go to the moon, the solar system. Blast off from your mediocre state to a state of grace and greatness. Lift the veil like Barack Obama and Oprah Winfrey. Leave no doubt like Dr. Cornel West and Dr. Neil deGrasse Tyson, with their knowledge, wisdom, and gift of gab. Through them we see that the pen is mightier than the sword. Be confident like King Akhenaten, Seti, Ramses II. Tut, Menes, Dsojer, and Tutmosis. The Egyptians brought us civilization in 3100 B.C. in a real blast off. They brought us science, mathematics, navigation, architecture, medicine, accounting, the first paper known as papyrus, and the illustrious pyramids and Sphinx. This was the Cradle of Civilization – greatness at its best. Today we strive to blast off like the Egyptians.

The mind was stretched to its limit in the case of brain surgeon, Dr. Ben Carson. The great Franklin Delano Roosevelt blasted off in bringing us out of the Big Depression with his New Deal and Keynesian Revolution. The great philosopher and economist, Adam Smith blasted off with his worldly philosophy. The U.S. women's track team blasted off in the summer Olympics. Carmelita Jeter in the 100m dash, Allison Felix in the 200m dash, and Sanya Richards-Ross in the 400m dash were rockets taking flight. Gabbi Douglass shined in gymnastics; she was on fire. Not to be outdone was Usain Bolt, the fastest man in the world. He blasted off out of the starting blocks and to the finish line in the 100m and 200m dashes.

Blast off like the great versatile and prolific actor Samuel L. Jackson. The highest grossing actor ever is a rocket in his own right. The Oscar winning actor Denzel Washington blazes in his role in *Training Day*. The things that you can do with your mind are astounding. We remember Dr. Daniel Hale Williams, who performed the first open heart surgery in America. We remember the African, Cesar, who developed a cure for rattlesnake bite and Imhotep, a physician who discovered the circulation of blood in the veins. He came up with the phrase, "Eat, drink, and be merry." Not to be outdone was another physician who blasted off beyond mediocrity, Dr. Charles Drew. Dr. Drew discovered blood plasma, a substitute for blood and the blood bank.

The great blasting rocket, Beyonce is a megastar. She sings harmoniously through the sound space of this atmosphere with splendor and grace. The Destiny's Child star has taken flight and soars like a beautiful monarch butterfly with a multitude of bright colors. We remember the blazing, Aaliyah. She sang beautifully to us in her young life. Her legacy of greatness will be in us forever. The king, Michael Jackson and his song and dance resonated greatness. He blasted off on stage and in the studio. People all over the world heard his music and he touched the souls of many. Selena broke barriers with her amazing vocals. She was the voice of reason in all of our ears.

A valedictorian is a rocket ship in his own right. He blasts off academically. Parents send their children to school hoping that they will get the lesson and pass the course. A valedictorian is a champ that blasts off in the classroom and masters the lesson. It all starts in the classroom. On the football field, the odds were stacked up against the young Russell Wilson of the Seattle Seahawks. Once a backup quarterback, Wilson led his team to two consecutive Super Bowls, winning one and becoming the rising star of the National Football League. My own story of blasting off is one of courage, determination, and perseverance. Being diagnosed with a fatal illness at the age of 21, I was told by a physician that I would never graduate from college. I didn't listen to him, graduating from an elite university and moving on to obtain from another elite university a master's degree. I was told that I couldn't, so I did. With three years as a Ph.D candidate, I blasted off into space with a studious mind and sharp intellect. After my sports and schooling, I now have a mind and a brain that knows no impossibility. I have self-actualized and fused with a higher energy in the form of a sudden awakening. This is called Satori. I have gone places and ascended mentally and in spirit.

The mental ascension of a rocket ship, Floyd Mayweather, Jr. is amazing. Undefeated and nearly flawless, Mayweather blasts off by lifting boxing out of the darkness. This greatly trained athlete brings light to the entire sports world and anyone striving to be great should try to emulate his greatness no matter what field it is in. It can be engineering, music, nursing, medicine, arts, acting, rocket science, teaching, psychology, or other endeavor.

Launching from the launching pad is Dr. Henry Louis Gates of Harvard University. This professor of black studies is a scholar and teacher and he helps people find out where they come from. The great comedian, actor, author, and talk show host, Steve Harvey has blazed the saddle. Making the transition from comedian to author, Harvey motivates millions with his insightful lessons on life. Harvey had humble beginnings and rose to the top of the entertainment world by being a multi-faceted talent.

From Harvard to the White House goes our president, Barack Obama. This intelligent man blasted off during his campaign and he ran a nation for eight years. With a litany of accomplishments, this great orator served our nation with enthusiasm, passion, and zeal. He stood by us when we were down. He was there for us when we had issues. He climbed with us as we reached our peak. The heavyweight champ of the world for so many years was Vladimir Klitko, a European. Following in his brother's footsteps, the 6'5", Klitko dominated the heavyweight division for a lengthy period of time. He was a champ and he blasted off. Often times we are in the shadow of greatness; we don't know how to be great. But this book teaches you how to be great. It transfers an inner feeling within you so powerful that you have no choice but to be great. Mediocrity is not wanted by anyone. It is something that keeps us unexcited and unaffected. We deserve more than that out of life. We want to go to the moon with our greatness, to outer space, to worlds untraveled to, to places unimagined.

It happens in the trenches. We must work hard and pursue our dreams. We must not limit ourselves. Like Dr. Neil deGrasse

Tyson said the sky is not the limit. The galaxy is big. We too must be big. It's our time. Evolution is upon us. We only use about 6% of our brain, imagine how great we can become. The world saw Michael Jordan win five championships in the NBA, leave to play baseball, and return to win another championship. We saw Dominique Dawes, the young gymnast win gold in the Olympics with style and grace. We saw the late Maya Angelou win a Nobel Prize in Literature with her great verses. We saw Toni Morrison do the same.

Someone who blasts off knows how to turn a crisis into an opportunity. The late Nelson Mandela, who became president of South Africa was an example of this. The one who leaves the battlefield first, loses. There are many others who have blasted off who inspire us all to do the same. Tiger Woods has blasted off as has Serena Williams. Lebron James has blasted off. Richard Sherman has done so. Payton Manning is a rocket ship who has separated himself from the pack. Derrick Rose has shined brightly as has Kevin Durant and Westbrook. Drew Brees has blasted off. In music, Brandy has blasted off as have 50 Cent, Eminem, Dr. Dre, Ciara, Janet Jackson, R. Kelly, T-Pain, Chris Brown, Usher, and Joe. The great producer Timbaland has blasted off. In acting, Halle Berry has done so as have Ving Rhames, Wesley Snipes, Sylvester Stallone, Taraji P. Henson, Kerry Washington, Terrance Howard, Don Cheadle, Tom Cruise, Tom Hanks, Russell Crowe, Mark Wahlberg, Matt Damon, Robert Deniro, Queen Latifah, and Ice Cube.

These people have reached greatness in their lives and should stand as an example of being great no matter what it is you do. The mind has the capacity to do amazing things. We all can't drive race cars the way Dale Earhardt and Mario Andretti can or play tennis like Venus Williams, but we can be great teachers, firemen, dentists, engineers, and leaders. The best way to be great is to follow the lead of someone else that was great. Evander Holyfield, three time heavyweight champ followed the lead of Mike Tyson and others. Kobe Bryant followed the lead of Michael Jordan, who followed the lead of Julius Irving. As a scholar in my own right, I follow the lead of Aristotle and Cornel West, great philosophers. In writing this book I follow the lead of the great Steve Harvey with my own insights on blasting off, becoming great in your quest for greatness, and being successful. If Aaliyah can hear me now, I would say you left us a legacy of greatness to follow and emulate. Oprah Winfrey has blasted off. This flawless communicator has reached a pinnacle of greatness and she joins the most elite group of businesspeople of less than 500 in the world.

Bill Clinton achieved the best economy our nation has ever had when he was president. This Rhodes Scholar of Oxford University and Yale University blasted off to his peak. Professor John Nash of Princeton University and the focus of the movie *Beautiful Mind*, was a mathematical genius, a Nobel Prize Laureate. His mind and brain was amazing. Albert Einstein was one of the greatest scientists ever to live. The physicist won a Nobel Prize in Physics and developed the theory of relativity. Scientist Sir Isaac Newton discovered gravity and developed the laws of thermodynamics. He authored the most scientific book ever entitled *Principia*. Charles Darwin wrote *On The Origin Of Species* later called survival of the fittest. We know what we know now because of this brilliant man.

What you need to realize about blasting off is that it is a choice. You have to be aware of the possibility first, then you must want it.

A great motivational author and race car driver once said in order to be successful, you must want something. Anthony Robbins said you must awaken the giant within. Dennis Kimbro said what makes the great *great* is courage and imagination. It takes courage and imagination to blast off and beat mediocrity. You have been called upon by the Universe to do something great and wonderful. Your family calls upon you to leave a legacy and lead the family. Humanity calls upon you to leave the world a better place than when you left it.

In this darkness, love is light. Nearly every great man has a woman behind him. Nearly every great child has a mother's or father's love behind him. King Akhenaten had Queen Nefertiti, King Ramses II had Queen Nefertarri. Superman had Lois Lane. Barack Obama has Michelle Obama. In your quest to blast off remember what monk Thomas Merton said. He said, "No man is an island." Although it can be done without a loved one, greatness should be expressed with someone you love beside you.

Love can lift you to greatness. It has no limits; you can take it as far as you can go. Move excitedly with love. Move with excitement and enthusiasm. Norman Vincent Peale wrote a book entitled, *Enthusiasm Makes The Difference.* Love enlightens the spirit. Love and greatness are juxtaposed. It is a positive trance to be in. You are mesmerized and also bewildered. Many great athletes or physicians are motivated by love. Roosevelt had Eleanor. Ronald Reagan had Nancy Reagan. George Bush had Barbara. The great computer whiz, Bill Gates has Melinda Gates. Love is a piece of the puzzle that makes us complete. We can be husbands and wives, fathers and mothers. Follow your heart. John Heisman said, "It is the heart that tells the story." Love is good for the heart, for the neurological system, and for our mind. And we need this in our journey up, our quest for greatness. So we blast off with others. Being in love is a state.

There are those who are in an undesirable state – our prisoners. There will come a time when our prisoners must get to a better state, a higher self, and blast off. Many have made major mistakes and their future doesn't seem bright, but 1.1 million prisoners must beat mediocrity as well. They must let freedom ring. They must become productive members of society. There is nothing written in stone that says that they too can't blast off. Remember the old adage, "What a man can be, he must be."

Our youth must take advantage of their youthful energy and spirit and blast off. They must strive to be valedictorians and leaders, champs and role models. They must have a mind of their own and launch from the launch pad and be great. The great Paul Robeson is watching us all. This great all-american was a rocket ship long ago. He inspired me to become a scholar-athlete and multi-faceted person. This gifted man loved humanity along with his many talents. He was an athlete, actor, singer, lawyer, linguist, and activist. The great football star played pro football to pay his way through Columbia Law School. His 298 appearances as the moor in Shakespeare's *Othello* is a record. I think fondly of his classic song "Ol' Man River". This great baritone-bass voice was gladiator-like, a sound of perfection. His King Kong presence is remembered by many.

So you blast off with role models. When I was in high school, a group of young men and I founded a mentorship program for freshman boys. In this capacity we served as role models for these young men. We read current events together, talked about sports, girls, career, and life. We were great mentors of theirs the way Robeson has been a mentor in my own quest for greatness. When Rome was at stake for being destroyed, they went to Cicero for advice. Cicero said gather all the children and dramatize the achievements of their ancestors and hope that they will emulate them. Rome was saved. Role models are key in this process of blasting off.

Imagination has no limit. Your mind is infinite. Use your imagination to the fullest extent. Homer, the great writer used his imagination as did Plato, the Greek philosopher. Mark Twain used his imagination as did Langston Hughes. You are capable of doing what you see in your imagination. Imagine a better world. Imagine a loving world, free of hatred and malice. Imagine a better state for yourself. Imagine self-actualizing. Imagine outer space, the moon, the place where you are blasting off to. Imagine writing a masterpiece, a thrilling movie or great book that inspires people to be great and reach their peak.

Courage is another key element in the greatness equation. We remember the lion in The Wizard of Oz. He lacked courage or at least he thought he did. He ended up saving Dorothy's life in the story. Even lions need courage. Our own hunt requires us to be courageous and brave. If you want to earn the love of someone special, you must be courageous. If you want to perform on stage or in front of a camera, you must be courageous. If you want to send your manuscript to demanding publishers, you must be courageous. Your dreams require you to have courage.

The bottom line is to never settle for less. Always believe in life, greater, broader, and fuller life. Analogously, greatness is to life as a sail is to a sailboat. If you listen to the voice of reason and let your mind and brain work effectively, blasting off is not rocket science. It just takes desire, ambition, and the effort of Hercules in Greek Mythology. In order to blast off and beat mediocrity in the 21st century, you must act like a champ and think like a king.

Chapter 13:
Survival

◇◇◇◇◇◇◇◇◇

This is survival. Survival was first proposed by Charles Darwin in his 1859 book, *On The Origin Of The Species*. His theory, natural selection, propositions that organisms that are able to adapt successfully to their environments have more offspring than those who are less successful at adaptation. In evolution, the giraffe an animal that once had a short neck, develops a long neck as the trees that bore fruit grew taller. This was the giraffe adapting to his environment. When it comes to survival, there are characteristics of the animal or in this case, man, and characteristics of the environment as it relates to man.

In the jungle or in nature, male animals compete to reproduce with female animals for their survival. It is the strongest male animals that get to reproduce with the female animals across all species. This phenomenon has been seen in lions, walruses, hippopotamus, etc. Man must adapt to his environment to survive individually as well as collectively. He must be in survival mode from birth until death. He must engage in the process of self-preservation.

The overall purpose of life is to survive. In Chinese the word, *douliu* means stay. We survived the American Revolution, the Civil War, World War I, World War II, and Vietnam. With the help of Franklin Delano Roosevelt's New Deal, we survived the Big Depression. In addition to war and depression, we are susceptible to famine, drought, disease, and natural disaster. These are threats to survival brought on by man and those brought on by the environment, in this case, the Earth.

What has surfaced as threats to survival in our society has been drugs, the AIDS epidemic, cancer, homicide, and suicide. There are two components of man's survival – mental and physical. Over 1.1 million people in America are in prison or jail. At the heart of the matter is their survival, both mental and physical. Man must be concerned with the survival of the U.S. ghettos as it was safer to be in Iraq during the Iraq War than the streets of Chicago. More specifically, there were more deaths by homicide in Chicago in a year than there were in the Iraq War.

Historically, attempts at genocide were attempted. Adolf Hitler and the Nazis exterminated 6 million Jews during the Holocaust and between 100 million and 500 million Africans died in the Middle Passage beginning in the 1600's. Today racism is a threat to survival, especially mental. In this scenario, man is indifferent to another man's survival on the basis of skin color. Man has been a conqueror since the beginning of time. Alexander The Great brought an end to the dynasties of Egypt. The Europeans nearly wiped out the Native Americans. The Roman Empire and the Ottoman Empire ended as well. Powerful forces of life come to an end. Man must coalesce so that he doesn't come to such a fate.

In the jungle, there is predator and prey. In our society we are dog-eat-dog which can be a side-effect of capitalism. In *Das Kapital*, Karl Marx said that capitalism was dripping with blood. The nature of the free market system is that there will be fierce competition and one man's gain is another man's loss. There are scarce resources that man is competing for.

Technology has sped up the pace of life for man. This has its benefits, but it can make survival more difficult as well. The faster the world is traveling, the faster it approaches destruction. Education is a tool for survival in our society. It is imperative in a capitalist society to be educated and/or trained to meet one's basic needs. Man must meet what is referred to as his Maslow's hierarchy of needs. Abraham Maslow was a psychologist who suggested that man had physiological and psychological needs that must be met in order to survive.

Man has survival as his basic instinct juxtaposed with his environment. His basic intelligence and wit allow him to adapt. He must continue this course for survival of the human race. Life has drama. Man must survive the drama of the day. He must meet his needs and flourish. He will face crisis after crisis and at times his life may be at a disjunction. He must evaluate his circumstances and overcome accordingly. He must remove himself from an unwanted and unfavorable state or condition.

Man will feel the raft of his own greed and hatred. There is abundance in our society, yet we have so many that have so little. Their survival is vulnerable – at stake. The common denominator in our society must be our survival. No man is an island as monk, Thomas Merton stated. Man's destiny is in his own hands, his course in history, his going concern for the future. He must successfully adapt to the nuances of his environment.

Drugs threaten the survival of man. In this society a mother would sell her female child to get drugs. This psychological state, to us, is mind-boggling. Drugs can change your life at many levels. It affects people from all walks of life: young and old, black and white, rich and poor. The behavior of addicts and fiends is erratic and irrational. The use of drugs diminishes the possibility of survival.

The widespread use of crack that began in the 80's has people mentally dead. Heroin, cocaine, PCP, and marijuana are also dangerous street drugs that permeate our environment. People use these drugs as a substitute for survival. Drugs interfere with mental survival. Many of the drugs like PCP are hallucinogens, having users see things that are not really there.

The widespread use of drugs has led to more violence, death, and prison. Many of our over 1.1 million prisoners are there due to drug related crimes. Experimentation with drugs has a domino effect; it affects the family, social, civic, and financial life respectively. For those who have an addiction, drugs become their way of surviving. This causes unpredictable conditions and circumstances and survival is at risk. Drug use causes users to be less responsible in their lives. Man must be responsible. He must function well in order to meet his physiological and psychological needs.

Experimentation with drugs and the usage of these chemicals disrupts the brain's processes. The brain is the most precious and complex organ man has and through drug use he is compromising the passage of electric messages from one brain cell and synapses to the next. It affects how the brain processes and stores information. This explains the change in behavior.

Drugs are indifferent and counterproductive to the survival of man. Man is drifting into a realm of unconsciousness. Thus, he becomes death, dumb, and blind. The ensuing result of drugs is poor health, both mental and physical. This is why America has declared a War on Drugs. A person may become unproductive and even destructive because of drugs. He may not value human life or man's survival. Many who use drugs have wasted ability and potential and one could lose everything he has worked for in one's life.

The possibility of overdosing on drugs makes it that more dangerous. We recall the story of Len Bias. Len Bias was the basketball star who was drafted in the first round by the Boston Celtics. After hearing about being drafted, Bias decided to celebrate by using cocaine. However, his body had an allergic reaction to the drug and Bias died before playing one game for the Celtics.

Man must be bigger than this. He must have character. His character must be too strong to succumb to drugs. In many cases the drug thinks for the man as the drugs have a mind of their own. Man must be too concerned about survival to take drugs in any form. Man must conquer his fears and cope with reality by means other than drug use. There is centripetal force pushing drugs on man. That force is money. Billions of dollars are being made through the sale of drugs. That is why even though it threatens survival, it is still strong in our society. Profit is being made. There are several players in the drug game. Each is motivated by self-interests. Not enough people are concerned with the fundamental survival of man – his mind, his body, his soul.

The violence in the U.S. cities is tremendous and it's mostly related to drugs. One must reminisce about the 1940's and 1950's when drugs did not dominate our society so much. Is there an end to this catastrophe? Will we survive this venomous enemy? Do not just focus on attempting to be great and succeed in life, focus on surviving. That is the ultimate purpose of life and being great, especially mental. Drugs are claiming the lives of so many with the potential of becoming great. Survival of the fittest means adapting and making the right choices in life. Say no to drugs and be great.

Survival of the fittest is about competition. Competition is supposed to make you better at what you do. There is competition in all aspects of life, it is ubiquitous. There is competition for education, careers, companionship, sports, and life in general. The first social psychologist was a man named Norman Triplett. Triplett was a cycling enthusiast. He found in his experiment that the presence of another cyclist caused a cyclist to have faster times in a race than when he raced alone. This process was called dynamogenesis. It basically states that the presence of competition makes you better. This should happen for you as you face survival. You should thrive off competition and not be crumbled by it. Don't be intimidated by competition, feed off it. Run for time as my track coach used to yell.

Apply the principles that we discussed in being great to your survival relative to others, i.e., competition. Juxtapose hard work with talent and you will be alright. Have determination and drive, desire and dedication. Remember struggle and sacrifice. You must prepare yourself for life's challenges. Seize opportunities. Learn and remember what you learned. Then use it for your survival. Take care of your mind and body and pass the tests that life offers.

Herculean effort is necessary. Remember that failure is not the opposite of success and that success is not finite but continuous. Keep striving and keep your eyes on the prize.

Be a realist. Base your life and your reaction on what is and not what should be. In other words, base your life and reaction on reality. A dose of reality always lets you know what to do; it lets you know how to react. Action and reaction is the key to survival. Movement along a progressive axis is the key to making it in life. The struggle for greatness is in essence the struggle for survival. After predators got sharper instruments to penetrate the shell of turtles, the turtle adapted by developing a harder shell. This is survival of the fittest. A young boy grows up in the inner city where there are less opportunities for mobility and more opportunities for danger. He adapts by learning to dribble and shoot a basketball. He emerges as a basketball star of the NBA where he now makes millions of dollars to do what he always dreamed of doing. This is survival of the fittest. A young girl grows up on a farm in Mississippi. She learns how to read with the help of her grandmother at the age of two and blossoms into a talk show host and actress of the greatest proportion. She adapted to her environment with her talent. Her name was Oprah. That's survival of the fittest.

It often takes for you to transform your mind fully to adapt to your situation. Malcolm X was a hustler in Detroit. He was sent to prison after committing a crime. He was introduced to information that transformed him into a thinker. He became a minister and leader of a religious organization. He adapted and survived a difficult lifestyle. It's not just drugs that can get a youth on the wrong path, but there are other distractions. A small boy grew up without many male role models in his life and gangs were recruiting him to join them. He adapted by going to college and becoming a school teacher, becoming a role model for others. A man was homeless, laid off from his job, tired of himself in general. He had goals of being on television one day. He adapted by relying on his ability to make people laugh and became a national comedian and talk show host. His name was Steve Harvey.

So if you can write a book, recite a poem, sing a song, shoot a basketball, solve a mathematical equation, then use your skills, your talent to adapt. Your survival depends on it. If you can act, communicate well publically, solve problems, teach, or speak languages, then do this for your survival. Go through the process of success in order to survive. Survive, succeed, and roar. If you want to take the cubs you have to go into the lion's den. If you want to climb a mountain you have to do what it takes to climb a mountain. It takes basic intelligence to survive. You have the power of life, use it to the fullest.

Mental survival depends on meeting your psychological needs. You must have activity and productivity and a certain level of success and comfort. You need a sense of challenge and accomplishment, self-efficacy and self-worth. We've talked about setting goals and shooting for the stars; this gives you challenge and when you are able to succeed at your lofty goals you get self-efficacy and self-worth. It takes ambition to survive in this world. They say only the strong survive. Be strong at all times in life. Think like a king with a kingdom at stake. Think like a valedictorian before an exam, like a president facing war, a heavyweight champ facing a top contender, a PhD observing a phenomenon that is a mystery, a CEO facing tough competition in his industry. Be strong in order to survive. Be wise. Be bold. Examine all the possibilities for greatness. Don't succumb to competition or adversity. Don't be encumbered by it. Don't be intimidated by it. Let it propel you to the peak, to your plateau.

A lot of times you will be in the trenches of life, the front line. This is where you have to fit yourself for survival especially. Pursue the most proven strategies, the ones that work. Have a plan and execute it. Focus yourself accordingly. Lift yourself up as if you were looking down at the world from the top of a mountain after a long climb. Know that you are connected to the greatness and complexity of the Universe, the galaxy, and even the Earth. Be into your dreams and let them guide your life. Have a purpose that comes from the Universe itself and fulfill it every chance you get. Have patience as you know a star doesn't become a star overnight. A boy doesn't become a man overnight. A student doesn't become a valedictorian overnight.

Let's talk about soaring. A bird can fly high in the sky. With the right prevailing conditions, man can soar high as well. He can soar as high as the track runner, Jesse Owens in Berlin, Germany. He can soar as high as Olympic sprinters Usain Bolt and Carmelita Jeter. He can soar like Barack Obama or Bill Clinton. This soaring is not physical, it is a mental high. It is the ascension from one condition of mind to the highest atmosphere possible – the highest level possible. Those who have ascended know what I am talking about. Jordan soared to the highest when he went for 63 points against Boston. Tony Dorsett soared to the highest when he went for a 99 yard touchdown. Barack soared to the highest during his first inaugural address.

Einstein soared above the clouds when he received the Nobel Prize in Physics. Homer soared to the highest in his writing. I soared to the stratosphere when I overcame the most fatal of illnesses to reach my full potential. Ascension is a state of mind. It happens once in a lifetime to those who work at it – to those who wrestle with the depths of their own minds. Potential is in all of us. It is up to all of us to tap this potential. You have to get to your greatest. You have the mind for great things to happen. It's up to you to activate it the way you turn on a switch. Give your dreams wings. Let your dreams flourish, let your dreams survive.

Chapter 14:
To Become Great

◇◇◇◇◇◇◇◇◇

There were kings and queens in Africa long before Europe got out of the Dark Ages. The Nile Valley featured the cradle of civilization, Egypt, also known as Kemet meaning "land of the blacks." Egypt was known for bringing mathematics, science, the fraternity system, navigation, accounting, and architecture into existence. Egypt became a civilization in 3100 B.C. when King Menes united Upper and Lower Egypt. He also established Memphis, a major city in Egypt. There were also empires in Africa such as Ethiopia or Kush, Meroe, Axum, Benin, Songhai, Mali, and Ghana. Songhai was an empire in Western Africa with its emperor, Askia Muhammad. There were other leaders of Africa in ancient times such as Mansa Musa, Soni Ali Ber, and Sundiata. The first university in Africa was known as the University of Timbuktu. The civilizations of Africa were as great as those of ancient Persia, Asia, Mesopotamia, and Babylon.

King Dsojer reigned in Egypt from 2668 to 2649 B.C.. Under his reign emerged his vizier, Imhotep, the first multi-talented and multi-faceted genius. Imhotep was a priest, a physician, philosopher, and architect. He created the first pyramid in Egypt, the Step Pyramid in Saqarra. He was known as the Father of Medicine 2500 years before the Greek father of medicine, Hippocrates existed. His name in Greek appears in the Hippocratic Oath. Also famous during the Egyptian dynasties was King Ramses II and his wife, Queen Nefertarri and King Akhenaton and his wife, Queen Nefertiti. Egypt was conquered eventually by Alexander The Great of Macedonia.

They were also invaded by the Arabs later. There were blacks all over the world in ancient times including Ancient China. The Moors in 1532 civilized Spain and Africans brought Europe out of the Dark Ages. Africa had a glorious past. The continent itself is made up of 52 countries rich in minerals such as gold and diamonds and natural resources. Known as the Motherland, Africa is home of the first human being as the oldest fossil of human remains was found in the Olduvai Gorge in Tanzania. General Hannibal of Carthage or what is known as Tunisia in modern times, was the greatest military genius of all time as he and his soldiers along with elephants crossed the Swiss Alps to surprise the Italians.

The Revolutionary War was our first pandemic. No longer under British rule, we strove for greatness. In America the Europeans had invaded the Native American or American Indian tribes. The Cherokee Nation was the most advanced American Indian tribe. Sequoya, a linguist translated the language from Indian to English. The Seminoles of Florida were a black-Indian tribe that were never defeated by the Europeans in America. They were the only Indian tribe that didn't sign a peace treaty with the Europeans. The first international conflict occurred when the Portuguese, namely, John Hawkins raided Africa and captured slaves from the coast of Africa. The Atlantic Slave Trade followed with millions of slaves being taken from West Africa. The Middle Passage the journey from Africa to America and the diaspora saw between 100 million and 500 million Africans die beginning in the 1600's. There were 11 million Africans brought to America to work as slaves on plantations. The plantations were located in the South. The African slave trade was our second pandemic. We emancipated blacks and they strove for greatness.

One of the most notable Black Americans during this time of slavery was Frederick Douglass. Born a slave in Maryland, Frederick Douglass or as he was originally known as Frederick Augustus Bailey first taught himself how to read as it was illegal to teach a slave to read in those times. He then physically fought his slave master and escaped to the North as became Frederick Douglass, the abolitionist. He founded his own newspaper, *The North Star* and spoke out eloquently against slavery all over the world. He published his autobiography, *The Narrative Of A Slave*. Douglass was the father of black history and he served as a role model to many black leaders to come throughout history. Also preeminent during slavery was Nat Turner, a major historical figure. Turner attempted to lead a slave revolt as he instilled fear in the hearts of slave masters. Although his slave revolt was unsuccessful he laid the foundation for resistance of African slaves for years to come and his sentiment was well taken.

Another great historical figure that rose to prominence was the abolitionist and women rights leader, Sojourner Truth originally known as Isabella Baumfree. Although Truth was illiterate, she could speak for hours on a platform on the issue of slavery and women's rights. She became a popular figure in history as she debated Douglass and was known to be a great speaker. Harriet Tubman or Moses of her people as she was referred to as, was the conductor of the Underground Railroad, a freedom organization founded by William Still. After escaping slavery, Tubman returned to the South many times freeing hundreds of slaves to the North. The African slaves learned the language of the land and cultivated the land, building America as slavery financed The Industrial Revolution.

The first person to die during the American Revolution was a black man by the name of Crispus Attacks. Blacks served America as soldiers during the American Revolution gaining independence from Great Britain on July 4, 1776. The issue of slavery caused the Civil War in the 1860's with President Abraham Lincoln issuing the Emancipation Proclamation, freeing the slaves. The Confederates or the South lost the Civil War to the Union states, the North. Blacks fought heroically in this war as well. Following the Civil war and the freeing of slaves in America was Reconstruction the rebuilding of the lives of free Black Americans in the country. From this the first black congressmen emerged in P.B.S. Pinchback and Hiram Revels. The position of blacks during Reconstruction improved greatly in America but there were still challenges.

During the Berlin Congress in the 1880's, the countries of the world partitioned the countries of Africa, i.e., colonization. Ethiopia and Liberia remained the only independent African nations. South Africa and Nigeria were colonized by the British. Ivory Coast was colonized by the French. Meanwhile back in America, Madame C.J. Walker became the first black millionaire.

She owned a grooming products company. There were many great black inventors in America in the 1900's. Elijah McCoy, whom the name "The Real McCoy" is named for invented the locomotive lubricator cup. Garret Morgan invented the traffic light and the gas mask apparatus. Jan Matzeliger invented a device that attached soles to shoes. George Washington Carver invented hundreds of uses for the peanut as he was a scientist for Tuskegee University. Dr. Lewis Lattimer invented the carbon filament that made the incandescent light work. Dr. Daniel Hale Williams performed the first open heart surgery in America.

One of the most prominent leaders of Black America during the early 1900's was Booker T. Washington. Author of the autobiography, *Up From Slavery*, Washington founded Tuskegee University and was the leader of the Tuskegee Machine. He was a proponent of vocational education for blacks during that era and he stressed accommodation as a political strategy. He was a powerful leader in the South. In the North was his adversary, W.E.B. Dubois, the first black Harvard PhD and co-founder of the National Association for the Advancement of Colored People (NAACP).

Dubois wrote *The Souls Of Black Folk*. He was an opponent of both vocational education for blacks and accommodation. He favored liberal arts education and political resistance. He and Washington had a major debate as blacks followed either one of these two interest during the early 1900's. Dubois was editor of *The Crisis Magazine*, the NAACP major political medium. He was mostly known for his theory known as the Talented Tenth, the notion that black people would have to be led by the most talented elite of black people in the country. Marcus Garvey was another great leader of black people during the early 1900's. His organization the Universal Negro Improvement Association or UNIA united 6 million blacks all over the world. Garvey led the Back to Africa movement in which he favored blacks returning back to Africa. This was a notion put forth by Abraham Lincoln and the American Colonization Society.

Paul Cuffee, a black leader financed his own ship to take blacks back to Africa prior to Garvey as well. Garvey had a fleet of ships known as The Black Star Line with the intention of sending blacks back to Africa. Paul Robeson said that America was black's home and they help build it so they did not want to go back to Africa.

Many other black leaders opposed Garvey and he was eventually deported back to Jamaica.

Blacks served courageously in World War I and World War II despite unequal treatment in America. They served their country well despite second class citizenship. World War I was the Axis Powers versus the Allies. Nazi Germany announced themselves to be the superior race and they tried to take over the world. America did not allow it to happen and blacks served significantly.

During the world war, the Tuskegee Airman, a group of black pilots headed by Benjamin O. Davis, Sr. supported by first lady, Eleanor Roosevelt, completed several air missions. Back home, the separate-but-unequal practice, Jim Crow was prevalent in the South. This was the practice of segregation in the South where blacks and whites had separate accommodations. One landmark decision that went against Jim Crow was Plessy v. Ferguson in 1896. Blacks suffered from unequal educational systems and housing throughout the country. However, there was the 1954 *Brown v. Board of Education of Topeka, Kansas*. This landmark Supreme Court case desegregated schools in America. Thurgood Marshall was the attorney in that case. He was later appointed a justice in the Supreme Court, the first black to hold such a position.

In 1956, Kwame Nkrumah led Ghana to its independence from Great Britain and Ghana became the first African nation to gain independence with other nations to follow years later.

The 1960's saw the emergence of Martin Luther King, Jr. as leader. This erudite leader was a Baptist minister and PhD, receiving his doctorate from Boston University. Dr. King led a nonviolent boycott in Montgomery, Alabama, the Montgomery Bus Boycott and a march on Selma, Alabama. He trained black leaders and blacks to follow Gandhi's nonviolent form of resistance to inequality. The result of his actions were the landmark Constitutional initiatives, the 1964 Civil Rights Act and the 1965 Voting Act. King won a Nobel Prize for Peace, the second black to receive such a coveted award following the great black diplomat, Ralphe Bunche who won the prize previously. In 1963, King led a march on Washington that brought hundreds of thousands to listen to his famous "I Have A Dream" speech.

As opposed to Dr. King's nonviolent protest was Malcolm X, formerly a gangster known as Malcolm Little and now a minister in the Nation of Islam. He favored black nationalism and militant resistance. The Nation of Islam was founded by Elijah Muhammad, formerly Elijah Poole, who with a fourth grade education received the teachings of W.D. Fard and founded the Muslim organization.

Malcolm became his national minister after making a transformation from prisoner to minister. Malcolm followed the lead of an earlier radical leader, Monroe Trotter and urged blacks to petition to the United Nations for human rights. Malcolm was a great orator and leader whose "By Any Means Necessary" proclamation laid the basis for black militancy in America and black power. The Black Panther Party, a group of counter-revolutionaries followed Malcolm's lead with founders Huey Newton and Bobby Seale. This movement raised the consciousness of Black America.

There was a tremendous amount of great black figures in history. Alaine Locke was the first black Rhodes Scholar. There were many notable blacks in science. Dr. Charles Drew developed blood plasma, a substitution for blood and the first blood bank. Ronald McNair and Mae Jemison were famous astronauts. The leading astrophysicist in the country is Dr. Neil degrasse Tyson. There was the biologist, Dr. Leonard Jefferies whose "Sun People" theory rocked the science world. In medicine, Dr. Ben Carson is a premiere brain surgeon.

In business, there was John H. Johnson, the founder of Johnson Publishing Company, publisher of Ebony and Jet Magazine. The first black billionaire was Reginald Lewis who completed a leverage buyout of TLC Beatrice Company. Russell Simmons is another great entrepreneur in America and Oprah Winfrey is a leading businesswoman in a class by herself. During the Reagan administration, there was the Black Capitalism movement where initiatives were made to increase the number of black entrepreneurs in America. There are many notable great blacks in sports.

The first one that comes to mind is Jesse Owens, won four gold medals at the Berlin Olympics in 1936 defying the Nazi Germany theory of the master race and superiority. Jack Johnson was the first black heavyweight champion in America. He was a flamboyant figure in the world of sports in the early 1900's. Female athletes like Wilma Rudolph and Althea Gibson dominated female sports in their era. In the world of basketball, Wilt Chamberlain was the greatest player in the NBA once scoring 100 points in a game and averaging over 50 points a game in a season. Bill Russell won eleven NBA championships with the Boston Celtics. Known to be an intelligent player with wit, Russell was a player-coach for the Celtics as well. There was the superstar, Julius Erving or Dr. J as he was called. He played for the Philadelphia 76ers and won a championship. He was known for his dazzling moves on the court.

UCLA won a national championship with Lew Alcindor, who later became Kareem Abdul-Jabar. Abdul-Jabar later starred for the Los Angeles Lakers and won a number of championships along with his teammate Magic Johnson. One of the most popular stars in the NBA was Michael Jordan who won six championships with the Chicago Bulls. Kobe Bryant of the Los Angeles Lakers was to follow his lead. Today the NBA is dominated by the play of Lebron James of the Cleveland Cavaliers.

In baseball there were stars such as Jackie Robinson who broke the color barrier in baseball in 1945 and Hank Aaron, the all time leading home run hitter. Reggie Jackson played for the New York Yankees and was a major league slugger. Rickey Henderson was an all-around great player who led the American League in stolen bases a number of times. Dwight Gooden won a World Series as a pitcher with two teams, the New York Yankees and New York Mets.

 There were a lot of great football players that people looked up to. They are Jim Brown, Gale Sayers, Franco Harris, Lynn Swann, Tony Dorsett, Eric Dickerson, Barry Sanders, Lawrence Taylor, Drew Prearson, Joe Green, Ed Jones, Reggie White, Randall Cunningham, Michael Vick, Michael Strahan, Richard Sherman, and Russell Wilson. In track there was Florence Griffith Joyner, Jackie Joyner-Kersee, Allison Felix, Sanya Richards-Ross, Michael Johnson, Carl Lewis, Michael Powell, and Usain Bolt, the fastest man alive. In golf there is Tiger Woods and in tennis there is Serena Williams and Venus Williams. Lisa Leslie and Cheryl Swoopes were great players in the WNBA. In boxing there were many great ones like Floyd Mayweather, Jr. and Lennox Lewis.

In entertainment blacks also do well. Actors Denzel Washington, Halle Berry, Jamie Foxx, and Jennifer Hudson won Oscar Awards for their acting. Spike Lee and Tyler Perry are famous movie directors. There are a myriad of great singers in Black America also. In politics Shirley Chisholm was a congresswoman as was Maxine Waters and Carol Mosely Braun. L.Douglass Wilder was the first black elected governor as he was governor of Virginia.

Colin Powell, formerly the highest ranked black man in the military as he was Joint Chief of Staff, was Secretary of State as was Condeleeza Rice under President George Bush. Jesse Jackson was the first black person to be a legitimate candidate for the presidency and Barack Obama followed by winning the presidency in the most recent election. The Black Congressional Caucus is a group of black congressmen who pass legislature for the benefit of Black America. In law there was the late Johnny Cochrane, an immense lawyer. In literature there have been some great writers like Langston Hughes, Ralph Ellison, James Baldwin, Gwendylon Brooks, and Noble Prize Laureates Maya Angelou and Toni Morrison.

In the past we had religious leaders like Father Divine and Noble Drew Ali and today the most prominent religious leaders are Minister Louis Farrakhan and T.D. Jakes. Mary McCleoud Bethune was a leading educator as she founded Bethune Cookman College with $1.50. Blacks have done so much with so little. Despite discrimination and an uneven playing field, we have soared high. Currently as a nation within a nation, blacks are 9th in the world in gross national product tied with Canada. This means that we are the 9th richest nation in the world as black people in America. This is tied with Canada and Australia. However, there is a paradox.

Despite such great aggregate wealth, 44% of black children grow up in poverty. So to be great as a nation, the wealth has to be distributed effectively. The 1960's Kerner Commission reported that blacks lagged behind in income as compared to whites and employment. In the 1980's there was a follow up report done, the Commission on Cities and it reported that blacks had double the unemployment rates of whites.

In order to be great in America, blacks have to demand equality and a level playing field. We continue to have pockets of progress but the economic disparities still exist. Education in the inner city lags behind in funding. In terms of business, 1 in 10 Koreans owns a business, 1 in 15 whites own a business, and for blacks that statistic is 1 in 64. We currently are the majority minority in America, 12% of the population at over 32 million people, but we only own 5% of the nation's wealth. We must continue to excel in sports and entertainment as that is our bread and butter, but we comprise only 6% of medical doctors in the country. We must increase that figure dramatically. We were successful in creating a 3 billion dollar rap industry and expanding the R&B category, but we must continue to strive for education.

As blacks we are a talented race of people. We must value intelligence as there are plenty of bright black people that can serve as role models. We must decrease the frequency of single mothers in Black America. We must master the art of choosing a mate just like we must master the art of business and finance. To the black youth of America: know your history, focus, persevere, be determined and shoot for the stars as this book advocates. Have the right role models. There is a great deal of police brutality that hinders black greatness. We must continue to mobilize the race beyond this evil phenomenon. Have racial pride; an Italian is proud to be an Italian, a Korean is proud to be a Korean, an Indian is proud of being from India, you must be proud of being an African-America. Long ago, Marcus Garvey said, "Up you mighty race!" We must increase the number of champs in Black America; the number of valedictorians, presidents, CEOs, PhDs, heavyweight champs, presidents, and even kings. Take your place in history. As we are drowning in the deep waters of blackness, we have to take our place in the ocean of greatness.

Chapter 15:
The Theory of Lay Epistemics

◇◇◇◇◇◇◇◇◇◇

We live in an information society in which the sum total of human knowledge is the highest it's been in the history of man. Knowledge is power. Your population of knowledge determines your opportunities and your leverage in the world. Be a sponge and absorb knowledge. Knowledge helps you rise. In Ancient Greece, Socrates, Plato, and Aristotle brought knowledge to the Western world. They each became famous philosophers in history. Knowledge is the beginning of wisdom. Wisdom is "wise dome" or wise head.

A PhD makes his or her living acquiring knowledge. Once he or she acquires knowledge, he or she disseminates this knowledge onto others. A PhD learns the Oppenheimer Scientific Method in which he begins with a hypothesis and ends up with a new piece of knowledge. Going to college or pursuing higher education is actually a quest for knowledge. Knowledge becomes know-how in career, business, sports, and life. Bill Gates had know-how in designing the most widely used software in the world.

In an information society, one must be informed. You must not let the world go on without you knowing what's going on. The information base is vast and filled with information about people, places, and things. At the stroke of a keyboard you can access information in seconds. Knowledge has to be discovered the way Sir Isaac Newton discovered gravity. He also wrote the most scientific book ever in *Principia*. His laws of thermodynamics are still studied in science today. Discover knowledge the way Imhotep, the Father of Medicine, discovered the circulation of blood in the human veins. This took intuition and insight of a rare nature and degree. Discover knowledge the way Cesar discovered the cure for rattlesnake bite. Discover knowledge the way of Dr. Daniel Hale Williams, the first person to perform open heart surgery.

Self-knowledge as encouraged by Socrates is also power. Knowing your strengths, weaknesses, interests, desires, and quirks are essential if you are to know thyself. Know what makes you tick. Know what is your rock. Know what is your mountain. Complete an inventory of yourself. Ask yourself the key basic questions about yourself. Knowing your body is important as well. What does it take to function well? To be healthy? Also, you must know your mind. Know what information or experience to take into it for positive results. Know what information you need to avoid. Know how certain things affect your psychological well-being. Furthermore, know your limit as to what you can take into your mind.

Self-knowledge allows you to know your talents and passions. This is helpful in deciding on a career, activities, a life plan, and other endeavors. It helps you set goals and even shoot for the stars. Self-knowledge lets you know yourself enough to adjust to circumstances and obstacles. A boxer with self-knowledge knows how to adjust to the punching power of his opponent. He has an inventory of his strengths so he uses his jab instead of going toe-to-toe with his opponent. A student given an essay assignment knows her strengths and weaknesses in attempting this assignment. She knows her own work ethic, her skills, and her stamina so she can plan accordingly to meet her deadline.

History repeats itself. One piece of knowledge that is power is knowledge of history like the historian Herodotus. History allows you knowledge of where you came from and from under what conditions you came from. It lets you know the experiences of the people who preceded you. I learned from history that American Indians had knowledge of the land in America. They knew how to live off the land and they appreciated nature. They were the first Americans, so what was their history? Not only is knowledge of history powerful, but it's fascinating. For instance, Harriet Tubman was so ingenious she knew exactly how much Mercury, the deadly chemical found in a thermometer today, to tap on a baby's tongue to knock out the baby when the baby was crying.

Thus, her group of escapees could stay quiet hidden in the brush as there were bounties on their heads. The history is that the Earth was once thought to be flat. The moon was unattainable and we knew nothing of the Cosmos. Now we have knowledge of the Earth being round and knowledge of the galaxy, the Universe, and the Cosmos. We have satellites that go 25,000 square miles in space. We have reached the moon with Neil Armstrong and the American astronauts. We know how to cure tuberculosis. Who is going to come up with a cure for cancer, for AIDS, or other disease that we now have no cure for.

We have advanced medicine, advanced theories and research in science and mathematics. Brain surgery is at its highest level of precision ever in history as is open heart surgery. People who would have died long ago are now living due to the advancement of knowledge in medicine. We have knowledge of the specifications that we can live under.

We live in the age of digital technology. Technology is tech "knowledge"y. Knowledge is being transmitted and shared electronically like never before in history. In science, we shall leave no stone unturned. We have knowledge of evolution and the infamous human tailbone. We know that life began in the ocean with an electrical storm acting upon a single-celled organism evolving into the first multi-celled organism according to biologists. Man is a multi-celled organism made up of 200 million cells. See how powerful knowledge is.

One needs knowledge of finance in a capitalist society. Financial literacy is the bridge to success in this type of market economy. Knowledge of how financial instruments and securities work is important. It is helpful to know how corporations finance their business through you, the investor or how the government finances its operations through you, the investor or taxpayer. In business, marketers must have knowledge of the market.

In war a general has to have knowledge and details also called "intelligence" about the enemy and battlefield. General Napolean Bonaparte was the greatest general ever because he had so much knowledge about the war. Life is a lot like war, you need knowledge to succeed and be great. You need know-how, the knowledge of how to execute a goal to the end. In life you need knowledge, wisdom, and understanding. That makes for a learned person or erudite. As a scholar I was hungry for knowledge, wisdom, and understanding.

There is a theory is psychology, Kruglanski's theory of lay epistemics. This theory states that man wants to obtain knowledge in order to be valid. He attempts to get knowledge to avoid being invalid. We seek knowledge for the power it puts in our head. A mind filled with facts is able to solve complex problems and complex situations and generate ideas. You have billions of brain cells or neurons, fill them with positive knowledge.

Knowledge turns potential energy into kinetic energy as the science metaphor goes. What's the use of having an automobile if you don't have knowledge or know-how of how to drive it and the driving rules of the road. What's the use of having all the ingredients of a meal to eat if you don't have knowledge of how to cook and prepare the meal. What's the use of being seven feet tall if you are a basketball player and you don't know how to put the ball in the hoop. Benjamin Banneker was full of knowledge. He created the almanac and was an astronomer. He also made the first working clock in America and laid out the blueprint for Washington D.C.. In order to make like Bannaker and acquire knowledge, you must read books. Words are the gateway to knowledge so read the dictionary. Reading comprehension and retention of what you read is very vital to putting knowledge together. Be able to give an overview of a newspaper article or encyclopedia article that you read. This is called synthesizing information. It is an important skill to a PhD or any student. It also applies to life as well – be able to take knowledge and tell the story to others. Go to the library regularly. Keep a knowledge journal featuring articles, statistics, quotes, and other forms of knowledge on a daily basis. I did this in high school and found that I had facts and statistics at my finger tips.

The opposite of knowledge is oblivion. Oblivion is burdensome. You can be the weakest link with oblivion. Let knowledge propel you to the top. You need knowledge of the classics, literature and philosophy, Homer and others. Knowledge leads to technical skills. These skills are essential in many careers and in life in general. A lawyer needs knowledge of the law, a doctor needs knowledge of medicine and the human anatomy, a chemist needs knowledge of the periodic table of chemicals, a basketball player has to have a high basketball IQ, an astrophysicist needs knowledge of the Universe, and a lion needs knowledge of the jungle in order to hunt and survive.

Let your brain wander off to places far away to places like Russia to experience the culture of the Russians, to China to have knowledge of their culture, to see how they adapt in South America, India, Africa, and other places. Once you know your own history, gain knowledge of the history of other places. Life is not simple, it is complex. Thus, you need knowledge to alleviate you from oblivion. The main way to knowledge other than empirical observation is through education.

Pedagogy is of utmost importance. Man cannot reach full emancipation without education. Civilization does not advance upward without education. America is twenty second in the world in math and science. It must improve this statistic in order to remain a superpower. The education of its masses is of vital importance as the nation's engage in survival of the fittest. A lack of excellent education puts a limiting threshold on a nation. Victory goes to the swift.

The intellectual capacity of a nation determines its fate. Destiny is in our own hands. We must teach our students how to use their infinite minds. Our curriculum must be adjusted in order to incorporate the fact that we experience a shrunken world, more globally competitive than ever. We must broaden the horizons of our students and their world views. Change is necessary. The key vicissitude of this change is the birth of a new nation. Then we realize the meaning of "America, the free."

From Harvard University to early childhood schools, we must dedicate ourselves to mastering the educational process. We must infuse our information into the minds of our students. Our students must absorb knowledge and apply it accordingly. Our institutions of higher learning must prepare our pupils for the competitive workforce. Schools should instill determination and drive into its pupils. We must grow economists and capitalists from among us. We must spring forth educators and scientists with original protocols. Our educational model must be improved. Mentoring must be utilized at every level of education. We must tap into the knowledge base. We must educate our pupils with proven methods of teaching. Teachers should be compensated commensurate with their achievement in advancing the minds of their pupils.

Education raises the consciousness of man. He becomes aware of his environment as well as his own strengths and weaknesses. He becomes capable of making the most of his environment and his opportunities. He becomes a product of his environment and not a victim of his environment. He increases his life chances and the probability that he will succeed. Education inherently trains a man how to think.

In America, our educational system should also be designed to match our students' skills with students all over the world. Students should be equipped with the ability to read, write, synthesize reading material, and do mathematics. Students should also be armed with the ability to verbally communicate. We must grow rational thinkers – a nation of rational thinkers. There is no limit to how far we can go.

There is a strong correlation between educational achievement and civilization. The more educated a nation, the more civilized it can be. A nation is only as strong as its scientists, its leading minds. We must reinforce science in the home and provide excellence in teaching it in school. Miseducation is a downfall. It correlates with violence, drug use, crime and other negatives in society. It goes against the norms of society as well.

We must build on our past successes. Advancement in medicine is one such example. Researchers and professors align to provide us with breakthroughs in science and education. We have trained generations of leaders for the betterment of our nation. The general psyche in our nation must be that it is positive to be smart. Schools must provide incentives and rewards for students who work hard and excel or a student who has improved from point A to B.

Education aids a student in the acquisition of the mindset needed to succeed in career and ultimately in the game of life. It allows for the transformation of man and the transition from dependent to thinker. Critical thinking is something that can be bred or taught in school. Analytical minds are needed in the workforce and in society in general. Students should be taught to make logical arguments and deductions. They must be trained to reason. Finally, man must have the ability to understand. That's the definition of intelligence – the ability to think, reason, and understand.

Knowledge is power as powerful as wind energy. Knowledge equips man with the ability to decide among alternatives. A stock investor makes investment decisions based on knowledge he has available to him. A parent makes decisions relating to her child based on knowledge available to her. Knowledge is uplifting; it helped Egypt rise, it helped Rome rise, and now America is likewise rising with ions of information. We live in an information age that followed quite naturally the industrial revolution, and the digital age. Man must tease out information, using only relevant information for a particular task. The sum total of human knowledge has increased dramatically over the last thirty years. There is more information than ever; that's where education comes into play. It teaches us how to use information effectively. It also teaches us how to disseminate information.

Education is not just an exercising of the mind, it allows man the ability to delineate the meaning of life. Through education, man discovers the purpose of life. He embarks on journeys otherwise unknown to him. Man uncovers unknown phenomena. Education helps him explain such phenomena. He learns how to write himself a dream and read his way to freedom. Education is a breakthrough of the mind. Through it man becomes master of his own destiny. A college degree is so important that it can separate the haves from the have-nots.

In mastering education at all levels, a student gains confidence. This confidence, he brings with him into his life. Confidence is a key antecedent of success. Education also builds character. Teachers, like parents, can instill character into students. In all education must let man know who he is. This is called knowledge of self or "ziji" in Chinese. Once man has this type of knowledge he can know how far he can go. Education is a long process. Thus, students who complete a significant level of it gain perseverance. They develop the attitude to never give up. Prime Minister of Great Britain, Winston Churchill, was asked to give a speech to Harvard University. He stood up and said, "Never, ever, ever, give up!" That was the entire speech. The learning process must teach students how to focus and not to fear challenges that surface.

Education must teach students to make something out of nothing, to make the best of a bad situation, to improvise. It must teach them to make the most of their resources. Learning has a role in meeting the Maslow Hierarchy of Needs. The more you learn, the better you are able to saturate your environment to meet your hierarchy of needs. Learning is in fact a need as you have intellectual needs. Man has the capacity to be intelligent. Education filters through man's mind like a white light through a spectrum of lights giving off a rainbow of colors.

Man has his own idiosyncracies, but his common denominator is the need for education. First, there is the preparation for life. Second, there is the broadening of his horizons. Third, if he is ever to exist as a free spirit, he must have a free mind. Finally, he is charged with taking care of himself and his family. Education allows man to get the most out of life. He seizes learning opportunities, designs an active life, and puts the pieces of the puzzle together. It also helps students discern the difference between right and wrong, positive and negative, good and evil. This is important for the society at large as we are engaged in an everyday struggle.

Education must teach man to be larger than his circumstances – greater than his state. If he is impoverished, he must be greater than that in knowing that he does not have to remain in poverty. In a capitalistic society, a market economy, you can go from rags to riches. You can make a dollar out of fifteen cents. However, you must have a competitive spirit. Every corporation must be competitive in its industry to gain a large market share.

College is supposed to teach you the language of the land. If you go into the jungle, you must speak the language of lions and tigers. If you are in America or other industrialized nation of the world, you must speak the language of capitalism. Financial literacy is the currency in a capitalistic society. The burden of financial knowledge has been on the student. This burden must be shifted onto the institution as everyone is expected to handle money in their lifetime.

One must understand the politics of inclusion. Those with education are more likely to be included in the plans of institutions. Those without education are left scrambling, left standing. Moreover, in the social arena, those with education have preemptive opportunities to be included. A lack of education cast a shadow of doubt on the minds of people as to their future, hope, ambitions, and dreams. He feels no confidence in obtaining goals if he has set them. He becomes complacent and even stagnant in life. His dreams wallow. His desires are stymied. His drive is decimated. He does not want a career, he wants a job. He does not want to be build, he wants to maintain. He does not want discovery, he wants status quo. He settled for immediate gratification and has no patience. The educated man knows that Rome wasn't built in a day, much like they were not educated in a day. The educated man knows that there is a pot of gold at the end of the rainbow. So he strives and strives.

Alexander The Great wanted to conquer Egypt because he knew they were rich in education. Education is power - from the small child to eldest person in the household. Reading is fundamental as a jump shot in basketball. Man must read himself to freedom and knowledge and peace. The only remedy to war is education and understanding. It was education that broke up the Cold War along with diplomacy among the educated elite. Let freedom ring in the minds of the educated masses.

Education allows for the metamorphosis of the human sprit. Education is refreshing to the human spirit. It is good for soul. It replenishes the mind. A caterpillar larvae first crawls for a period of time before it builds a cocoon in which it meditates and grows. The cocoon protects it from its environment. Once the caterpillar matures and grows wings it breaks out of the cocoon and takes flight as a beautiful butterfly. Man matures the same way. Education not only protects him, but it matures and develops his wings. Once his mind is educated and his spirit is invigorated, he takes flight into the air.

Lever means to put into action. Education is in fact the lever man uses to overcome obstacles in life. We know life is about ups and downs. The environment presents you with certain stumbling blocks or obstacles. Man must use his instincts along with his education to overcome such obstacles. When man has financial woes, he can look to education to dig him out of such a hole. Because a more educated man takes better care of himself, the obstacle of poor health can be overcome. When in an environment is not conducive to his development, he can use his education to remove himself from it and mobilize into a more productive environment.

Education is a pilgrimage into another realm of consciousness. Education and knowledge illuminates man's mind. Consciousness is thinking. If only man can be conscious of how powerful he can be. It is through education that this takes place. If he can conquer exam after exam, he can conquer challenges in life. Education must test the common sense of man. It must be something that the student can relate to. The process of education must facilitate a positive attitude in a student. Much can be borne of this attribute in a person. He becomes positive and sets goals for himself. His outlook on life is also positive. He must rise up like a plant. He must absorb knowledge like this plant's chlorophyll during photosynthesis, absorbing light.

Through education a man develops a mentality. This is his mindset. Everything flows from his mindset - his actions, dispositions, and behaviors, his beliefs, and practices. Enter into this calculus, his philosophies and opinions. Education and knowledge allow man to climb mountains, to obtain greatness, and to amass glory. No mystery shall be left unsolved. No mouth shall be left unfed. No mind shall be wasted.

Chapter 16:
Have A Job

◇◇◇◇◇◇◇◇◇◇

    Does it seem that the stars have to be aligned correctly for you to be happy? The elements have to be lined up. The chemistry of happiness is one in which your makeup, i.e., mental and physical, must be in sync with your external world, your environment. You must have a job. Life is a mountain and happiness is the plateau, the peak. How do you reach the top? Regardless of what's happening around you, how do you obtain happiness?

Let us use the Socratic method: what is happiness? Happiness is being content about your life and not depressed. It is a mental feeling or state. It is being in a positive and peaceful state of mind. Additionally, it is having control over one's life. Happiness is an extension of the type of person you are. For instance, if you are a negative person, inner happiness may be more difficult to obtain or maintain. However, if you are a positive person, this lens allows you to be happier as long as the elements line up.

The antecedent to finding happiness is meeting your needs. There are physical, physiological, and spiritual needs. This means one's environment must provide for all of these elements and more. Much like a fish needs water, people need economic stability for this precursor of needs. For example, it is difficult to focus on your spiritual needs when you haven't eaten for a week or have no roof over your head. Thus, it is difficult to hone in on happiness when you are preoccupied with survival. The climb is steep, but once you lay the foundation for happiness, the peak is attainable.

Life is about circumstances. You have to be greater than your circumstances. Part of happiness is knowing what you don't want. Many of the circumstances you have are unwanted. You must alleviate these circumstances or they may cripple your chances of happiness. This is the process of overcoming obstacles to achieve your goals. Adversity will permeate your psyche. Once you have laid the foundation to have control over your life, then adversity can be subdued.

Setting goals is a key phase to the happiness process. If you want to be an astronaut, set the goal of becoming an astronaut and do everything you need to do to accomplish this. If you want to climb a mountain, set the goal of climbing that mountain, and do everything you need to do to climb that mountain. If you want to be a doctor, then set sail and head in that direction to that destination. It starts with a goal. Philosophically, happiness occurs in the mind. The prisoner's dilemma is being imprisoned and still trying to be happy. In this case he is free in his mind despite his body being incarcerated. This requires strong mental ability and happiness does as well. A lot of people have a prison in their mind. They must free themselves.

Amidst the storm, one must have peace of mind. There are disturbances in the world, calamity, and adverse conditions. One must not let this alter one's peace of mind. Topsy-turvy is the world, but the mind is capable of achieving peace of mind and happiness. You must reach for the stars to find serenity. You must tap the secret valleys of your mind to find peace and happiness. You must lay to rest your negative past and move forward. Conditions are prevalent, you must adjust. Positive thought is the mechanism to peace of mind. As a man thinketh, so shall he be. If the seed is positive, the root of the plant will be positive. If your thoughts are positive your mind will be healthier.

I solve my problems using my intellect. The use of rational thinking allows me to have peace of mind and happiness. My mind ventures into worlds unknown. I have engaged in the process of discovery. The more I discover, the more this makes me happy because that's what is important to me. Mental anguish comes to those who don't use their minds effectively. There is chaos in the minds of those who don't have peace of mind. This is a struggle. Thus, happiness is a struggle. Many a man is at war with himself.

He battles on a daily basis. He struggles with the real world. He finds it hard to set goals. He faces crisis and does not know what to do. He needs happiness to have peace and needs peace to have happiness. If you have inner peace you have inner strength. One must be able to cope with stress in life. Stress can have an effect on your neurological system. Don't be nervous, be at peace. Many things may be unsettled within you. You must make amends.

Life is a puzzle. You are required to find the pieces of the puzzle and put them together. The pieces are your infrastructure, the infrastructure of your life. This may include a career, a family, friends, a hobby or project, a social life, etc. The first type of humans were gatherers. You must gather the pieces of the puzzle along with pursuing your ultimate goal. In order to gather an infrastructure, one must have awareness. You must be aware of what your surroundings has available and the opportunities it offers. You have to be aware of your strengths and weaknesses as well. Finally, you must be aware of what it takes to meet your goals and needs.

Being what you want is a key to happiness. I wanted to be a college football player and I was able to do that. This made me happy. I wanted to be a college professor and I did so. This made me happy. I wanted to be a writer and did so. This made me happy. I wanted to be a world traveler and accomplished that. This also made me happy as did being a mentor. Being what you want to be takes focus and determination as well as perseverance. Meeting your goals is a key to happiness. You put the effort forth and you want a positive outcome. Here, the sky is the limit. You can become great if you put your mind to it. If you can conceive it, you can achieve it.

Happiness can lift your spirit and invigorate your soul. You perform better at whatever the task may be when you have happiness. One element of happiness is excitement. Nothing ever happens until you are excited. Excitement or zeal for something is the spark that ignites everything. Imagine a world with no excitement. Being excitable is a prerequisite for happiness. Man doesn't really have the capacity to be bored. He needs activity, new horizons, new experiences and adventures. What was the last time you were excited? When was the last time you were inspired?

To the highest of mountains and the deepest of seas to be happy, we seek inspiration. With inspiration, we withstand the mightiest of storms. With inspiration we become great. Many are called upon by the Universe to do amazing things and they answer the call. It is with this inspiration that they are lit up like a light to do the impossible. They advance the cause of mankind, of civilization.

This book by the author is to help you ascend to your highest level of happiness and satisfaction. It is to inspire you to be great and to overcome whatever is in your way of reaching your peak.

The motion that you make defines your chances. Inspiration rejuvenates your spirit, your human spirit. Your spirit carries you through the world. Your mind needs a spark to do great things and achieve your ultimate goal. Watching others in motion do amazing things transcends to you and you wish to emulate them. Like in Rome, Cicero told the children to emulate the achievements of their ancestors and Rome was saved. You have to use inspiration as a force . This is a force that drives you to grab hold of your destiny and put your happiness in your own hands.

Inspiration awakens the giant within you. It has a chemical and electric effect on the brain, its impulses, its reaction to the external world. When a man runs the 100 meter dash in 9.5 seconds, it inspires the world, when a man composes beautiful music without the benefit of sight, he inspires the world. When two brothers invent a way for man to fly through the sky, they inspire the world. When we complete a journey of our own, we inspire. A poet inspires us with her verses, a doctor with his medicine, an architect with his pyramids. We look for others for inspiration in our daily lives.

The great Pharaohs of Egypt left monuments in Egypt to inspire generations to come. Writers like Mark Twain leave written words for people to be inspired by. Scientists like Albert Einstein, creator of the theory of relativity, inspired us to discover more than what we now know. There is nothing more inspiring than human progress. I recall when I was sick and could hardly walk. My wife would walk with me around a pond of geese at the park for weeks. I would get my walk back. This was progress. I was happier. Progress is the key to happiness. It empowers you. When you set a goal you must monitor your progress and progress one step at a time. Progress allows you to endure for life is not a sprint but a long distance run. Often times it requires you to transform your mind to progress. This is progress of your mind in the way you think. Like a caterpillar larvae, man undergoes a metamorphosis. This is the maturation and development of the mind. The mind is the key element in happiness.

Education is important. When you are educated you can extract more out of life. Your horizons are broadened. You develop a world view. You start formulating theories about life. I recall in college I would walk across the campus and look up at the stars and theorize about life, the big picture. The big picture is you want to be happy. You develop theories as to how to do this. This book develops keys to happiness in which I reflect on my lessons in life and theories. If you follow the keys you can develop a life plan for yourself and your loved ones.

The wind blew in a piece of knowledge to me: knowledge and the acquisition of knowledge has meant being in a position to be successful. You're only as strong as your knowledge. Reading has infused knowledge in me and I like to carry facts in my head. The psychology theory called lay epistemics says that people acquire knowledge to be valid. They acquire knowledge for fear of being invalid. It is also the cornerstone to happiness because knowledge becomes know-how and when you have know-how you have valid solutions to problems however complex. When you have tacit knowledge, deep inner knowledge you can solve problems that surface. Solving problems is important to being happy because reality is that problems will come in cycles.

Fulfilling your passions make you happy. First you have to do an inventory of yourself to find your passions. Then you have to make them a part of your life plan. Thomas Edison had a passion for inventions. He was so determined that although he failed 10,000 times in trying to invent the light bulb, he eventually invented the light bulb. Your passions make you glow. It takes exploration and exposure to find your passions. I was exposed to higher education and eventually discovered that I had a passion for learning. Thus, I went to college for nearly 10 years and I was happy. When I was 19 years old I had the opportunity to travel to Russia and many other countries. This exploration helped me realize my passion for world traveling culminating into a trip to Egypt at 24 years old. I have been to the Lovre Museum in Paris, the Hermitage Museum In Russia, the British Museum, and the Egyptian Museum. I have made going to museums a part of my life plan as it became a passion of mine. You have to design a life plan for yourself and your loved ones. It has to have activity that represents your passions. You have to make like Leif Erickson and be an explorer of life.

The monk, Thomas Merton said that no man is an island. I agree completely. Love plays a key role in happiness. The objective is to share your passions and your life plan with someone else. You can love a spouse, you can love a friend. You have moments together and the sum of the two of you is greater than the two parts if left separate. The union between to people is a beautiful thing. It is a chemical and psychological process. Love nourishes your soul. A man without love is a ship without a rudder.

One aspect of a life plan is a social life. This aspect is often overlooked when it comes to happiness. Lasting relationships are important. Activity is key. It's about people, places, and things, the fundamentals. Much planning should take place when designing a social life. Networking must be pursued. You must get rid of xenophobia, fear of strangers and meet new people. A good social life allows you balance and relaxation.

Many people say money can't buy you happiness. To a degree I agree, but the lack of financial security can be a handicap to happiness, a road block, a glitch. A life plan requires money for the most part. The hierarchy of needs require finances. And once you have money, you must be financially literate enough to keep it. There are 9 million millionaires in America so there is money available. One must be career-oriented and business savvy to become financially independent. Happiness is about having a piece of the pie.

Self-worth is important to being happy. This is a feeling of worth that comes from *abintra* or within. This element weeds a lot of people out when it comes to happiness. Self-worth starts during childhood and continues during adulthood. It is a process, psychological in nature. Setting goals and obtaining them is a good way to gain self-worth. Juxtaposed with happiness is good health. One must maintain optimal health. Heart disease is the leading cause of death in America. Cancer ranks among the leading causes of death as well as diabetes. Eating the right foods and exercising is one way to maintain good health. Regular checkups with a physician are another good practice. Another aspect of happiness is having control over one's own life. You can only be as happy as the control you have over your life.

Chapter 17:
Infinite Greatness

◇◇◇◇◇◇◇◇◇

In mathematics, infinite is defined as lacking limits or endless. Greatness is defined as a high level of excellence. The concept of infinite greatness is that there is no limit to how great one can become. After all there are levels to greatness. Martin Luther King, Jr. won a Nobel Prize at thirty five becoming the youngest person ever to receive this award. He was the pinnacle of success and reached a high level of greatness. There are those who reached an astronomical proportion of greatness in their lives. Frederick Douglass was born a slave. He fought his slave master and escaped to freedom. Prior to escaping he learned to read and write. As a free man, Douglass became the leading abolitionist, writer, and orator in America. He spoke out eloquently against the evils of slavery and alienation. Many regard Frederick Douglass as the father of black history.

Those that are infinitely great affect people around them. They break the chain of mediocrity. Becoming infinitely great is like becoming free. The strive for infinite greatness is equivalent to the strive for freedom. Greatness is a chemical, psychological process of the mind. Yes, it is a process. Harriet Tubman wasn't infinitely great overnight. First, she went through the process of struggle. She had inherited a state that was unwanted and she dedicated herself in her mind to doing something about it. She freed herself and later came back through the Underground Railroad to free hundreds of others from bondage. She was the conductor. She also served as a spy and nurse in the Civil War.

W.E.B. Dubois was an intelligent man who became a Harvard PhD. He was a historian and sociologist. He was also a writer, leader, and one of the founders of the NAACP. Dubois reached such a high level of greatness during his time that he is regarded as one of the greatest scholars ever to live and the Father of Sociology. There are stories told about the amount of effort Booker T. Washington put into getting educated and becoming a leader after the turn of the century. He was one of the most famous black leaders of his era and leader of the Tuskegee Machine.

Those that are infinitely great bring light to a dark world. They illuminate us with their charisma, their dynamicism, their magnetism, their talent, their intelligence, their presence. To become great takes exponential development. Exponents are numbers raised to a higher power or degree. Those that are infinitely great are raised to a higher level. Their minds, bodies, and spirits are lifted to a higher exponential degree. One such person who was lifted to a higher level was Henry Ford. An inventor, Ford invented the first car in America, the Model T. He was successful in his invention and became one of the richest men in the world.

Infinitely great men and women fascinate us, lift us, they encapsulate us, enthrall us. There are a lot of great athletes, entertainers, doctors, inventors, leaders, and teachers and there is room to be infinitely great in the area of lifting humanity. As a humanitarian, I have a love of humanity. One must declare a cause and have conviction to pursue it. My cause is human development and development of the mind. That is why I wrote this book to stimulate the minds of my reader - intellectually, psychologically, spiritually, and emotionally.

To achieve infinite greatness, greatness that no one can limit, limitless greatness, it takes ambition, mindset, courage, and focus. You have to be ambitious to desire something important or big for yourself. You have to strive in other words. Here you shoot for the stars or higher, as high as you can imagine. It takes imagination to be ambitious and self-esteem and positivity. It takes mindset to achieve infinite greatness. Your brain is already wired for you to strive for your goal; you must program your mind to acquire the necessary characteristics needed to pursue your endeavors. There is a lot of pressure and backlash in pursuing your goals and pursuing leadership and greatness, so it takes courage an inner condition of the heart and mind to achieve infinite greatness. Finally, one must keep the main thing the main thing. In other words, one must remain focused or remain on the path toward greatness. This way you sustain your effort, your Herculean effort.

Speaking of Hercules, Hercules was infinitely great in Greek Mythology as was King Perseus, Atlas, Apollo, Hedes, Poseidon, and Zeus. King Perseus saved Mt. Olympus by defeating the evil Medusa. The others were offspring of Zeus as well; gods. Those that have reached infinite greatness have reached the pinnacle of success and shown great courage. For instance, General Hannibal of Carthage, Africa once battled in a war with one eye. He surprised the Italians by crossing the Swiss Alps with elephants. Since the mind is infinite, intelligence is infinite, and the imagination is infinite, man can be infinitely great. To be infinitely great in our society you must act a certain way and think a certain way. In this case you must act like a champ and think like a king. Think like Hannibal, a soldier of fortune.

Infinite intelligence is the ability to think, reason, and understand. Man's understanding can be beyond the basics or the surface; he can get deeper and more tacit. He can acquire tacit or deep knowledge. Man has gone up in space, created digital technology, advanced in medicine and science, education and business, entertainment, and leisure. He has challenged his mind do delineate the mysteries of the Universe which are so mysterious and complex. But his brain is also complex and up to the task at hand. He is an engineer who builds bridges, an astronomer who maps out the solar system, a scientist who experiments with the unknown. He is infinitely great and astounding. Man has infinite power. History has proven that. He has risen to the occasion time and time again as he perpetuates civilization. From the beginning of civilization in 3100 B.C. with the uniting of Upper and Lower Egypt by King Menes, to the civilization of America, a superpower with the greatest infrastructure and economy in the world.

Man has infinite resilience. Resilience is the ability to bounce back. The mind can weather turbulent storms and natural disasters. In my personal life I faced many obstacles that I had to battle mentally and practically to become successful. Martin Luther King was arrested several times and pressured greatly by society before becoming a Nobel Prize Laureate. Frederick Douglass was born in captivity and he rose to fame as a leader. Muhammad Ali was put in prison at the height of his boxing career. He was resilient and rose again to be champ. General George Washington faced a harsh winter in Valley Forge with limited resources and not many men to help win the American Revolution in our nation's history. He became the nation's first president after overcoming many obstacles and being infinitely resilient. He was infinitely great.

Abraham Lincoln was the nation's sixteenth president. He had health issues, but he embarked on one of the nation's most important pursuits in history – the preservation of the union. Lincoln beat the odds and got his emancipation proclamation signed into law and he preserved the union despite much backlash in doing so. He was infinitely great. A man who is infinitely great also has character. A person who is infinitely great, the world can hear him roar. We use this metaphor because we know that a lion in the jungle is infinitely great, the king of the jungle. She raises her cubs to be great as well. She hunts and leads the jungle. She is a beautiful creature with a strong essence. Man is not unlike the lion in many ways. He can be a king in his own right. He can be a leader and a person with a strong essence.

Benjamin Franklyn was infinitely great. He flew a kite in a thunderstorm to invent electricity. What would make a man fly a kite in a thunderstorm? The imagination, intellect, and intuition of man would. Benjamin was a statesman as well and a key person in the history of this country. Another person in history who was infinitely great was physicist, Albert Einstein. Albert Einstein was born at Ulm, in Wurttemberg, Germany on March 14, 1879. In 1896 he entered the Swiss Federal Polytechnic School in Zurich to be trained as a teacher in Physics and Mathematics. In 1905 he obtained his doctorate degree in Physics. In 1916 he published his paper on the general theory of relativity. Einstein contributed more than any other scientist to the modern vision of physical reality. He received the Nobel Prize for Physics in 1921 making him one of the greatest scientist ever.

A man who is infinitely great is excellent. He is excellent in the process of life. He has mastered his environment, his Universe, his domain. He has made something of himself. He doesn't surrender to his fears, to mediocrity. He himself feels his greatness. He resonates greatness. His climb of the mountain was very steep.

He has infinite and perfect ambition. A mathematician appreciates infinity, an onlooker appreciates those who are infinitely great. When a baby comes out the womb, he can be infinitely great. Those that are infinitely great inspire others to be great. They inspire us in our daily lives. You ever seen Usain Bolt run the 100 yard dash in 9.58 seconds or hear Beyonce Knowles sing or watch her dance, or see Lebron James play basketball? It is inspiring. We too can be inspiring. There is nothing greater than inspiration. Nothing more lifting. The capacity of my own mind inspires me and lifts me. It also fascinates and empowers me. I have ascended to higher heights. We must emulate this infinite greatness to be free.

Those that are infinitely great are amazing. Sue Cobb was a great mountain climber, Julie Krone was a great jockey, Tiger Woods was a great golfer, Michelle Obama was a great first lady, Lennox Lewis was a great boxer and champion, Malcolm X was a great leader, Bruce Lee was a great martial artist. Their greatness was infinite, limitless. They lift the spirits of the people. When I was a mentor as a senior in high school, I lifted the spirits of my freshmen males. I was a leader, an athlete, a great student, and they could relate to me. I showed them the way and inspired them to be great in their own lives. When I was a teacher, I instilled ambition in my students. I always asked them what they wanted to be and told them to aim high and never limit the circumference of what they could become.

There is a certain chemistry in the minds of those who are infinitely great. The brain is electric and it works well in the external world. Each person who is infinitely great must have first examined the possibility of their infinite greatness. In many cases they surprised themselves, but for the most part they believed they could be infinitely great and amazing. To them greatness is within their reach.

To talk about a spark that someone else gives you, you must talk about the infinite greatness of Moses. Moses said, "Let my people go!" He led an exodus of the Jews out of bondage in Egypt and Pharaoh's grip. He was simply on another level. The story goes that Moses showed courage and a powerful mindset in leading these people to freedom. Freedom is a theme in this book because the purpose of being infinitely great is to be free ultimately. We set goals and we strive for them. We are preoccupied with pursuing these goals. Only the accomplishment or attainment of these goals can set you free like Moses in Egypt. You have to part plenty of Red Seas in your life and deal with bondage whether psychological or physical of some type as well. But you must have courage along the way.

In terms of greatness, there are levels. The level you are on is determined by your level of intensity, your level of mastery. It takes persistence to be infinitely great. Denzel Washington was persistent in working on his craft. He became a master actor. This infinitely great actor won an Academy Award. He has a perfectionistic orientation and this is reflected in his work. One of the greatest actors ever, Denzel inspires and entertains millions. Lebron James is one of the best basketball players ever to play. Recently winning a championship for the Cleveland Cavaliers,

James scored 41 points in consecutive games. James rose to the occasion to be infinitely great and his greatness transcended onto his teammates. He plays at the highest level. He first examined the possibility of his own greatness then he pursued such greatness.

Floyd Mayweather, Jr., is another perfectionist. In his case he is a perfectionist in the ring. The undefeated pound for pound best fighter in the world has marveled millions with his flawless performances time and time again. He fights on the highest level. He shows the importance of being confident, physically fit and well trained. Floyd is infinitely great and intense. With his impeccable jab and his cunning defense, Floyd may retire undefeated.

I am fascinated by the infinite greatness of sprinter Usain Bolt. Bolt is lightning in the flesh. He has the world record in the 100 yard dash at 9.58 seconds and he is the favorite to win three more gold in this upcoming Olympics. Described by Olympian great Michael Johnson as the greatest sprinter ever, Bolt is in his infinite glory. Talented and hard working, Bolt is the ultimate athlete. One characteristic of these infinitely great people is inner strength. They possess the inner strength of Moses and Harriet Tubman in getting others out of bondage. They possess the inner desire of Frederick Douglass to be free and in this case to be great.

One thing that the infinitely great do is seize their opportunities, seize the moment. When it is time to perform, they are ready. They trained all their lives for their big moment and when it was time to perform, they did it to their best capacity. Blast off, they did. Excite their onlookers, they did. Make history, they did. We can't forget the exploits of Detroit Lions running back, Barry Sanders. This former Heisman Trophy winner once scored two eighty yard touchdowns in the same game and rushed for over 2,000 yards in one season. With his amazing moves and blazing speed, the infinitely great running back is in a class by himself. Perhaps the greatest back to put on a uniform, Sanders was humble and determined. I always wondered what was in the mind of this great athlete. He thrilled millions of fans throughout his lifetime of playing football and he was a great man as well.

My little brother Darryl was a great athlete in his own right. Growing up he played baseball, football, basketball, soccer, ran track, and did karate. In karate he had perfect form. In baseball he could catch, hit, and run with excellence. As a high school football player he was remarkable at running back and corner back. He ran like Terrell Davis and Barry Sanders combined. On defense he was impeccable. I remember him lifting me up with his play on the football field. I was his greatest fan and supporter. My brother Darryl is infinitely great.

One thing that these infinitely great people have is excitability. They get excited when they are in the midst of their passions. Nothing else matters in the moment. Denzel, Usain, Lebron, Einstein, my little brother, they all get excited when doing what they do. We know from my first book, "On the Wings of Perseus", that nothing ever happens until you are excited. This is a chemical, psychological, and spiritual process. The body lights up. The mind lights up. You become an incandescent light. You grow wings and you fly or soar high. Take flight and be glorious. Be majestic, be intense. The laws of nature are in your favor. The characteristics of your brain, the makeup of your mind are in your favor. Your brain is servo-mechanistic; it is a machine that is wired for success. It is infinite and it is wired for infinite greatness. There is nothing like glory. We all want to be appreciated for what we can do with our mind and body. We all want others to admire and be fascinated by us and our abilities.

When there is an intersection between your goals and your obstacles, push on. Push on and you too will be great. When you face unsurmountable odds, push on, when things go awry, push on. When everything seems dark and there is no sign of light, push on. You have to believe that you can be infinitely great and you will be. Ascend to your highest level. Your ascension will be your glory. You will be infinitely great.

Chapter 18 :
My Story

◇◇◇◇◇◇◇◇◇

I was born March 26, 1973 in New Brunswick, New Jersey. New Brunswick is a health care hub located one hour from New York City and one hour from Philadelphia. It is known as a major health care hub because of its famous hospitals, Robert Wood Johnson University Hospital and St. Peter's University Hospital of which I was born. New Brunswick is also known for its universities, Rutgers University – the State University and the University of Medicine and Dentistry of New Jersey. I was born to Theresa and Roosevelt Harris, two working class parents who were separated around the time of my birth. I had seven brothers and sisters and at the time my mother was a single mother.

As a youth I recall my city being permeated with gangs and drugs; it was a street life. My mother worked two jobs often walking miles to and from work to support the family. Muhammad Ali was world famous and I remember one Christmas receiving a Muhammad Ali doll as a gift. He was the first famous person I ever knew and I knew he was something special even as a young boy. I knew he was a boxer and I knew he was great. He was my introduction to greatness at an early age. My mother was in fact my first introduction to greatness. I always looked up to my mother and she would take good care of me. She talk me early on the lesson of respect and trying to do something for oneself.

The inner city had its various paths that one could take, but Obi Linton, one of the older boys in the neighborhood had introduced me at age 8 to the Pop Warner football team that played down the hill from my house. He was a member of the team and he encouraged me to join. I joined. My first coach was Audrey Blue, an educated young man who took personal interest in his players. At first they were going to position me on the offensive line, but I remembered my excellence as a running back in street ball, so I urged the coach to let me run the ball at practice to compete for the fullback position. He allowed me to and I ran with tenacity, skill, and grace refusing to go down. It was my audition and I succeeded in getting the fullback position.

My team was called the New Brunswick Raiders, an organization that was known for having talented players. At age 8 we won the championship and again at age 9 we won the championship. We went 11-0 each year. I excelled at fullback and middle linebacker. Not only did I excel on the football field, I excelled in school as well. I was an honor roll student. I remember my seventh grade teacher, Ms. Willie Mae Jeter who would teach me about making choices in life so that you would end up alright in the future. She was a great teacher and she instilled in me greatness at an early age. I remember my eighth grade teacher, an ex-nun by the name of Sally Saharko. The first thing she asked me was, "Do you like learning?" I surprised her by saying yes. She and I got along very well and when my standardized test scores came in she contacted the mayor of New Brunswick to honor me with a Mayor's Proclamation at the age of 13. That year I was named Pop Warner National Scholar, the first from my town. My mother and I was invited to an awards banquet in Philadelphia for this honor. In order to gain this honor I had to excel in school, football, and write eight essays to be judged.

I graduated from eighth grade with honors and made the graduation speech. In 1987, I entered New Brunswick High School as a freshman. Immediately I made impact on the football team even as a freshman. My coaches were John Parker and Odie Paige. My team was talented but there was a lot of competition from bigger schools that year. I was the backup tailback. I played basketball that year as well. In the classroom I made the National Honor Society. My Biology teacher was Mr. Russell. Mr. Russell was a great teacher who always told us life stories. I learned lessons about life from Mr. Russell. My sophomore year my team made it to the playoffs and won nine games. I scored my first touchdown that year.

My junior year I was the starting tailback on the football team and was the student council vice president. I was a member of the track team as well. My coaches taught me the value of responsibility and discipline. My coach Odie Paige believed in me and always taught me to take leadership. My family was supportive of my success in school and on the football field. My little brother, Darryl Germaine was my pride and joy. I wanted to be a great role model for him as I was ten years older than him. From a small boy I would take him everywhere with me and I would let him receive my trophies at my awards banquets so he could get the idea at an early age. My hope was that he would want to emulate my success and attempt for his own greatness and he did just that playing many sports at an early age including football, baseball, basketball, soccer, and karate.
My senior year was an awakening for me. I was MVP of the football team, making All-Star and All-State. I was accepted into the Peer Leadership, a group of peer counselors that mentored freshmen students. My teachers were Janet Obzut, Karl Bernstein, and Donnie Collins. Through this organization I founded a male

mentorship program that was for students by students. For this I was featured on the front page of the newspaper, my picture with a motivational quote. These teachers taught me the value of service to mankind and love of humanity.

I was selected keynote speaker to the National Honor Society Ceremony that year and my advisor told me that my speech was better than Avery Brooks himself. I became an orator for the Martin Luther King Players, an oratorical group that performed oratorical speeches and songs all over the country. This was a national oratorical group. My leader was Louis Dunbar, who had led this group for decades, and Bobbie Brown who was once in the group. These two men became my mentors and they supported me throughout high school. I performed the speech of Langston Hughes entitled, "Let America Be America Again." I won the school's essay contest that year and had an over 4.0 grade point average. I won the Highest Achiever Award, "Mr. NBHS", finished third in Central Jersey in the 400 meter dash in track, and I graduated with high honors.

The culmination of my achievements was a full football scholarship to Lafayette College in Easton, Pennsylvania. I was recruited as a wide receiver and kick returner. Lafayette was a highly selective, highly elite, top 1% small liberal arts college with a great reputation. In football one of their players was featured on the cover of Sports Illustrated and the team won the NCAA Patriot League Championship.

So in the fall of 1991 I entered Lafayette College with determination and dreams. Dreams of graduating and finishing the course. I wanted to be the first in my family to get a college degree. I would major in Economics, Accounting, and Black Studies at Lafayette. My first semester I excelled both in the classroom and on the football field making varsity. I made the Dean's List with a 3.8 grade point average including the highest grade in a Biology lecture hall of 300 people. This was my first sign of greatness in college and it catapulted me to more great things. I received a Silver Medal for academic and athletic achievement that semester and was sent to West Point to a prestigious student conference for my exploits in Political Science. At this conference was the best students in the country and I was among them. I was published in the conference book as well.

My sophomore year my team won the NCAA Patriot League Championship and went 8-3. I was a vital member of the offense that year. I was a champion once again, the first time since Pop Warner football. My mentors in college were Dr. Gladstone Hutchinson, Professor Curlie Holton, Dr. Rexford Ahene, and Dr. John McCartney. Dr. Hutchinson instilled in me the importance of demonstrating my ability in tangible ways. Professor Holton told me to write. Dr. Ahene was my advisor to my senior thesis and Dr. McCartney taught me the importance of mastering the material and becoming a master in academics.

So I wrote. I wrote for four newspapers on campus and edited another. I was also a peer counselor on the dean's staff. My writing was very well received by faculty and staff and I was named Unsung Leopard. That spring I attended a year abroad in London, England where I attended the University College London, the college that Charles Darwin author of "Natural Selection" attended. This was the third ranked university in all of England after Oxford and Cambridge. I studied Economics, Math, and Social Geography there.

While in Europe I took part in a traveling expedition that covered Csech Republic, Poland, Romania, Lithuania, Latvia, Estonia, France, Amsterdam, Ukraine, Russia, Bulgaria, Austria, and other countries. I was exposed to the culture and the lives of the people in these countries. I was exposed to their economies as I had learned in school. Russia had just opened up to the world since the fall of the USSR. We were there. We visited Moscow and St. Petersburg. In Moscow I went to the Kremlin, Russia's equivalent to the White House and in St. Petersburg I went to the famous Hermitage Museum. Although Russia was underdeveloped I saw a lot of greatness there including the Pushkin Palace named after the great poet Alexandre Pushkin.

My first three years in college I worked also at Johnson & Johnson Worldwide Headquarters as an accounting intern. When I returned to college in America and midway through my third football season, I was diagnosed with a fatal illness by a doctor. I had to stop playing football and I became ill. After leaving school for the remainder of the semester and being in the hospital, I returned home to New Brunswick with diminished hopes. A professional doctor told me that I would never graduate college.

I spent the rest of the semester with my mother and little brother, Darryl. My father had come to see me as well. I was glad to see him for it had been so long since I had seen him. I had to rebuild my health back up with hopes of returning to college and graduating, proving that doctor wrong. I remember my little brother carrying me on his back figuratively. He would play baseball twice a week and this became my favorite event. He and I spent a lot of time together; I even went up to his school and sat in on one of his classes. He was my savior. I built my health up with the help of my brother and mother and returned to college the next year.

I made it through mid-terms that next semester and my illness came back. I returned to the hospital and lost almost all hope. I returned to college that winter and climbed through three feet of snow to get to my classes and with determination I finished the semester. I even had all A's and B's that semester. After returning the following two semesters of college I graduated at the top of my class and received a graduation award and a double major in 1996. Through this experience I learned the importance of perseverance and will and determination. I also learned never to give up on your dreams. I graduated.

After graduating from Lafayette, I received a fellowship to attend Purdue University's Krannert School of Management, a top business school in West Lafayette, Indiana. This would be for the Master's degree. My best friend Jevon, a Rutgers graduate and great student in his own right, attended with me. Prior to my first class at Purdue, I had traveled to Rome, Italy and Egypt in 1997. I saw the great pyramids and the Sphinx, the Tower of Kings, and the Egyptian Museum. It was my first exposure to kings, an exposure that would influence my notion of greatness and majesty.

Once I returned to Purdue I realized how rigorous the curriculum of the business program was. I had to dig deep to excel. At Purdue, I managed to win the best speaker award and appeared on the Dean's List and Honor Roll. I was also an instructor of a Finance class. Every February I gave a lecture for Black History Month sponsored by the dean of the business school. Both were very successful. I ran my own personal development firm, worked as a marketing director of an engineering firm, and became a success coach. My experience at Purdue taught me the importance of hard work and dedication. I had a chance to feel my own greatness at Purdue.

I graduated from Purdue in 1999. Upon graduation I took on a sales consultant position with a Fortune 500 subsidiary. I learned a lot about psychology in this job and excelled to be a top sales consultant, nationally ranked. After a number of months I was accepted into a PhD Program in Marketing. Here I was a member of the PhD Project and the American Marketing Association. After obtaining a 4.0 grade point average and being on the faculty which required me to teach and do research in Marketing for three years, my fatal illness recurred and I had to leave the PhD Program with no idea of whether I would finish.

I ended up in the hospital again with diminished hopes. It was very severe. I could hardly walk and talk and I didn't have my little brother to be there for me this time. Then after getting out of the hospital I returned to New Jersey to rebuild my health and strength. I was able to build my strength back and my body and I even pursued boxing after recovering. Although my PhD career was over I was motivated to build up my body and pursue being like the great Muhammad Ali. I excelled in training and many felt that I could become a champion if I worked hard enough.

I trained hard. I ate, drank, and slept boxing. I had been a football star, but football was a team sport. Now I was training for an individual sport. I loved the boxing culture. I felt boxing was a way to make a way for myself in this world. A few weeks before I was supposed to spar the top amateur boxer in New Jersey, a boxer who was a top candidate for the Olympics, my health regressed and I missed out on my chance at something big. I had to give up boxing. Then after getting my health better, I pursued writing. I remembered what my mentor Curlee Holton said to me. He told me to write. So I wrote and wrote and before you knew it I had a finished manuscript. In 2007, I got my first book published entitled, "On the Wings of Perseus: The Life of the Athlete After Sports."

Through my successes as an athlete, writer, scholar, businessman, and success coach I learned the importance of struggle. My life was indeed a struggle. Everything in my youth came easy to me, school, social, athletics, etc., but after being diagnosed with a fatal illness things became a bit of a struggle. I had to press on, persevere, weather the storm, and stay dedicated. In fact, 1 in 3 people with my fatal illness dies. I had come so close to death and that made me value life. I had mastered the art of not giving up. I have the training of a doctor of philosophy and I use it in my writing. I have been on top of the world and on the bottom of the barrel and my lessons on life are drawn from this paradox.

In my youth I learned the importance of role models beginning with Muhammad Ali. My coaches and teachers were role models as were my mentors. I remember my sophomore year when I had met the great Dr. Cornel West. I was in the presence of a great man, infinitely great, there was no limit to how great this man could become. I wasn't intimidated though. I debated him ferociously on his best-selling book. I had the opportunity to meet Angela Davis, author Nathan McCall, and leader Al Sharpton during my years in college. I felt the presence of greatness. Many of these great people had to overcome grave obstacles to achieve greatness much like myself. Mine was a fatal illness among other life obstacles. However, I took from my experience lessons to live by and share. In my infinite wisdom, I have reached thousands of people whether as a teacher, professor, or presenter.

I have learned to be bigger than my illness and that greatness will not evade me because of the illness. In fact, I believe that in many ways the fatal illness made me deeper and greater as a result of me fighting so hard and seeing death and suffering. Never underestimate the power of a suffering soul. When times got hard. I looked to the stars. I looked to the sky, the phenomenal sky. I remember walking the campus at night asking the question, "What is the meaning of my life?" And now I went from near death to the process of self-actualization.

I thought about what would have happened had I given up in college. Had I listened to the doctor that said that I wouldn't graduate. Where did I get the strength to persevere? I got it from the desire that I possessed to make something of myself at all cost. I got it from my inner ambition. My spirit pierced through all the poor health and was resurrected.

Chapter 19:
The Master of Home Life

◇◇◇◇◇◇◇◇◇

One thing I charge you to master is home life. Master home life the way a sailor masters the wind when he sets sail. You get only one life, so it is essential that you advance along the horizontal axis of existence. Survival is the very basics, but mastery is the ultimate ambition. The nuances of home life can get very complex, but this can be made worse by lack of an intellectual project and other activities.

We have seen masters at work and we marvel at them. However, how many of us are masters of home life? How many of us get beyond our circumstances to prevail. Mastery is the process of understanding and excelling in life to the highest degree possible. Every individual must examine the possibility of his mastering home life. Every individual must secure his place in life.

Life offers various stimuli. Man must respond accordingly. An artist masters the art of design and creativity. Man must master the art of responding. Man must respond to turbulent storms. He must gather his internal resources and inner strength to respond effectively. This requires the energy within his being to do so. This requires the effort of the 12 gods of Olympus. The quest to master the response is what gives life meaning. It gives life purpose. A difficult task indeed, but man has the obligation to try.

So life can be thought of as a response to storms. It can be thought of as climbing a mountain whether it be Mount Everest in excess of 29,000 feet or the Rocky Mountains. Furthermore, life can be viewed as a race with obstacles and you are charged with mastering the course. To master the race, man must have mindset, ambition, drive, and effort. This is the creation of power by man in attempt to master his external world.

Man's internal world, i.e., his brain contains one hundred billion neurons that are capable of sending response messages to the body. The brain cells process information and survival becomes its message. The brain stores this response for the purpose of mastering life. So anatomically one has the capability to master life by responding to the storms and circumstances of life.

Man uses his mind to think. In order to be a master of home life, career, finance, social, family, love, and the physical, one must be a powerful thinker. Thoughts are the seeds of plants and they protrude through the soil to reach sunlight. The ability to think is an antecedent to understanding life and its nuances. An elevated mind is the most powerful weapon in this battle we call life. This means thinking on a higher plane, thinking deeper. An elevated mind seeks understanding of complex concepts and phenomena. Philosophically, thoughts determine destinies. Thoughts precede actions and actions determines one's state.

In life man is given a state – a state of being or existing. This often can be an undesirable state. For this state, man must master the conditions that cause such a state. A bird just hatched is in a state of danger. He must master this state in order to survive. A man who has hit rock bottom can rise by mastering his state. He requires

Herculean effort and drive. He must be driven by his unwanted position.

Reaching one's destiny means being given a state, responding to this state, and mastering the process thereof. Mastery means advancing to the highest degree. The state is a part of self, *ziji* in Chinese. It is a rigorous journey to master self, but this is an essential process. In order to master life, one must master self. This is your state, your idiosyncracies, your strengths, and weaknesses.

In order to master self, one must constantly evaluate one's own responses to his state and the turbulent storms or adversity in his life. Do you have what it takes to respond effectively to the storms? Are you resilient enough? What are your strengths? Your limitations? If your response is not optimal it may be something about you that causes this. This may require adjustment.

There is hardship in life; you must adjust and respond to it. Along with hardship comes circumstances that must be dealt with or lived with. Much hardship is outside of your locus of control. You must battle the elements. You must take the bull by its horns. How much control you have over your response to hardship determines your state. You will gain resilience from the process of responding to hardship. The process is as follows: you exist, you flourish, you face hardship, you adjust, you learn from the process, and you perpetuate further.

Hardship can come in many forms. The loss of a spouse, a financial crisis, a health catastrophe, a loss of hope. The elements of life can be entrapping. They precipitate change in your state. Mastery involves being resilient despite hardship and making a calculated adjustment. Hardship may be as wide as the river; you must be ready. Readiness, an important attribute, involves being mentally prepared for what's to come however unexpected. One does not get results without response and adjustment.

There is something, some atom within the process of hardship if responded to effectively that enhances one's mental powers. One develops will and wit and a capacity to overcome and rise even higher than before the hardship occurred. Mastering the sail of life and what it has to offer involves strong will and wit. Included in this is the capacity to think. A beautiful rainbow appears after the storm; you become stronger when you respond well to the storm. You weather the storm with tenacity and form models for dealing with similar disturbances in the future. After all, your survival in the future may come as a result of something you learned in the past.

The energy of your anatomy provides you with the prerequisites to adjust to the manifestations of storms. You have the innate makeup and ability to handle disturbances. Measure up to your own makeup. A soldier at war must use all of his weapons at his disposal. You must use all of your innate capabilities and armament. There are those capabilities that you develop with training also. The ability to problem solve or communicate is an example of this. An innate ability is exemplified by your memory. Philosopher, Plato said remembering is learning. Your memory is an important tool in mastering life or in

Reality is one element of life that pervades. Often reality or the metaphysical is harsh and must be dealt with realistically. This requires for one to put life in perspective. One must think of life as a race with realistic obstacles that must be circumvented by any means. Can you beat reality? A master ponders this question seriously and knows his obligation to try. A master withstands the heat of reality and controls his own destiny. This requires mastery as well.

One way to respond is to live a principled life. The multiplicity of principles guide your actions and reactions to stimuli. The principles will be based on your knowledge of self and your environment. They have to be compatible with yourself and your environment. The success of your life and your mastery are predicated on such principles. The principles are a road map for your civic life and your personal life. They allow you to respond to road conditions. Also, they help guide decision-making and choices. One example of a principle to live by is love for humanity. Another example is never cheat to achieve gains. The principles may vary, but they should cater to your responsive needs.

Life is not a sprint, but a long distance race. Thus, man needs everything that a good long distance runner possesses: perseverance, endurance, and stamina. Like a runner, in life, man must pace himself, i.e. manage his energy. His mindset must be long term and not myopic. Although he lives in the present, he must keep an eye toward the future. In addition, he must be poised under the pressure of the turbulent storms.

A man is only as great as the precision of his thoughts. If the seed is positive, the root is positive, and the plant is therefore positive. A man must have positive thoughts in order to master life. A man's mind incubates his thoughts. They then develop.

You must develop your mind to the fullest. A man's thoughts are an extension of himself. If he has a preponderance to be positive, his thoughts will likewise be positive. What a man encounters influences his thought process. What he sees impacts his mind. If he sees nothing but negative, his thoughts will be negative. Thus, it will be difficult to master life as life is in itself is positive.

In mastering life, wisdom is necessary. One must develop his own philosophy on life. This insight will then guide him through life like a lighthouse to a ship at sea. Man must reflect on his life and create lessons from his past. When a storm hits, wisdom is invaluable. It forges resilience in the wake of the storm. A king in his kingdom has wisdom. A teacher to her class has wisdom. You must seek wisdom for the mastering of life.

You must have the yearning to master life. The possibility is eminent. You must realize this and proliferate the effort necessary to make it a reality. You have looked in the mirror and mastered yourself. Now you must master the possibility of mastering your environment. What opportunities does your environment have for you? Does your environment nurture you? The elements of life are diffuse. You must master the elements of life. They are crisis, obstacles, change, and progress. The stars above must be aligned in order for you to master these elements. The chemistry must be right in order for this to occur. You must be active and reactive for this process. For every action, there is an equal positive reaction. It must dawn on you to react to prevailing conditions.

Mastery is first planted or rooted in the mind. It is then moved to action. You must move clockwise in the direction of progress. Crisis will be manifested in every turn. First, brace yourself from it. Then react positively, productively, and constructively to it. Problem-solving acumen is pervasive at this point. Creative thinking must persist without limit. Creativity is infinite; the population of creative ideas is infinite. A crisis is a way to test your mind's capacity and your resilience. Don't be uprooted by the tornado of crisis and the gusty winds of adversity. Remain intact. Embedded in the difficulty of it all is the ability to get stronger and wiser. The journey has its lessons. Surrendipity is at hand through crisis. Crisis has led to many discoveries.

Obstacles are not an apogee, they are close to us in everyday life. This is an element of life that is unavoidable. There is an axis of action that must be taken. Again creative rationality is needed. Assert your power, your inner strengths, your wit, and your fortitude. Your aura has within it the ability to respond to obstacles. It's not a haphazard response, but a calculated, mathematical response. Mathematical response separates the civilized from the barbarous. When you face an obstacle, blast forward with a response. The way you and others have responded in the past may serve as a basis for your response in the future. The continuum of obstacles that you are presented will create the material that is in your brain. Heighten and elevate your mind to analyze your position and eradicate yourself to a more stable position. The wavelength of your brain's activity is expanded by the prevalence of obstacle messages. You know when you are in danger. When a baby bird comes across a predator, she knows her life is in danger. The brain thus responds. Like a sailor facing a tidal wave, man knows his destruction is eminent or at least possible. The threshold of his response, his reaction determines his fate.

Rise above the trinkets of adversity in your thinking. Be two steps ahead of the adversity. Be proactive. Focus when facing a problem, on obtaining the right answer the way a student answers a mathematical problem in class. Often times there is only one right answer; you must arrive at it often in the blink of an eye. The ability to think fast, to think under pressure and with time constraints is an immense skill. It is one that is basil to survival. Let's not forget the importance of memory. You must remember how you got in a particular position in order to get out of that position. Adjust the way giraffes have adjusted by growing longer necks to reach taller fruit-bearing trees. Adjust the way a turtle has developed a harder shell to protect itself from sharper instruments on the part of predators.

Rise above the destructive forces of life. Negativity in the form of people and counter-productivity can be impactful. You must avoid the tenets of this destruction at all costs and by any means necessary. The recklessness of your surroundings should move you to better surroundings. A fish cannot thrive out of water. Man cannot survive without air. When your environment deprives you, you must mobilize yourself out of it.

Progress is the most inspiring attribute to man. A man who could not walk is inspired by his new ability to walk. Life must be built one brick at a time. A twenty five mile marathon starts with one step. Progress elicits hope and hope fills man's heart with air and power. Hope is like a windmill, power generated from within. Hope is like a steamship powered by steam. When man progresses, his response is reinforced. Hope and progress keeps one afloat in the thunderous storms. Progress keeps one on track with one's goals and aspirations. Crystallization of these goals and aspirations doesn't occur overnight. They run in stages. Be progressive in each stage or phase of the goal. See it through. There is light at the end of the tunnel. When you see things through you will master life.

Mastering the elements of life radiates masterful performance. This life is a stage and you must perform. You must perform in career, social, financial, spiritual, and intellectual life in order to master it. Thus, you must rehearse for your performance. A piano player rehearses over and over again before performing a recital. An athlete rehearses his vision over and over again prior to his performance in front of thousands.

You must perform or act productively in the midst of competition. Dynamogenesis is the improvement of performance as a result of the presence of competition. You must be made better as a result of competition. This is your response to competition. Competition is ubiquitous; it's in every corner of our lives. There is competition for love, for money, for jobs, for space, for attention, etc. If you are to master life, you must master this element of life.

You must be able to move and shift with change. The only constant in life is change. There is change of geography or environment, change in job, change in rules, change in goals, etc.. Society changes over time. You must adapt to these changes. Often times you saturate the effects of the changes and its vicissitudes. You must not allow change to diminish your position or state. Change affects one's state proportionately. Change is an important element of life that must be mastered.

Many of us are able to ascend or get to their highest level or peak in life. This takes chemistry and power. A man is only as powerful as his mind allows him to be. He can climb higher mountains to higher peaks and become his higher self. Mastering life is part of ascension as an equation. The more your mind is stretched to its limit, the more you are empowered, the greater your chances to ascend to your highest. Self-actualization is a theory in humanistic psychology. It occurs when one reaches one's full potential and finds meaning. It is characterized by moments of ecstasy.

A cardinal part of mastering life is similar to self-actualization – meeting a hierarchy of needs. There are physiological and psychological needs that must be met. In my experience, self-actualization does not occur without the battling with deep adversity and adapting to it positively. In the heat of adversity, you must be progressive. In any event the mind goes through the intricacies of life and adversity. It is adjusting or mental adjusting to the adversity and the settling of needs that self-actualization occurs.

I experienced self-actualization in June of 2014. I was wrestling with extremely difficult conditions and I had to some soul searching. I settled in on a state that was comfortable and a surge of power went through my brain. It was god-like, powerful, and intense. It was like no other experience I had ever imagined. Life had meaning for the first time and I saw my potential skyrocket to the top.

I now know how powerful the mind is. In addition, I battle the elements, difficulty, and adversity with this crucial weapon. Armed with a powerful mind, I am possessing of hope. I don't give up. I press on with my mind as a compass seeking my way. This book is destined to help you find your way in life by mastering this psychological journey with me in the pages of this small important book.

Your mind has the ability to untangle the mysteries of life – people, circumstances, and reality if there is such a thing. This book helps you ascend. It will get you to your peak, your highest, your best, your ultimate. After all, what individual purpose is greater than that? As we unravel the complexities of life, we will discover that which will help us progress or succeed. Progress or success is not finite, they are continuous processes. In all you must measure up to your own design or live up to your full potential. How it darkens our light to see so many people in life who don't live up to their full potential.

I am a scholar, an athlete, a thinker. I play chess with the deep concepts of life like self-actualization and response. I have been on top of the world and on the bottom of the barrel. As far as I have gone up is as far as I've gone down and I learned about life from that perspective. I have faced challenges as wide as the sea and have had successes that have allowed me to master the elements. I have often asked myself the question, "What can this mind do?" It is an encompassing question, fully loaded, and it puts things in perspective.

Explode with curiosity. What verses, what concepts can help me master life? How can a book help me master life? Books can help you think more effectively. This book was designed to penetrate your neurons or brain cells; you have 100 billion of these to work with. Store the concepts in your brain for use in life. The brain is the most complex entity that exists, more complex than any microcomputer with its bits and bytes, circuit boards, and diodes.

We have satellites that are 18,000 square miles in space and they are not as complex as the brain. When you take in information, the brain automatically processes this information. Process the information in this book and become a master.

Chapter 20:
I Remain

◇◇◇◇◇◇◇◇◇

Champ

With every flex of your brain,
You are a champ,
With heavyweight dreams you move mountains,
With intellectual zeal you have power,
You blast off like a rocket ship,
You beat mediocrity,
You win the battle and the war,
You astound those who watch you,
You are a king, a CEO, a PhD, a president, a valedictorian, and of course, a heavyweight boxer,
You have reached greatness,
Your highest plateau,
The climb was steep,
You had to persevere,
You did it, you made it, you're a champ,
You overcame a force of some kind,
Reality was succumb,
Ascend. Take flight.

Resilience

Much like the way we attract,
Resilience is the ability to bounce back,

Facing obstacles in the heat of the day,
We adjust to the obstacles' dismay,
Turbulent storms and an oasis of pain,
We can withstand ourselves in the rain,
Lift yourself,
Seek refuge,
React,
Respond,
You must be ready for the outpour,
What does life have in store?
For us, our people, our bodies, our minds,
What can we find?
Great resilience in space and time,
There's nothing we can't take,
From a bad dream we must awake,
Greatness is abound,
Can you hear the sound?
The sound of birds chirping, the sound of the wind's breeze,
Let's get off our knees,
And continue to breathe,
The air is free, our minds are free,
Our resilience was tall as the tallest tree.

Beyonce The Great

That woman can sing and dance,
Her greatness can put you in a trance,
Lifting hearts, inspiring souls,
She may go platinum, she may go gold,
Her charm, her grace, her sound we hear,
She's raising the spirit in the atmosphere,

Undaunting, uncompromising greatness,
I lived to see her so I'm a witness,
Beauty encapsulates her,
Every time she performs, it's an adventure,
I'm caught in her rapture,
The imagination of fans is what she captures,
Excellence is in her blood,
She's misunderstood but full of love,
Her music is in syncopation,
We are astounded by her formation,
She works hard and grinds it out,
To be the best we all must shout,
She's Beyonce The Great like Alexander The Great,
She's manifesting her destiny, taking control of her fate,
The passion of this mighty woman,
She came. she saw, she conquered,
A star gleaming in the dark distant night,
She's the greatest star in this here light.

Resurrection

Metaphorically, you go from death to life,
You go from giving up to striving,
From extinction to surviving,
The darkness surrounds you,
You are at your lowest point,
You need something to resurrect you,
It is your dreams that lift you,
Grab hold of the wind and live again,
A new life from goals you will win,
They counted you out, ordered the casket,

But you lifted your head, the code you cracked it,
Numerous times you were lifeless,
Spirit down,
mind boggled,
dreams deferred,
but life is what you preferred,
so dig yourself out of this deep hole,
and understand your motivation and role,
exasperated,
enthralled,
capitulated,
you must abruptly emerge,
from the dust, greatness on the verge,
resurrect yourself through your dreams,
look in the mirror and have self-esteem,
I hear the clamor of man's ideal,
You can live again, great and real,
I got your back, your vision is what I feel.

Mountain Peak

True to life, the mountain is steep,
But through my greatness, I'll reach the peak,
A champ, a king, I must climb,
Like Mt. Everest at 29,000 feet, it is time,
Tap into the secret corridors of your mind,
Don't be victim of the sublime,
The climb is steep, you can't be weak,
The peak is your highest level of peace,
The mountain represents achievement,
The climb is your very statement,

To the world you express yourself,
There's the mountain, the valley and nothing else,
As ambitious as you are, you look to the star,
But you realize that you must go very far,
Outdistance your circumstances, your obstacles,
Win rather than lose,
Finish what you started,
The urge to quit is truly departed,
Where is the mountain peak?
You must go up,
Your excellence must be abrupt,
Like a volcano you must erupt,
So scale this mountain and greatness will come,
Then you will realize that you are the one.

I Remain

The tumultuous storm of adversity blew my house away,
The gusty winds of crisis uprooted the trees that
Overlooked my dreams,
They nearly came tumbling down,
Chaos and confusion struck the place where I dwelled,
And even blurred my vision,
Obstacles struck my foundation one after another,
I remain!
The ferocious hurricane of problems swept across my land,
And concealed the clarity of my master plan,
Its force was crushing to any efforts to exit,
Its compassion null,
Its impact encompassing,
Its relentlessness unwavering,

It came inside my dream and tried to sweep that away too,
Tried to make my dream dull,
My dream remains,
I remain.
Adversity comes storming in on my sunshine,
In the shadow of the storm,
Obstacles surround my soul,
Circumstances surround my dreams,
The earthquake of crisis shatters my stability,
The momentum of my dream is stymied by the tornado of setbacks,
I weather the storm,
I remain!
I remain!

Perseverance

Illuminated minds, excited hearts,
Souls that clamor, you must persevere,
The storm has come, you know lightning and thunder,
The formation of clouds, a disturbance in the atmosphere,
You must persevere,
Stick with your plan,
A master plan, follow your gut,
The best in you will truly erupt,
Quitting is not an option,
A ship can't go halfway across the ocean,
Allow yourself the opportunity,
To move forward with your own destiny,
In order to master life, you must persevere,
In order to make your dream come true, you must adhere,
To whom and to where,

Will you cast a shadow of doubt in the air,
You must measure up to your own design,
Will the stars align?
Be ahead of the game and not behind,
Examine the possibility of your own greatness,
You can elevate your thinking and your mind's richness,
When the birds sing, lift your head and never give up,
Perseverance will make you great and your skin will be tough.

The Great Mind

With infinite intelligence and infinite imagination,
The mind is great and you must be told,
Like a champ, a king, you must be majestic and bold,
For the mind there is a ribbon in the sky,
The stratosphere is not the limit,
It's super,
It's powerful,
It's amazing,
It's infinite,
It's great,
The complexity of your mind is a mystery,
To look at great minds, look at history,
It is your mind that is responsible for your destiny,
Nothing can outthink you,
Out of life experiences, your mind grew,
There is no equal, there is nothing like it,
Keep your body and your mind relatively fit,
Creativity is born from this entity,
It is your mind that lifts you to ecstasy,
So don't limit the parameter of your great mind,

Yourself, I charge you, you must find,
Exactly what is your purpose in life?
With the use of your mind your future is bright,
Let your mind ascend to the highest,
Seeing things you never imagined would be in sight,
It is mind over matter a powerful trait,
Through the activation of mind you lift the gate.

Look to the King

It is with the wisdom of a king that I start my journey,
The majesty of greatness that is the key,
Lifting the veil of society I feel the need,
To take heed to a king's lead, I will succeed,
A king runs his kingdom and runs it well,
The great pharaohs of Egypt got a story to tell,
Capricious as he may be,
Decisive as he may be,
A king implements greatness and that's his legacy,
Down in the valley, o'er the mountains he goes,
Look to the king and listen to my prose,
In the height of the climb,
It was King Ramses' time,
The kings of the earth come from a great line,
In modern day we must look to the king,
Emulate his character and get into the swing,
When you are down and out raise your head,
The king is alive and never dead,
His spirit lives on, you're not a peasant,
Once you're successful, life will be pleasant,
Rule great lands, reign supreme,

A king to be that is the dream,
Blast off like a rocket ship,
Kings come from vast lands, let's take a trip,
To his greatness, I do not exaggerate,
Protect your own kingdom, don't let anyone infiltrate,
Wear the crown over your head,
You have to make it, babies need to be fed,
Look to the king,
Look to him,
Look to the king,
You will win,
You'll be mesmerized by him, he has no equal,
Rise up and be a king; this is your sequel.

Metamorphosis

From a caterpillar to a monarch butterfly,
You metamorphose from the ground to the sky,
Fly, soar, get all the way up,
At first they didn't like you now they love,
You've developed into a great one,
Your time is soon,
You beat your wings out of the cocoon,
Now you're not crawling, you're too much for that,
Your mind is complete, right and exact,
As a crawling caterpillar you imagined greatness,
Now you're like a bird with its own nest,
Science says you're one of a kind,
This is as true as these words rhyme,
Every time you beat your wings,
You represent the greatness of kings,

I can't imagine anyone more graceful,
You took flight now you're very playful,
An intelligent creature is what you are,
There's nothing stopping you from being a star,
Metamorphosis, man can do it too,
Develop your wings and keep your mind true,
Fly as high as the clouds, the sky is blue,
In order to succeed you must move,
Sir Isaac Newton discovered gravity,
Keeping us on the ground, but do we?
The sky is the limit we must manifest,
Keep it in stride we are the best,
The salvation of my soul depends on wings,
My time has come, this is what this means,
Keep the faith you're the way,
On this great path you must stay.

The Power of Life

Man asks me what motivates me,
I say life,
Man asks me what excites me,
I say life,
The power of life is very enthralling,
So much so that it is sprawling,
Like a crawling caterpillar or a soaring butterfly,
Life is about reaction,
A life in motion stays in motion unless acted upon by an external force,
They ask me what is the source,
You only get one life, that is enough,

Your life is a diamond in the ruff,
As imperfect as your life may be,
You can still be great until eternity,
Life is a game, a battle, an uphill climb,
You must be aware and read between the line,
Make your life worthwhile, don't waste time,
Make sure you're not a victim of the sublime,
Like an artist with his canvass,
Be a master of life,
Like the love between husband and wife,
What's the foundation of life,
Love is, it's all about strife,
Complete your ultimate journey of life,
Open your eyes, never be blind.

Usain

He is a lightning bolt,
He runs as fast as a colt,
100 yards, he covers so fast,
There was Jesse and Carl in the past,
This sprinter is world class,
The fastest man in the world, no one can pass,
Greatness doesn't evade him,
He's an athlete who is a gem,
From Jamaica he hails,
Everyone has witnessed his sails,
Flames,
Exploding out of the starting blocks,
9.58 seconds, he's a different stock,
Gold medals in the Olympics,

He's so fast it makes us sick,
He flies,
He dashes,
He sprints,
That's his reaction,
His power is unbearable,
His skill is impeccable,
We watch this man – he's sensational,
We've heard of the story of the tortoise and the hare,
This man's so fast that it's unfair,
Blazing, he is a rocket,
Blasting off on the track,
There's no one like him,
He leaves the rest behind,
He breaks from the pack,
Bolt is a great runner, he never lacks.

Peace of Mind

In life there are turbulent storms,
You must have peace of mind be true to form,
Be still, have a quiet mind,
Be patient it's a virtue of time,
There's a lot going on in the world,
Chaos,
Adversity,
Problems,
We need tranquility,
That's the reality,
But who can beat reality?
On the surface you may be happy,

But do you have peace of mind that you can see,
Grab hold of the wind and go for the ride,
Your path of achievement, take it in stride,
Your inner peace versus your inner volcano,
It erupts and you are free,
Peace of mind is not a matter of degree,
So be still mankind,
And relax until your time unwinds.

Infinity

In mathematics, infinity means lacking limits,
You are this platform of greatness, you are in it,
Endless,
Limitless,
Boundless,
We explore the corners of the earth,
Infinity, we can count and it doesn't end,
The memory in our brain, we must expend,
People don't know how great they can be,
But I remember the great ones, I did see,
The song is in our ear, we like the melody,
Of infinite greatness that inspires me,
Once we reach our glory we will know,
We are no longer amateur, we are pro,
Ambitious minds are unstoppable,
Infinite greatness is educational,
Let me hear the sound of greatness,
Ringing loud and clear in my ear,
I did all that I could, this is my year,
Infinite intelligence is what we possess,

Like Hercules we pass a series of tests,
It was a crucible, we had to make it,
The power of our minds has no limit.

A Lion's Roar

To capture greatness one must look to a lion,
The king of the jungle, he is the one,
A beautiful creature, this is no pun,
Can you hear the lion roar,
Much like the wolf howls and the birds soar,
He is calling to the Universe, he wants to be great,
So this creature I can relate,
A Japanese proverb states that in order to get the cubs, you must go into the lion's den,
We need to analyze the lion, we must begin,
His roar is powerful,
We hear him miles away,
Gallantly,
Enthusiastically,
Perfectly,
He is a picture of greatness,
The roar of lions is our fate,
He hunts, he raises his cubs,
He roams,
Much like we strive to be something,
We must make like a lion and be like this king.

Full Potential

Self-actualization means reaching one's full potential,
Getting to this point in life is essential,
The power of your self is in your grasps,
Develop your mind and work on your craft,
A proportion of your greatness is not enough,
You fight to be great it gets very tough,
Moments of ecstasy you feel,
A surge of power you will never kneel,
The mind is your foundation,
Being your best in my estimation,
The great Paul Robeson did his best,
The linguist, athlete, and actor was ahead of the rest,
Don't be half of yourself, be whole,
This is the greatest of stories ever told,
Reach your full potential, until then do not rest,
Realize that life is your final test,
The flames of greatness heat up the path,
I'm at my greatest, feel my raft,
Don't just exist, you must live,
Don't just take, you must give,
At the turn of the century there were many,
Men who were at their best,
Women who made the grade,
Being your best is an uphill battle,
Over time you will complete yourself,
Rise to the occasion and nothing else.

The Coliseum

I am a gladiator and this is my coliseum,
The greatness of my work will be in a museum,
There are thousands watching this great soldier,
I think of my past, present, and future,
Swords clang and gladiators fight,
The cast of battle day and night,
America is but a coliseum,
An oasis of cultures in a melting pot,
We can't afford to be mediocre, certainly not,
Draw your weapon or forever hold your piece,
The tension of life here we must release,
What does it take to be a gladiator?
It takes the mind, its elevation,
The coliseum,
A place where the great ones roam,
The coliseum,
A place only for the strong,
Determination is the key to success,
With desire and dedication you'll pass the test,
Complete the cycle of life; it is time,
Gladiators conquer their fears; they're on the grind,
Whatever you want in life you must fight,
So lift the gate with all your might.

Look to the Stars

Like a slave following the stars,
You must look to the stars in your life,

Up and away,
With the stars you can stay,
You must remain,
Your vices, you must refrain,
For peace and joy look to the stars,
For serenity look to the stars,
When I wanted to know the meaning of life,
I looked up,
In life there is no crutch,
They're luminous,
They shine,
Bright as can be,
And intertwined,
Look to the stars and make a wish,
To be your greatest, highest self,
Ascend in orbit,
The galaxy is yours for the taking,
These are the dreams were making,
Excellence is in the balance,
It takes Herculean effort this instance,
The stars will guide you, they will light up your dark world,
You can be among the stars,
Just think like a king and act like a champ,
Infinite greatness, your life you must revamp.

Mind Over Matter

With the athleticism of Lebron James and the ingenuity of Einstein,
It's mind over matter,
With the intelligence of Robeson and the charisma of X,
It's mind over matter,

Man's Divine Nature

We must visualize our greatness with our minds,
Picturing success one at a time,
Day and night we work real hard,
With our mind we go real far,
It's mind over matter,
It's motion over inertia,
It's light over darkness,
It's success over failure,
When you see yourself gleaming,
The tide will turn for your self-esteem,
Knowledge is power, don't you know?
You mustn't stop, you must go,
The world is your oyster,
Take the bull by its horns,
The mind has something great in store,
Thinking requires thought,
Think of the wars you fought,
Your destiny is in your own hands,
It's up to you, your best you ought.

The Pharaohs

Akenaton changed man's thinking,
Ramses II led the people,
To the gods Osiris and Isis,
And the kings of Egypt,
This is the way of the Pharaohs,
King Tut was a boy king,
Dsojer had Imhotep invent the first pyramid,
This was the way of the Pharaoh,
Queen Nefertiti was a great one,

Queen Nefertari made her mark,
At first it was dark,
But with science and architecture they gave off a spark,
The wisdom of the Pharaohs,
The majesty of kings,
The people loved them they were the link to the gods,
The way of the Pharaohs,
Intelligent,
Keen,
Wise,
Powerful,
That was the way of the Pharaoh,
Can we reminisce on the beginning of civilization,
Through their minds, there was elevation,
Let's remember Memphis,
Let's see the monuments,
The way of the Pharaoh was their statement,
The originators of mathematics,
That was the blossoming of the Pharaoh,
The eighth wonder of the world,
That's the way of the Pharaoh.

Chapter 21 :
Apotheosis – Man Elevated to the Divine

◇◇◇◇◇◇◇◇◇◇

Despite the pandemic you can experience apotheosis – man elevated to the divine. You worship Elohim, Yahweh, Jehovah, Jesus, Mohammad, etc., but when you worship others you never get too see how great you in your own right are. When Muhammad Ali proclaimed to the world that he was the greatest, he was divine. The divine are the top 5%, highly powerful and effervescent, spirited and energetic. King Akhenaton equated himself to the divine long ago in Egypt. Kings are divine, champs are divine. Many self-actualize the way I did and reach their full potential. Self-actualization is the highest level you can get to; it's the highest on the hierarchy of needs. When you self-actualize you feel god-like. You feel a power surging through your body. You tap into a higher energy and power. Your greatness is amplified. Remember you already have a force – your mind. Your mind is infinitesimal. Your spirit is a force too. You have high powers. The energy of your brain and body must be used effectively.

The divine have magnetism like the tide of the ocean. They have effervescence and dynamicism. The belief is that man can be god-like, a god with a body, in the flesh. His productivity and capabilities warrant such a description. He amazes those who watch him or experience his Godliness. Perhaps the Pharaohs and the Egyptians when they proposed multiple gods or polytheosis were really talking about the divine when referring to Osiris, Isis, Horus, Thoth, Ra, and others. Perhaps the creators of Greek Mythology when talking about Greek gods were really talking about the divine when talking about Zeus, Hercules, Appollo, Atlas, Hedes, and Poseidon. The Romans followed with their mythical god, Jupiter, who is equivalent to the Greek god of thunder and lightning, Zeus. The Hindus have their gods as well in Hinduism.

A divine person has a mentality and self-esteem that are powerful - god-like. He believes in themselves and their abilities and that no scenario or condition can prevent them from rising. Their ability is astounding and fascinating. How can a man run the 100 yard dash in 9.5 seconds in Usain Bolt. That's divine. Carl Lewis ran the 100 yard dash in 9.8 seconds as did Jesse Owens. These God Bodies defied gravity. When Michael Johnson ran before the world everyone felt his god-like ability; he was divine. I'm not saying never be a Christian, Muslim, Jew, Buddhist, Hindu, Taoist, or other follower, but you can be divine in your own right. Never sell yourself short. Your ability is your power and it speaks for itself. The rays of the sun will beam on you.

The world may have begun in darkness, but with the divine, there is light. The divine give a large part of themselves to humanity. Bill Gates has donated over 24 billion dollars to charity. Divine persons like him are called upon by the Universe to lift the world with their heart and soul. The athletic ability of Serena Williams, the number one tennis player ever, is divine; as is the powerful boxer Mike Tyson, the youngest heavyweight champion ever at 21 years of age. We saw with our own eyes the impeccable speed of Florence Griffith Joyner or Flo-Jo on a track and the versatility of Jackie Joyner-Kersey in the Olympic heptathlon. British heavyweight champion Lennox Lewis is divine. His powerful fist and superhuman physical ability allowed him to dominate boxing. The belief is that man is more powerful than any hurricane. The divine overcome supreme obstacles that seem to boggle the average man. They are psychologically impeccable, mentally impeccable. Many believe that General George Washington, later the first president, experienced apotheosis or elevation to the divine. Imhotep was deified 2500 years after his death and referred to as the God of Medicine. The intensity of the divine or those that are god-like, those in the top 5 percentile is felt by those in contact with them; those who witness their performance. The stories of these men and women are astounding; their impact on the world is impeccable. They make the difference. Man is capable of miracles and history is a witness to that fact. The divine have raised the roof, they have elevated the status of the world. As the world is going the wrong course, it takes the divine to turn it around. Their greatness cannot be denied. Many say that 5% of the population are divine. This is not because they say they are but because of what they can do and what they are about. They are champs and they think like kings –majestically.

Patrick Mahomes is a divine person with superior physical ability. This Kansas City Chief at the age of 22 threw 50 touchdown passes in a season. He can run the ball and throw precision passes. Deion Sanders who played in the Super Bowl in the National Football League and the World Series in Major League Baseball. He too had god-like speed and abilities as an athlete. The physical prowess of running back, Eric Dickerson was seen throughout the National Football League. With blazing speed and power rushed for 2,105 yards in one season for the most of all time. However, it was the way he ran that stood out most. Today there are several professional football players, the best athletes in the world, who are divine. Richard Sherman, the All-Pro corner graduated with a 4.0 in a Master program at Stanford University. He is intelligent and athletic. This All-Pro is a divine person.

The divine come in all nationalities. President Bill Clinton was a Yale Law graduate and a Rhodes Scholar. This intelligent and charismatic leader was divine in his own right. His ability to persuade and lead was remarkable and his mind was powerful. He was at one time the most powerful man in the world. The divine are destined for greatness. Those who are already great will magnify their greatness. We heard the harmony of singer, Paul Robeson, divine in all dimensions. His amazing voice is god-like and the way he elocutes and lifts people from their state is tremendous.

Perhaps Jesus, Mohammad, Buddha, and Confucius, those who have religions based on their lives were God Bodies of ancient times. The beauty and talent of songstress, Beyonce is divine. She is the greatest entertainer in the world the way Michael Jackson used to be. She is also divine. She is the exception to the rule. A born star, Beyonce captures the imagination with her vocals and her dancing of all those who bear witness of her greatness. The performer of Me, Myself, and I, Dangerously In Love, and Girls Run The World, fascinates and excites millions and she is also a humanitarian as well. Rapper Jay Z is a divine person as well. The blazing Olympic Gold Medal sprinter, Florence Griffith Joyner was also a divine person.

I am a divine person myself. I have self-actualized and experienced Satori, a sudden awakening and momentary fusing with a higher energy. My mind has been taken to the limit and being powerful it has allowed me to overcome the most venomous obstacles over and over again. I experienced apotheosis like these men and women. I had a fusing with an indirect channel and energy during my battle with a brain disorder combined with my intense athleticism, intellectual capabilities, and my life experiences. My light shines on. I have watched the great ones like Joe Louis, the Brown Bomber and the great leader, Malcolm X, who had one of the most devastating transformations in history. I have seen men do amazing things and it has impacted my life. I know who and what I am. The great Paul Robeson, who taught himself Chinese and sang songs in other languages and stopped a Civil War for a day by singing for enemy lines, was divine.

We go beyond the concept of greatness. There is the concept of superhuman intellect and superhuman physicality and powerful essence. I overcame a fatal illness in life to succeed when I was told I wouldn't. In terms of superhuman physicality, we witnessed Bruce Lee, a God Body astonish us with his martial arts. One of the three dimensions of man as noted by divine philosopher, Socrates, was intellect. We witnessed his intellect and the intellect of Albert Einstein whose Theory of Relativity was god-like. We are marveled at the depths of their minds.

Millions witnessed a man run 100 meters in 9.5 seconds. Millions can hear the divine voice of Beyonce harmonizing to the depths of the Earth. A lack of historical confirmation questions the so-called savior of man from 2,000 years ago, but we witness the great feats of the divine in contemporary society. The divine are a sign that you will be everything you ever wanted to be. They're the world's real saviors. Religion is man-made and the heroes they have put on a pedestal are mythical in nature, but today's divine have shown us greatness that we can see with our own eyes. Divine persons do things that astonish the human mind. They have ascended to the highest of heights, the peak of the mountain. Like in a flower garden, there is always a budding flower that stands out among the rest. A divine person is such a flower, more powerful than what conventional wisdom purports. They became great and casted a shadow of greatness onto the world. They feed the hungry, educate the ignorant, excite the masses, heal the sick and shut in, and eliminate the despair. We must walk with the divine ones. We must not be depressed. Hand over your life to the divine and count your blessings one day at a time. This has been the outcome of my own experience. Man is capable of great stature and prowess. You have the power of life.

So whose going to save us now. Doctors of psychiatry and psychology? Politicians and presidents? Men and women of the clergy? The divine are masters of their own destiny. They were born to be great and to cast a shadow of greatness on the world. They lift the world with their bare hands. They feed the hungry, entertain the bored, inform the ignorant, heal the sick, and calm the savage beast. Steve Harvey, a God Body in his own right has written three books that have informed millions on how to relate to others and how to succeed. I have followed up by taken it a step further, increasing the awareness of those who read and helping to transform minds. Walk with these divine. Let them guide you, let them rejuvenate and invigorate your spirit. Walk with these god-like men and women and in your stride never look back. Remember that the lion is not just the king of the jungle, he is God of the jungle. I want to hear you roar.

Acknowledgements

I want to thank the following people: my mentors: Paul Robeson, Dr. Gladstone Hutchinson, Louis Dunbar, Bobbie Brown, Curlee Holton, Rexford Ahene, Dr. John McCartney, Coach Audrey Blue, Coach John Parker, Coach Odie Paige. To my family, my dad, the late Roosevelt Harris, my mother Theresa Harris, brothers: Sherman Harris and Darryl G. Harris, sisters: Angela Hargrove, Constance Harris, Scarlet Harris, Sheree Harris, Elva Richardson. My nieces Kiara M. Harris, Jamiah Thomason, Joevannah Harris, Samiyah Hargrove, Alana Richardson, Jayla Harris, Zoria Richardson. My nephews: Sherman Harris, Jr., Deandre Taylor, Samir Hargrove, Kobe Williams, Nasseem Richardson. Brother-in-laws: Minister Linnie Muhammad, Nathan Richardson. Best Friend: Jevon Gordon and his wife Dominique Gordon. My professors; Dr. Doug Bowman, Dr. Cindy Emrich, Professor Rosie Bukics, the late Dr. Cornell Bell, Dr. Marc Weinberger, Dr. Bill Diamond, Dr. Msamo Mangeliso, Dr. Vanitha Swaminathan, Dr. Ron Karren, Dr. Eshwar Iyer. My teachers: Mr. Vaughn Russell, Ms. Janet Obzut, the late Karl Bernstein, Mr. Reginald Johnson, Ms. Willie Mae Jeter, Ms. Kathryn Szep, Ms. Sally Saharko. My friends: Lola Stewart, Stephanie Stewart, Robert Montgomery, Harrison Bailey, John Kahn, Jamal Jordan, Netfa Slaughter, Erik Marsh, Tom Kirchoff, Jafir Young, Jamal Young, Jamal Taitt, Quincy Miller, Eddie Pailen, Chris Taylor, Jojo Herndon, Chris Everett, Tremont Evans, Jarrett Shine, Alvin "Black-Nom" Miller, Tom Caldwell, Kenny Davis, Eugene Colvin, Jamal Schaife, Lawrence Patterson, Spel, Jeffry Crawford, Mr. Dunton, Mr. Washington, Brian Teel, Milton Davis, Johnel "Stress" Gibson, Officer Ron Reid, Officer Valentine,

Officer Mason, Vivian Aberra, Mark Baskin, Vonn Johnson, Sonya Johnson, Terrell Williams, Dirby Williams, Serena Baskin, Tamika Williams, Tanisha Baskin, Shawn Thompson, Clyde Sullivan, Dorine Sullivan, my aunt Victoria Baskin, Uncle Michael Sullivan, Paul Williams, Emendo Thomas, Brian "Amir" White, Dr. Stuart Ascher, Dr. Sheldon Stearns, Dr. Chacinski, John Rametta, Selvin Padilla, Damion Montgomery, Dwayne Leslie, Tony Wiggins, Anthony Shields, Eric Cromedy, my quarterback, the late Travis McCalreth, Tommy Wright, Shane Spells, Bobby Spells, Prosanto Weaver, Mr. Campbell, Coach Smith, Willie Weaver, Mr. Blount, Coach Shivas, Coach Jeff East, Timothy "Dip" Wilson, John Wilson, Lou Williams, Heather Williams, Wendy M. Williams, Vonetta McDonald, Lisa Perez, Dr. Dionne Johnson, Coach Bill Russo, Coach Frank Tavani, Coach Whalen, Coach Mancini, Darius Robinson, Christopher Badger, Rachel Wellington, Maghdi Barber, James Edwards, Eric Messam, Rondell Holman, Wiley Smith, Nina Wallace, Tammy Allen, Yolande Mcbride, Dametrius Mose, Greg Turner. And for their inspiration: Eric Young, Imamu Mayfied, Magic Johnson, Michael Jordan, Lennox Lewis, Mike Tyson, Floyd Mayweather, Jr., Muhammad Ali, Leila Ali, Roy Jones, Jr., Evander Holyfield, Sugar Ray Leonard, Pernell Whitaker, Terry Norris, Bernard Hopkins, Lisa Leslie, Rebecca Lobo, Allison Feaster, Sheryl Swoopes, Denzel Washington, Will Smith, Ving Rhames, Martin Lawrence, Eddie Murphy. Lawrence Fishburn, Kevin Hart, Terrence Howard, Don Cheadle, Dwayne "The Rock" Johnson, Mr. T., Michael Jai White, Chuck Norris, Jean Claude Van Dame, Sylvester Stallone, Jet Li, Carl Weathers, Tom Cruise, Tom Hanks, 50 Cent, Wesley Snipes, Oprah Winfrey, Steve Harvey, Montell Williams, Dr. Phil, Dr. Oz, Russell Simmons, Hillary Clinton, Whoopi Goldberg, Raven Simone, Iyanla Vazant, Serena Williams, Venus Williams, Lebron James,

Derrick Rose, Isiah Thomas, Russell Wilson, Richard Sherman, Payton Manning, Ray Rice, Adrian Peterson, Desean Jackson, Michael Vick, Bo Jackson, Marcus Allen, Lawrence Taylor, Tony Dorsett, Eric Dickerson, Barry Sanders, Deion Sanders, Dwight Gooden, Jim Brown, Gale Sayers, Earl Campbell, Franco Harris, Lynn Swann, Terry Bradshaw, Joe Morris, Gabrielle Douglass, Dominique Dawes, Usain Bolt, Jackie Joyner-Kersee, Marion Jones, Sonya Richards-Ross, Allison Felix, Carmelita Jeter, Lauren Jones, Carl Lewis, Michael Johnson, Cuba Goodie, Jr., Tyler Perry, Spike Lee, Bill Clinton, Barack Obama, Condeleeza Rice, Colin Powell, Michelle Obama, Jesse Jackson, Al Sharpton, Alexander O'Neil, Joe, Keith Sweat, Brian McKnight, Run, Monica, Janet Jackson, Mary J. Blige, Ciara, Ashanti, Mariah Carey, Keri Hilson, Keisha Cole, Erykah Badu, Kelly Rowland, Michelle Williams, Brandy, Ray J, Omarion, Marques Houston, Patti Labelle, Gladys Knight, P. Diddy, Dr. Dre, Ice Cube, Queen Latifah, Jamie Foxx, Boys II Men, Donnell Jones, Usher, Chris Brown, Neyo, Teddy Riley, Dave Hollister, Rihanna, Nicki Minaj, Ice T., Eminem, Lil' Wayne, LL Cool J, Jay Z, Nas, Busta Rhymes, T.I., TPain, Stevie Wonder, Kanye West, Timbaland, Angela Basset, Meagan Goode, Kerry Washington, Tyra Banks, Gabrielle Union, Tiraji P. Henson, Halle Berry, Elizabeth Taylor, and Beyonce Knowles.

Printed by Libri Plureos GmbH in Hamburg, Germany